Labor Movements in the Common Market Countries

Marguerite Bouvard
foreword by
Stanley Hoffmann

The Praeger Special Studies program—
utilizing the most modern and efficient book
production techniques and a selective
worldwide distribution network—makes
available to the academic, government, and
business communities significant, timely
research in U.S. and international economic, social, and political development.

Labor Movements in the Common Market Countries

The Growth of a European Pressure Group

Praeger Publishers New York Washington London

PRAEGER SPECIAL STUDIES IN INTERNATIONAL ECONOMICS AND DEVELOPMENT

PRAEGER PUBLISHERS
111 Fourth Avenue, New York, N.Y. 10003, U.S.A.
5, Cromwell Place, London S.W.7, England

Published in the United States of America in 1972
by Praeger Publishers, Inc.

Library of Congress Catalog Card Number: 78-189302

Printed in the United States of America

FOREWORD
Stanley Hoffmann

Marguerite Bouvard's book constitutes a thorough, painstaking, and balanced effort to describe the relations between the labor unions in the several countries of the European Economic Community (EEC) and the institutions of the EEC. Hers is the first attempt to cover completely a much-neglected aspect of Western European integration. Her case study shows how the creation of new institutions above the nation-states has led the labor movements to carry their demands and pressures to the new, supranational level, what role they have been able to play in the decisions of the Western European bodies, and what kinds of measures these agencies have taken in the broad area of social policy.

Readers interested in the slow establishment of what two distinguished scholars have called "Europe's would-be polity" will find Dr. Bouvard's account a most useful contribution. Until now, in the study of Western European integration, theory has somewhat run ahead of empirical data presentation for two reasons. First, many of the most challenging analyses, although based on exhaustive research, were more concerned to provide the reader with a conceptual framework and a theoretical model than to describe the (frequently technical or tedious) facts that the framework and model were supposed to order and explain. Second, the treasures of intellectual ingenuity and analytic ambition lavished on the theory of integration often have been far more impressive than the achievements of integration; scholars have worked harder than statesmen--or at least they have tried harder to be constructive.

Stanley Hoffmann is Professor of Government at Harvard University.

Dr. Bouvard's study provides a clearly presented
mass of data that can be used not to test existing
theories of integration but to show their limits.
The story she tells is essentially a negative one.
Here we find, indeed, new institutions with rule-
making powers and national pressure groups that have
understood the need for a supranational echelon. And
yet we find neither a transfer of allegiance to the
new Western European political system, nor any functional expansion of the EEC over the years, nor any
strengthening of the institutions. Why? Some of
the answer can be found in the basic treaties, which
created the Coal and Steel Community, Euratom, and
the Common Market: Labor policy and social policy
were never considered crucial concerns. However,
vagueness of initial commitments has not impeded
spectacular progress in integration of agriculture,
for instance. The deeper answer, then, must be found
in the attitudes of the governments. For while it
is true that skillful leadership and the pressures
and imbalances of the process of integration may ob-
lige the member states to go beyond their earlier
expectations and calculations, it is just as true
that the process itself does not really begin--and
leadership at the European level does not have any
fighting chance--unless the member states give a
strong push, beyond the treaty commitments, and want
to keep the process going.

    In some areas this push has been provided by a
common will or by the convergent interests of the
six governments, which are convinced that the advantages of integration for their respective economies
far outweigh the risks: for instance, in the establishment of a common market of industrial goods or
in the definition of a common external tariff. In
agriculture the push has been provided essentially
by one of the governments--the French--which skill-
fully and ruthlessly made its participation in all
other joint undertakings dependent on the creation
of a preferential and protected common market of agricultural products. Today the drive toward a common
currency and closer fiscal, budgetary, and monetary
cooperation derives from a shared conviction that
the national governments cannot, in isolation, stop

or control inflation or prevent the monetary disruptions for which the existence of a prolonged U.S. balance-of-payments deficit and of a capricious Euro-dollar market is very largely responsible. But there has been nothing comparable in social policy matters.

Here European integration finds several major obstacles. In the first place, no government has any strong incentive to establish a powerful Brussels echelon above it; no government faces, for instance, the problem faced by the French state with respect to agriculture--the evidence that an essential economic activity can be modernized and saved only through the elaboration of a common European policy carried out by central institutions. We may posit that as a rule a government will want to keep the monopoly of distributing benefits to its citizens as long as possible. It will give it up only when otherwise faced with a serious domestic crisis _and_ when there is a visible supra- or transnational alternative (for whose creation it will then try to take credit). Now each government may have its own labor troubles and may find its social security system increasingly costly and heavy. But the setting up of a strong Brussels echelon in these areas would weaken the hold of the governments on their citizens without solving any of the problems. For, in the second place, the whole logic of the European enterprise, so far, is one that treats social policy as a dependent variable. What matters is economic growth, productivity, industrialization, and financial stability; consequently, in most of the countries "incomes policy" has been little more than an attempt to keep wage increases reasonably low and to minimize labor pressures. This concern is both too important for each country's economic policy to be delegated to a supranational bureaucracy and too restrictive to provide this bureaucracy with any real incentive for functional expansion. Each government finds in European economic integration a host of reasons or rationalizations for resisting social demands. A strong Labor and Welfare Ministry in Brussels would either make it impossible for the governments to plead necessity or deprive them of one of the most important remaining areas of political control and social experimentation.

Third, governments have been under no domestic
necessity to heed labor pressures in favor of a more
active European social policy. The peasants, although
their numbers are dwindling fast, constitute a stra-
tegically most sensitive part of each electorate.
But in countries whose governments have, on the
whole, been based on a coalition of middle-class and
peasant elements, labor unions have had much less access to, and blackmailing power over, cabinets whose
survival often depends more on their ability to re-
sist labor demands than on their willingness to accommodate such pressures. Even when the governments
are well disposed, the labor unions' counterparts,
more often than not, are not the state but the business associations. Thus, there has been little incentive on labor's part to ask for a reinforcement
of supranational authority that would be both too
distant and irrelevant. Indeed, the technocratic
nature of the European institutions (toward which
peasant unions tend to feel a mixture of lingering
suspicions and high expectations) has served to re-
move whatever strong incentive labor groups could
have had.

Fourth, the political, religious, and ideological divisions of the labor movement, well documented
in this volume, have weakened its effectiveness,
splintered its reactions, and scattered its efforts
at the European level. Fifth, the new kinds of demands that labor unions, more or less clearly and
swiftly reflecting the desires of the workers, have
begun to present in recent years--concerning the
rhythm of work, the length of the work week, the
need for leisure, the "quality of life" in general--
are of a nature that supranational authorities would
be just as little equipped to handle as are national
bureaucracies and management in industrial societies
marked by increasing conflict between the hard logic
of economic rationality and the much softer one of
cultural claims for a more humane rationality.

These are the reasons why, in the field studied
by Dr. Bouvard, enormous efforts have produced negligible results. But readers aware of the complexity
of the facts the author had to organize and to present,

and grateful for the lucidity of her account, must
recognize that she has been a masterful guide to the
top of the mountain. Arrived at the summit--or at
the end--we may contemplate once again what might be
called the original dilemma of Western European integration. "Pure" federalists were not at all wrong
in arguing that only the establishment of a full-
fledged federation could bring under the jurisdiction
of central institutions realms that the process of
functional integration, for all of its dynamism and
spill-over effects, would otherwise avoid or neglect.
But functionalists were right in pointing out the
political resistance of governments and of powerful
groups within the states to such a sudden mutation.
The beneficiary of this deadlock between the two
sets of arguments remains the nation-state, especially
in the realm that this book studies; and a fine irony
dictates that the nation-state's resilience be no-
where more salient than in one area: labor, where
internationales have proliferated and where the
search for transnational loyalties has taken some of
its most ardent forms.

CONTENTS

xi

LIST OF TABLES

LIST OF FIGURES

LIST OF ABBREVIATIONS

CAP	Common Agricultural Policy (of EEC)
CDU	Christian Democratic Union (Germany)
CFDT	French Confederation of Democratic Trade Unions
CFTC	French Confederation of Christian Trade Unions
CGIL	General Confederation of Italian Labor
CGT	General Confederation of Labor (France)
CGT-FO	General Confederation of Workers' Organizations (France)
CISL	Italian Confederation of Trade Unions
CNPF	National Council of French Employers
CNV	National Organization of Dutch Protestant Trade Unions
COCCEE	Committee of Commercial Organizations of the EEC Countries
Confindustria	Confederation of Italian Industry
COPA	Committee of Agricultural Associations of the EEC
CSC	Confederation of Belgian Christian Trade Unions
DGB	German Labor Organization
ECFTUC	European Confederation of Free Trade Unions in the Community (ICFTU)
ECSC	European Coal and Steel Community

EEC	European Economic Community
EO	European Organization (WCL)
ERO	European Regional Organization (ICFTU)
FDP	Free Democratic Party (Germany)
FGM	Federation of Metalworkers
FGTB	General Federation of Belgian Workers
ICCTU	International Confederation of Christian Trade Unions (renamed WCL in 1969)
ICFTU	International Confederation of Free Trade Unions
ILO	International Labor Organization
KAB	Netherlands Catholic Workers' Organization
MRP	Popular Republican Movement (France)
NVV	Netherlands Federation of Free Trade Unions
OECD	Organization for Economic Cooperation and Development
OEEC	Organization for European Economic Cooperation
SFIO	French Section of the Workers' International
SPD	Social Democratic Party (Germany)
TUC	Trade Union Congress (Great Britain)
UIL	Italian Union of Labor
UNICE	Union of Industries of the EEC

WCL   World Congress of Labor

WFTU   World Federation of Trade Unions

In October 1971 both houses of the British Parliament approved the entry of Great Britain into the EEC on the terms negotiated between Geoffrey Rippon for the British government and the EEC. The success of the negotiations is significant not only for their potential political and economic impact on the international system but also because they constitute Britain's fourth attempt to gain entry into the Common Market in the past decade. Britain's first request for membership occurred in 1961. Two years later French President Charles de Gaulle pronounced his historic veto of approval to Britain's application; and in 1967 Harold Wilson, Labour prime minister, made another unsuccessful attempt to gain entrance to the EEC.

However, the vote within Britain was subjected to the strains of diverging interests and judgments as severe as those that occurred on the international level. Although the Conservative government won approval for entry by a majority of 112 votes, debate was long and bitter, the longest on a single subject since World War II, and the speakers numbered close to 200. Moreover, despite the repeated exhortations to international solidarity and responsibility by Continental Socialists, the Labour Party cast only 69 out of its 287 votes in Parliament in favor of entry. Since the British Trade Union Congress (TUC) is heavily represented in the Labour Party and supplies 80 percent of its funds, labor clearly revealed its predominantly negative attitude toward membership in the European Community.

The fears and suspicions expressed by the TUC and the Labour Party over Britain's impending membership are reminiscent of the opposition expressed by the Socialist parties and some of their labor counterparts two decades ago at the inception of the European Coal and Steel Community (ECSC). If one

were optimistic, one could carry the analogy a bit
further and conclude that since yesterday's opponents
have become the staunchest supporters of Europe a
similar positive attitude might be expected from
British labor. The Continental Socialists discovered,
to their gratification, that the European structure
could serve as a useful source of information and
support to wield against their own governments. The
British unions might also discover that, rather than
having their role in the play of national interests
weakened, their bargaining power might be enhanced
by the weight of the European trade unions and the
interests of the EEC in search of a role.

However, the cooperation of the Continental
parties and unions within the European Community has
been greatly facilitated by the fact that they share
common political cultures and traditions that transcend the bounds of their national polities. The
fragmentation of the national political cultures of
the Six into Christian Democratic, Socialist, and
Communist movements differentiates them from the
homogeneous Anglo-Saxon political culture. Moreover,
all three subcultures in the Continental political
systems have European dimensions, which had been expressed in a variety of ways before the establishment
of the EEC.

INDUSTRIAL RELATIONS
IN GREAT BRITAIN

If the British political culture is differen-
tiated from that of the Six through its consensus
and pragmatism, the trade union movement has a set
of traditions, practices, and objectives equally different from those of the EEC trade unions. Industrialization was accomplished at a much earlier date
in Britain and the trade union movement developed
well before the extension of the franchise to all
adult males. Because of this and also because of
the unions' strength, legislation plays a relatively
minor role in British industrial relations.

In Britain the trade union movement is not
divided along political or religious lines. The TUC

encompasses 160 unions, includes 90 percent of union membership, and is the recognized national spokesman for industrial labor. Although it has no direct control over the collective bargaining of its members, it advises them, coordinates their activity, and provides important services for them: conciliatory, arbitrational, educational, and informational. It is regularly consulted by the government, and its members and nominees participate in the network of advisory, consultative, administrative, and adjudicative bodies that prevail throughout the British political system.

Collective bargaining in Britain is highly decentralized and characterized by great diversity. The unions coordinate bargaining at the national level; but the resultant agreements constitute broad guidelines, and the negotiated benefits are floors to be built on by additional bargaining at the plant level. Collective agreements at the company or plant level are negotiated by union branch officials, shop stewards, a plant council of stewards, and sometimes by joint consultation councils. As plant politicians the stewards of the unions who have members in the plant generate many claims. British collective agreements are not legally binding contracts between employers' associations and the unions. Agreements negotiated at the plant are oral memoranda based upon past practices.

Collective bargaining in West Germany and in Italy has features similar to the British system, with negotiating power and prestige moving more toward the factory and company level. A trend in this direction has been apparent in France since 1968. However, the union organizations in that country are top-heavy and weakest at the level of the enterprise.

IMPROVEMENTS IN THE
STANDARD OF LIVING

Have the EEC unions realized substantial benefits as a result of twelve years of economic integration? A reasonably accurate comparison of living standards between Britain and Western Europe can be made by looking at average incomes, price levels, and trends in social welfare. (See Figure 1.) Such a comparison demonstrates that living standards have risen rapidly in the EEC and are now equal to, or higher than, those in Britain and that wages have risen faster than prices in all of the Six. Since 1958 workers' real incomes rose 54 percent in France and 95 percent in Germany, compared with 30 percent in Britain. The fact that the rise in real wages was highest in Italy and the Netherlands, which had the lowest wages at the formation of the EEC, points to a narrowing of the gap between living standards among the Six.

The more rapid growth of wages in the EEC compared with Britain is due partly to a sharp increase in industrial productivity in Community countries in recent years. From 1958 to 1967 industrial productivity increased by 70 percent in the Six and by only 32 percent in Britain. In the same period EEC imports were up by 140 percent, compared with 57 percent in Britain; and exports increased by 139 percent in the EEC and 32 percent in Britain. The more rapid increase in economic activity permitted wages to rise relatively quickly without leading to the same degree of inflation as in Britain.

Wages do not tell the whole story, however. Paid holidays, social welfare payments, and other fringe benefits also make a substantial contribution to real income.

There are broad differences of principle between social security systems in the EEC and in Britain. More than half the state cost of British social security (National Health Service, family allowances, supplementary benefits) is financed by general taxation. Social security is considered a charge on society, which must guarantee minimum subsistence to all citizens. It is a universal and uniform system based on flat rates and relatively low benefits. In the Six, social security is based mainly on the insurance principle; benefits are in most cases related to earnings and frequently are higher than in Britain. The EEC was not intended to develop uniformity among

social security systems but to achieve a gradual
leveling up of benefits and the adoption of common
rules of eligibility with procedures for mutual consultation to ensure that national legislation accounts
for the goal of harmonization.

Both the EEC and Britain are experiencing trends
toward shorter working hours as a result of either
legislation or collective bargaining. Although patterns of average hours in different industries are
similar among the seven countries, working hours are
slightly longer in Britain.

Paid holidays for industrial workers are much
longer in the EEC than in Britain; holiday bonuses
are common throughout the Community but an exception
in Britain. Both the European Organization (EO) and
the European Confederation of Free Trade Unions in
the Community (ECFTUC) have adopted a common program
for the EEC that includes a forty-hour week and a
minimum of four weeks' annual holiday with pay.
(See Chapter 2.)

Certainly a careful examination of living and
working conditions within the European Community since
its establishment points to a steady improvement in
labor's share of the national pie as a result of integration and also to the fact that the Continent's
rate of improvement has exceeded that of Britain.
However, this finding has not influenced the general
attitude of the TUC toward Europe. Rather, the TUC's
views are based upon its assessment of Britain's
economic weakness vis-à-vis her European partners,
revealing the nationalist underbelly of labor's official international ideology.

THE POSITION OF THE TUC

The enthusiasm demonstrated by the EO and the
ECFTUC for the entry of Britain into the Community
is hardly matched by the TUC. Both European labor
organizations have dispatched welcoming declarations
to the TUC at regular intervals, the latest on the
very eve of the 1971 TUC meeting at Blackpool, which

announced a strongly negative attitude toward Europe.
Despite the overtures of their European partners and
the internationalist bias inherent in labor's interest, the British unions have adopted a strongly
nationalist stance.

The TUC's position on entry was set forth in
its General Council's supplementary report to the
1970 congress, which spelled out in great detail labor's basic objectives for negotiations with the EEC.
Labor's main concerns were defined as the effect of
entry on Britain's balance of payments, the extent
of Britain's contribution to the Community budget
(with from 6 percent to 10 percent set as a limit),
and full compensation for workers affected by the
higher food prices and the value added tax. The TUC
considered that the June 1971 negotiations failed to
achieve these objectives and therefore declared labor
solidly against entry. The TUC's objections to membership in the European Community are based upon a
number of assumptions concerning Britain's contribution to the EEC budget, the higher cost of importing
food from the Six, and the net effect of the free
movement of investment capital within the EEC.

The French condition for opening negotiations
with Britain was that the EEC would determine first
its financial arrangements on a permanent basis, a
condition met at The Hague summit meeting of the six
heads of government, called at France's initiative,
in December 1969. The EEC position during the June
negotiations was that these financial arrangements
could not be changed and would have to be accepted,
subject only to transitional measures. Labor considers the contribution rate set for Britain (from
8.64 percent to 18.92 percent of the budget by 1977,
with some limits placed on the rise in her share in
1978 and 1979 but not after 1980) disproportionate
and unfair, for while she will be the largest con-
tributor to the EEC budget, she will draw the lowest
receipts. In addition, Britain will have to pay
revenues raised from levies on food imports and customs duties on industrial goods. The TUC is concerned that the terms of entry will involve high
balance-of-payments costs and that these would not

only cancel out the expected dynamic effects of integration but also condemn Britain to economic stagna-
tion and create unemployment.

Given Britain's slower rate of growth, the TUC
is worried that, with the free movement of capital,
the large international firms might switch their investments to the Continent and that even British firms
might contemplate expanding in the Milan-Turin-Ruhr
area. And, regardless of the European Investment
Bank's activity and the EEC's demonstrated concern
for regional development, labor fears that integration will have an adverse impact on Britain's underdeveloped areas in the Midlands and in the South.
The TUC's fears of unemployment and an outward flow
of capital were experienced to some extent by the
left-wing unions of the Six in the early 1950's.

One of the most serious objections to the EEC
raised by labor is that the workers' standard of
living will suffer from the higher food prices incurred by switching from a system of low food prices
maintained by deficiency payments to the Community's
Common Agricultural Policy (CAP). The CAP supports
prices for the EEC's main agricultural commodities
(cereals, milk products, beef, veal, pork, sugar,
poultry, and eggs) at high levels without production
controls. To prevent imports from cheaper suppliers,
import levies maintain the prices of imports slightly
above domestic price supports. The system, in conjunction with technological change, has stimulated
an increase in production and the consequent need to
reduce surpluses by export. The agricultural fund
yielded by import levies provides export subsidies
in order to meet world competition at world market
rates. The British labor unions believe that there
are better ways to support European farmers than at
the expense of the agricultural nations of the world,
notably by adopting a variant of Britain's system of
differential payments. One can safely assume that a
future Labour government would seek to modify the
CAP, particularly since the small farmers in western
France and their German counterparts complain that
the CAP benefits only the large, already wealthy
farmers and are considering the British system of
support with some interest.

On the basis of its General Council's study, the TUC has concluded that the British economy, and hence its workers' living standards, would fare much better if Britain remained outside the European Community.

THE POSITION OF THE
LABOUR PARTY

Given the intensity of opposition to Europe within the TUC and the largely negative vote of the Labour Party in October 1971, an examination of that party's position is in order. The majority of the party, including former Labour Party ministers Denis Healey and Peter Shore, supported Harold Wilson's strong objections to entry. They are opposed by Roy Jenkins and Michael Stewart, who consider that entry would further Britain's cherished goals of a more equal Atlantic partnership, relaxation of East-West tensions, and a Europe responsive to the needs of the developing world.

The arguments ventured by Labour's anti-Europeans are both economic and political. The economic case for entry is not obvious to most Labour members of Parliament, for the high costs are immediate while the potential benefits are uncertain. In exchange for membership, Britain must give up all preferential arrangements with the Commonwealth, pay the largest contribution to the EEC budget, harmonize British corporation taxes with those of the Six, and accept the free movement of capital (and hence constraints over a broad range of future tax policy). Because growth rates and corporate profitability are higher in the Six than in Britain, the Labour Party expects a substantial net outflow of capital and pressure to effect plant expansion on the Continent. These probable occurrences, plus Britain's serious regional unemployment, might anchor Britain outside the EEC's center of gravity.

The political objections to an enlarged Community are based upon fears of a loss of national sovereignty, a loss of democracy, and a bias against the Conti-

nental political culture, which differs so clearly
from the British political culture. The concerns
over possible loss of sovereignty loom out of proportion to the actual power of the EEC. Although Parliament's role in enabling European measures will
depend upon its own vigilance and flexibility in
coping with new tasks (see Chapter 3), Labour's members of Parliament fear that Parliament will cede
its sole right to levy taxes and spend the proceeds
to an unrepresentative European Commission and that
the sole right of Parliament to pass laws enforceable
in Britain will be abrogated. One can assume that
participation in the EEC's institutions will yield
a clearer view of the centrality of the national governments in European policy formation and will help
dispel concern over European encroachments on national
institutions. This has proved to be the case with
the Six.

The Labour Party shares the concern of the Socialist parties in the Six for the lack of democratic
accountability in EEC decision making. However,
while the Continental parties believe that they can
exert a beneficial influence on the problem, the
Labour Party is not as optimistic and would prefer
to remain outside the "European technocracy" altogether.

Finally, Labour casts a rather jaundiced eye on
the state of democracy within the Six. Seen from
across the Channel, the size of Western European
Communist parties and the labor disturbances of 1968
and 1969 are dim indicators of the prospects for
democracy within the European Community.

These fears are familiar to historians of European integration, and their evolution is predictable
within well-defined limits. The December 1971 elections of Labour's shadow cabinet registered a more
even balance of forces on the subject of the EEC than
in October. It is conceivable that, once within an
enlarged Europe, the Labour Party will seek out converging interests within the Community in order to
influence European policy rather than seeking to with-
draw Britain altogether.

PROSPECTS

If the remaining obstacles are overcome and enabling legislation is passed in Britain, that country
will become a member of an enlarged Community by
January 1, 1973. What will be the effects of this
step on the Community's position in world affairs,
its social policy, and its labor organizations?

The political arguments for British entry have
changed as the international system has undergone
far-reaching transformations. A decade ago a unified
Europe was considered a possible third force in a bi-
polar world. With the end of a bifurcated world and
the emergence of China and Japan as major centers of
power, Europe has become one of five major clusters
of power. An enlarged European Community will enhance Western Europe's role in the international system and thus increase Britain's influence, which has
waned since the end of World War II and the disinte-
gration of her vast empire. Although EEC members
have been pursuing independent foreign policies,
there have been serious attempts to cooperate more
closely in this area recently; and with the addition
of Britain a strengthened EEC could act as a unit
not only toward the United States but also toward
the Soviet Union, Eastern Europe, and the developing
nations of the world.

Significantly, while British labor has rejected
the economic arguments for the EEC--a larger economic
space and an enlarged market--it has manifested no
opposition to the Community's social policy. As a
result of full employment and the increase in bargaining power of labor at the plant level, the British
worker has undergone a transformation in attitude
and expectations similar to that of his Continental
counterparts: the desire for a progressive and sustained rise in living standards and the willingness
to strike for this goal. This paradox of discontent
amid prosperity is exploded if one accepts that the
sustained rise in real wages that has been experienced
by labor on both sides of the Channel has generated
a rise in expectations of living standards and a

blending of the sense of the possible with a desire
for equality. Among the Six, rank-and-file members
of the trade unions are threatening to paralyze their
respective institutions in search of a great equality
and participation within the national policy.

Within the EEC social concerns are no longer
considered palliatives but chief modifiers of economic policy. The EEC has responded to recent developments by revising and enlarging the European
Social Fund and by creating the Standing Committee
on Employment, a source of satisfaction for both
the TUC and the European labor organizations (see
Chapter 3). The TUC stands to benefit from the Social Fund, readaptation aid, regional programs, and
the information services of the European Commission's
Social Directorate. The only area of social policy
in which membership could conceivably pose problems
for Britain concerns social security for migrant
workers. However, adoption of this policy will not
pose major administrative or financial burdens, especially since Britain already has some reciprocal
arrangements with the Six on this matter.

What will be the impact of an enlarged Europe
on the European labor organizations? Since 1967 a
member of the TUC's General Council has participated
in the ECFTUC's Executive Committee, and therefore
the addition of an important new member will not
necessarily involve far-reaching reorganization.
Moreover, British workers have already participated
in activities of the industrial committees of that
organization, notably the 1968 coordination of support for striking Belgian workers at the Ford plant
in Genk.

Nor is it likely that the impending merger of
the three Italian labor confederations into a single
trade union front or the recent cooperation of rival
unions in Belgium and in France will precipitate a
reorganization of the European labor groups, although
such developments might produce stronger cooperation
between the EO, the ECFTUC, and the Confédération
Générale du Travail (CGT)-General Confederation of
Italian Labor (CGIL) liaison group. Strong unified

national labor movements do not preclude multinational unionism as the German Labor Organization's (DGB) role in the ECFTUC amply confirms. Once British entry into the Community is finalized, the TUC will adapt rapidly to the demands and rewards of a new political setting. Certainly the TUC will add strength to the European labor organizations, mitigating their minority position in the EEC and increasing their leverage to achieve their social aims.

Labor Movements in the Common Market Countries

1

BACKGROUND:
LABOR MOVEMENTS
IN FIVE MEMBER COUNTRIES
OF THE EUROPEAN
COMMUNITIES

The labor movements in the member countries of the European Communities operate in widely varying economic and social conditions; consequently, there are considerable differences among these countries in the configuration of labor relations. In Belgium and Germany collective bargaining procures most of the goals of the labor force, and in both countries the legislature has been concerned mainly with providing the institutional framework for worker-employer confrontation. In France, Italy, and the Netherlands the determination of wages and working conditions is characterized by a heavy degree of governmental intervention. In Germany, Belgium, the Netherlands, and Luxembourg the trade unions are strong, well organized, and adequately financed. In France and Italy non-Communist unions suffer from a lack of adequate financial resources, loose structure, and poor discipline; and the strong and efficient Communist trade unions dominate the labor movement. In all of these countries the labor movement is ideologically oriented and split between rival Socialist and Christian confederations. Although these differences may underlie the initial attitudes of labor toward European integration, a sufficient body of shared values has enabled the trade unions to transcend their purely sectional aims and to collaborate within the European framework. Moreover, as a result of participation in two decades of European integration, differences in industrial relations among the member countries of the European Communities have become less marked and the social policies of each country have exhibited gradual convergence.

THE NETHERLANDS

In the Netherlands the trade union movement is split on the basis of religion and ideology. The Netherlands Federation of Free Trade Unions (NVV) is the largest labor union. It has Socialist tendencies, has close relations with the Netherlands Labor Party, and is affiliated with the International Confederation of Free Trade Unions (ICFTU). The Netherlands Catholic Workers' Organization (KAB) and the smaller National Organization of Dutch Protestant Trade Unions (CNV) are affiliated with the World Congress of Labor (WCL). Together the confessional unions are stronger than the NVV,[1] and they find much of their political support in the left wings of the denominational political parties. All parties in government coalitions have maintained close ties with the trade union movement.

Although separated by religion and ideology, the three trade union federations have managed to cooperate effectively for the purposes of collective bargaining. Agreement on important social and economic questions is usually hammered out in a joint consultative organ prior to negotiations at the national level, and the NVV generally acts as spokesman for the entire labor movement during negotiations. Since 1967 the three federations have developed common platforms in a joint committee consisting of the presidents and general secretaries of each federation.[2] In the absence of strong Communist trade unions, as in France and Italy, plural unionism in the Netherlands has not proved divisive.

In the Netherlands the need for economic reconstruction after World War II was more pressing than elsewhere in Western Europe because of the simultaneous loss of colonial empire. Therefore, the integration of the labor movement into the social and governmental system has occurred more rapidly and

more extensively than in other Western European
countries. A highly structured system for dealing
with economic and social pressures has emerged out
of the Netherlands' postwar experience.

The trade unions participate in economic planning,
and this has made them highly conscious of wage-price
relationships. More than their counterparts in other
countries, the Dutch trade unions have been forced to
recognize the relevance of balance of payments to
wage settlements and, until recently, have generally
refrained from making demands that would lead to
price increases with a consequent decrease in exports.[3]
They have had no desire to assume responsibility for
raising the price level to the point of reducing the
competitiveness of Dutch industry in international
markets. In an economy heavily dependent upon international trade, the preservation of a low price level
has been deemed imperative. The stable price level
has eased the burden on trade union leaders to re-
strain rank-and-file pressure for higher wages based
on cost-of-living arguments. On the other hand, the
labor unions have not opposed measures to increase
productivity, provided the government exercises its
powers to remedy any unemployment effects and increased per capita output is reflected in a higher
standard of living.

The machinery governing wage formation in the
Netherlands is highly structured. It consists of
the Council of Mediators, the Foundation of Labor,
and the Economic and Social Council. The locus of
power and decision making has shifted among these
bodies at different times in response to changes in
policy and in order to assert control over wage
movements.[4]

The Council of Mediators, an independent body
of professional men, was established by royal decree
in 1945. Collective agreements are enforceable by
law only after its approval, and the Council is en-
powered not only to approve collective agreements
submitted to it but also to make them compulsory for
firms that have not subscribed to them. Since 1963
the Foundation of Labor has assumed the responsibility

for approving collective agreements and the Council
of Mediators has become responsible for examining the
general effect of collective agreements on total
labor costs.[5] Any agreement considered excessively
costly is referred to the Minister of Social Affairs,
who may reject it.

Management-labor cooperation is institutionalized
in the Foundation of Labor, which has been the scene
of centralized wage bargaining and has had a powerful
advisory role in the adjudication of wage claims in
various industries concerning requests for wages
above or below the national pattern. Thus, it permits industrial self-policing to prevent inflationary
accords. The Foundation acts as a channel among
labor, management, and the government and as an advisory body to the Cabinet. It was one of the primary influences inducing the government to end its
strict controls over wages and prices in 1968 and to
allow the adoption of a relatively free wage system.[6]

The Economic and Social Council is an autonomous
body composed of representatives of the government,
the employers' organizations, and the trade unions.
The Cabinet must request the Council's opinion on
all economic and social legislation contemplated.
However, the Council is not dependent upon the Cabinet and may issue unsolicited opinions on economic
and social matters at any time and, thus, can stimulate action by the Cabinet. In order to enlist additional pressure upon the Cabinet in favor of its
initiatives, the Council sends copies of all its reports to members of the Parliament.[7] This practice
has been highly effective, for the Council representatives form an important portion of the Parliament's
national constituency.

The Dutch wage control policy, which had made
the wage structure in the Netherlands one of the
most stable in the world, was recently discontinued.
The Netherlands' participation in the EEC is partially
responsible for the liberalization of the wage control system, for its economic partners in the EEC
pursue less controlled wage systems, thereby posing
the problem of a serious exodus of skilled workers

from the Netherlands to other member countries, especially Germany. Moreover, the two parties in the
Foundation of Labor were unable to hold down the
level of wage increases because of the tight labor
market and the high level of demand. Employers were
able and willing to pay higher wage increases, and
the trade unions realized that they could get higher
wages by trying to opt out of the national wages
policy. The unions therefore served notice that they
no longer wished to participate in the process of
centralized wages policy and that they preferred
free collective bargaining with the Minister of Social Affairs, retaining the right of rejection in
certain circumstances. As a result, an agreement
between the government and the Foundation of Labor
in 1968 assured freedom in wages policy.[8] Now the
social partners can determine wages and working conditions without governmental intervention, although
the government will retain supervisory power to
avoid wage increases endangering the general economic
situation of the country.

Since World War II the trade union movement has
obtained increasing influence over the level of
wages, the employment situation, and economic and
social life as a whole. Recently the unions have
proposed retained profits and wealth-sharing schemes,
"investment wages," in addition to normally negotiated
wage increases. This is an indication of the labor
movement's increasing attempts to influence nonwage
decisions and to initiate changes in the content and
form of bargaining.

The three Dutch trade union federations have
been strong and consistent supporters of European
integration. The NVV was one of the first labor
unions to call for an integration of national trade
union functions in order to meet the new conditions
brought about by the economic and political trends
in Western Europe. At a special NVV congress concerned with European problems in 1954, a resolution
was passed calling for European integration to preserve freedom and welfare in Europe and to remain
abreast of the production increases in the Soviet
Union and the United States.[9] The NVV has always

favored the creation of European organs of economic
control advised by representatives of the various
economic interest groups, as well as political union
to assure the concomitance of social and economic integration.[10] It lent its full support to the Rome
Treaties although it felt that the trade unions were
insufficiently consulted during their drafting and
deemed them insufficiently strong to achieve full
policy coordination of the member countries. In
order to strengthen the European Communities, the
NVV considers it indispensable to coordinate monetary
and fiscal policies within the framework of medium-
term planning for the Community as a whole.[11]

The attitude of the KAB toward the Paris and
Rome Treaties reflected the position of the WCL,
which regards integration as necessary for keeping
European political influence strong and for improving
European welfare. However, although the KAB believed
that the policies of the European Communities should
benefit the economic welfare of the workers, it opposed the creation of what it termed excessive uniformity in the social systems of different countries.

What matters is that the workers have an
equal share of the increasing prosperity.
The form of this share, either through
increases in wages or in social benefits
should be decided by the labor unions
themselves, not by supranational measures.[12]

The CNV also believed that European integration
would produce higher living standards and increase
prospects for economic and social cooperation. As
did its Catholic counterpart, it considered that social harmonization should come after economic integration and that it should not undermine the right
of each member state to express its individual aims
in this field.[13]

The initial attitude of the Dutch trade union
federations toward European integration mirrored
their privileged national situation: participation
in economic planning through the national Economic

and Social Council and excellent relations between
workers and employers. They wished the Consultative
Committee of the European Coal and Steel Community
(ECSC) to have a parity of representation between
Committee members with a background in trade unions
and those representing industrial enterprises. They
favored a strong Economic and Social Committee for
the EEC and wanted it to be able to offer unsolicited
advice to the European Commission and the Council of
Ministers. Their national aim of full employment was
reflected in their demand for a full employment policy and an investment policy on the European level.

Over the years the trade unions have developed
a detailed blueprint for a European Community commen-
surate with labor's aims. The three trade union federations favor an enlarged Community, including all
democratic European countries and capable of wielding
considerable influence in world affairs, particularly
able to forge satisfactory relations with Communist
states and to contribute substantial trade and aid
to the developing countries.[14] They believe that
the EEC should be strengthened and democratized:
strengthened in order to develop regional and structural policies and to permit the coordination of cyclical and fiscal policies essential to the maintenance of full employment, and democratized in order
to permit labor's full participation in European
policy making. Dutch labor feels that the EEC will
remain a technocracy too subservient to narrowly defined national interests unless its institutional
structure is transformed.[15] It has consistently applied pressure for revision of the EEC in order to
strengthen the European Commission and to confer
budgetary, supervisory, and legislative powers on
the European Assembly, since it has found the Commission and the Assembly the organs most amenable to its
influence.

BELGIUM

In Belgium economic interest groups are aligned
according to religion, ideology, and geography; and
the trade unions are enmeshed in Catholic, Socialist,

or Liberal subcultures. The labor movement includes
the Socialist-oriented General Federation of Belgian
Workers (FGTB), the Confederation of Belgian Christian
Trade Unions (CSC), and a small liberal union. The
rivalry between the FGTB and the CSC is not so intense as that between Christian and Socialist trade
unions in other countries, partly because their influence is geographically defined. The FGTB enjoys
a near monopoly in the Walloon South, whereas the
CSC is dominant in the North and in Flanders. Although these two organizations are equal in strength,
the FGTB is more influential among blue-collar workers, and the CSC organizes a slight majority of the
white-collar workers.[16] The liberal trade union has
a negligible influence over the labor movement because its members are spread thinly over the country
and over many industries.

The CSC is motivated by Christian social doctrine.
It aspires toward the gradual establishment of a social and economic order characterized by a fair distribution of wealth and equal opportunity for all to
develop their personality and aptitudes.[17] While
the CSC rejects Marxism, it also repudiates the
hegemony of a capitalistic policy as a leading principle in economic life. Its long-term program includes the achievement of economic democracy through
the participation of the workers in managing economic
and social life in all sectors and at all levels.
It advocates comanagement for the workers but opposes
nationalization. Despite its ideological differences
with the FGTB, the CSC has demonstrated an increasing
willingness to cooperate with it.

The FGTB is committed to a planned economy, including the establishment of an investment institution and public control over investment policy,
trusts, and holding companies. It regards the nationalization of the energy sector and the setting
of production targets for the private sector as the
only means of achieving economic expansion and full
employment.[18] It also believes that the workers
should participate in the direction of all phases of
the economy.

In Belgium the government does not intervene in the formation of wages. Wages and most working conditions are obtained by collective bargaining conducted autonomously by the social partners. In contrast with the situation in other member countries of the EEC, the Belgian Parliament has been concerned mainly with creating a framework for the conclusion of collective agreements and with making the norms included in these agreements obligatory for all enterprises of a sector.

Collaboration between workers and employers throughout the economy was established by the 1948 Law on the Organization of the Economy, which created a hierarchically coordinated system of bipartite or parity commissions.[19]

At the top of this hierarchy in the social field is a consultative body, the National Council of Labor. This organ enjoys the right to propose opinions on general social problems to the Ministry of Labor and the Parliament. It has prepared most of the legislation on paid vacations, family allowances, accidents at work, safety, and hygiene.[20] It has also been instrumental in the conclusion of two national agreements that have all the characteristics of collective agreements. One of these relates to the works council and the other covers accidents at work.

Parallel to the National Council of Labor is the Central Economic Council, which has consultative competence on problems of the national economy. Directly below this organ are joint industrial councils with consultative status.

Bipartite commissions at the industry level are the units of collective bargaining. They are composed of an equal number of heads of enterprises and trade union officials, headed by an independent president and vice-president. Their tasks include the establishment of general bases for remuneration corresponding to various degrees of occupational qualification, deliberation on working conditions,

and assistance to government officials in preparing
and executing social legislation for a particular
sector.[21] They are also concerned with apprentice
training and with maintaining close relations with
institutes of vocational training and orientation.
In addition these commissions play an important role
in the conciliation of conflicts. Collective agreements in Belgium cover a wide variety of matters
that in other countries are usually dealt with by
legislation, including the determination of minimum
wages and the variation of wages in relation to the
price index, the relation between wage increases and
increases in productivity, the establishment of wage
categories, and even supplements for unemployment
compensation.[22] Decisions within parity commissions
are taken unanimously and made obligatory for an entire industry by royal decree.

Outside of parity commissions, collective agreements may be concluded for a group of enterprises
or within a single enterprise. In the latter case
agreements frequently set forth modes of applying a
collective agreement emanating from a parity commission. In most cases they provide for additional
benefits, such as yearly bonuses.

At the level of the enterprise, workers and employers collaborate within the works council. This
organ has consultative status only: the right to
give opinions and suggestions on all measures pertaining to the organization and productivity of the
enterprise. It also has the corresponding right to
receive information and reports on the financial
situation of the enterprise. The principal activity
of this organ, however, is the modification and formulation of shop regulations. Among its other duties
are the review of criteria for hiring and firing and
the management of social services established by the
enterprise for the welfare of the workers.

Outside of the parity commissions, employers
and workers have periodic recourse to national agreements or recommendations defining principles of social and economic action. The first instance of
such an undertaking was the Agreement on Social

Solidarity, concerning social and economic problems
of the postwar period.[23] Belgium's present system
of social security and of wage determination and its
complex of parity commissions are the result of this
agreement. A similar agreement instituted and defined the works council.

Parallel to this practice on the national level
has been the tendency of workers and employers to
pursue unofficial negotiations within a small committee outside of the industry-level parity commissions.
The ability of workers and employers to collaborate
fruitfully outside the institutional framework provided for this purpose is evidence of the excellent
state of industrial relations in Belgium.

The FGTB lent its enthusiastic support to the
Schuman Plan for economic and ideological reasons.
It has consistently demanded, however, that welfare
policy and labor standards be considered among the
major purposes of the Paris Treaty and not merely
as adjuncts of economic policy.[24] Parallel with its
demand for a supranational welfare policy has been
its campaign for the harmonization of wages, social
security, and working conditions throughout the ECSC.
Given the high cost structure of Belgian coal and
steel, the workers were unable to achieve their goals
of a shorter workweek, higher wages, and improved
working conditions without undermining Belgium's
trade prospects. The answer was found in the harmonization of social conditions throughout the ECSC
and in the demand for the strengthening of supranational institutions.[25]

The FGTB's espousal of supranationalism is also
a result of its internationalism and its Socialist
commitment to a cooperative raising of living and
working standards. Its economic and social doctrine
dictates its view of European integration; it approved
the creation of the EEC because it regarded it as a
force potentially capable of opposing cartels, and
it supports planning at the European level through
the creation of public enterprises and of a public
investment fund capable of neutralizing cyclical
fluctuations.[26] Given these ambitious goals, the

FGTB has always considered the structure and powers
of EEC institutions inadequate. It argues that the
powers of decision of the Council of Ministers are
too great for an organ so susceptible to national
interests and that the powers of the European Assembly and the European Commission are too limited.
The latter should have the power requisite for a
true executive, and the European Assembly should be
financially independent of the national legislatures.[27]
As do other trade unions, the FGTB would like the
Economic and Social Committee to enjoy the right of
initiative for problems within its competence and to
be obligatorily consulted on every decision or recommendation of the European executives.

The FGTB has often criticized the lack of provision for an active social policy in the Rome Treaties
--i.e., the assumption that social progress will automatically result from the functioning of the Common
Market. It complains that the few concrete measures
on social affairs included in them were inserted
mainly to placate France, and it urges the drafting
of a detailed harmonization program and a timetable
for its implementation.[28] However, while this labor
union may criticize gaps in the Rome Treaties, its
strong ideological commitment to Europe has led it
to demand increasing doses of supranational power
rather than to reject Europe altogether. Moreover,
the FGTB has always distinguished itself from its
counterparts in other EEC countries by its frequent
appeals for strengthening the European trade union
organizations and for forging a common front with
the Christian and Communist labor movements.

The CSC supports European integration for essentially the same motives as the FGTB. For the CSC,
as for other Christian trade unions, Catholic labor
doctrine provides the ideological basis for support.
When the Schuman Plan was proposed, the CSC feared
the possible effect of the ECSC on the high wages
and social costs in Belgium. It was equally reticent
at the prospect of social harmonization within the
EEC. It soon reversed its position, however, and
now considers integration a positive factor for progress in wages and working conditions.

Unlike their Christian counterparts in other EEC countries, particularly the French Confederation of Democratic Trade Unions (CFDT), the CSC is convinced that free play of competition and prices is incapable of ensuring optimal production or full employment. It believes that enterprises on the European level should be managed by organs composed of public authorities and has seconded the FGTB's demands for a strong supranational welfare policy.[29] Initially it did not share the latter's enthusiasm for extending supranational authority; a politically united Europe now has become one of its basic objectives.

GERMANY

The German Labor Organization (DGB) includes 87 percent of all organized workers in the German Federal Republic.[30] Its highly effective organizational structure and considerable financial resources make it the most powerful labor union in the EEC. Among its material endowments are banks, housing projects, and insurance societies. In addition, extensive resources have enabled the DGB to establish a separate career structure and to form a strong bureaucratic elite within its ranks.

Although the DBG's constitution proclaims its independence vis-à-vis the government, local authorities, and political parties, it has close affinities with the Social Democratic Party (SPD). Nearly all DGB leaders are Social Democrats, and a majority of its membership has similar political inclinations. However, since the SPD revised its program at its Bad Godesberg congress in 1959, eliminating the last vestiges of Socialism and endorsing free enterprise, the DGB has stood to the left of the SPD. The DBG's program places more emphasis on planning and suggests that some transfer into public ownership must be included in measures required for public control of economic power. Although the DGB leaders are active in the left ranks of the SPF, the organization cannot maintain overly close connections with the latter for fear of alienating the large minority of its

members who have Christian Democratic leanings. DGB
leaders have been able to maintain the unity of its
politically diverse elements by their nonpartisan
attitude and by espousing codetermination as their
central rallying point. Since the experience of collaboration between Marxist and Christian unionists
is of postwar origin and has no basis in tradition,
it is justified in terms of the goal of codetermination, a social theory on which both labor camps can
agree. Although the WCL has worked vigorously to
reestablish a German affiliate and a new German Federation of Christian Trade Unions was founded in
1955 with strong financial backing, it has attracted
only insignificant defections from the DGB.

In Germany collective bargaining is conducted
autonomously by the social partners. Bargaining
produces two types of agreements. "Manteltarif,"
or blanket, agreements are concluded at the national
level between employers' organizations and the industrial union. These agreements regulate overall
conditions for a period of several years. However,
industry-wide bargaining does not result in wage
uniformity; it sets only minimum terms of employment,
what the marginal firm can afford to pay. Supplementary "Lohntarif," or wage and holiday, agreements
are annually negotiated closer to the point of productivity, at the local level. Deviation from the minimum rate is a normal practice, and the spread is
often substantial.[31]

The postwar establishment of codetermination
remains one of German labor's most significant
achievements. Codetermination was introduced in the
steel industry at the time of decartelization in
1947 and was instituted in the coal-mining and iron
ore-mining industries through the Special Codetermination Law of 1951. Under its terms the supervisory boards of the coal-mining and iron- and steel-
producing companies must be composed of representatives of the stockholders and the employees on a
parity basis. The employee members of the supervisory board must include representatives of the
wage-earning and salaried personnel employed by a
company. They are nominated by the works council

after consultation with the trade union representatives within the company and with the trade union federation. The wage-earning and salaried members of the works council then meet separately to conduct secret elections.[32]

The managing board of a company subject to special codetermination must include a labor manager with equal rights. He can be neither appointed nor dismissed against the votes of a majority of the employees' representatives on the supervisory board. Nominations for the position are made by the mine workers' or metalworkers' union and submitted to the works council and supervisory board of the company. The labor manager has special responsibility for almost all questions within the competence of the works council. He spends most of his time supervising the staff departments under his direct control. The personnel department for which he is responsible may include such sections as job placement, job evaluation, labor law, and wages and salaries. The social department usually includes family welfare, housing, a clinic, accident prevention, and a shop for disabled workers. However, the establishment of the true collegiality of the labor manager with other members of the management board has been problematic.[33]

General codetermination was created by the Law on the Constitution of the Enterprise of 1952, which applies to virtually all private corporations except those subject to the Special Codetermination Law. The DGB's draft for a general codetermination law, sponsored by the SPD, would have extended almost all aspects of the Special Codetermination Law to the rest of the economy and to the entire administration at all levels of the government. These proposals were also designed to give greater influence to the unions by granting them the right to convene the works council and to participate in its meetings without the council's request. However, the employers were unwilling to make the concessions into which they had been forced in the special cases of iron, coal, and steel. The final and milder version of the bill was passed by the Christian Democratic Union (CDU). In enterprises within the scope of this

law, only one-third of the supervisory boards must
be representatives of the employees. They are elected
by the employees in general, equal, and direct elections and are not appointed by the works council, as
under the Special Codetermination Law.[34]

A further gain in industrial democracy was
achieved in 1956 through a law applying a modified
form of codetermination to holding companies of coal
and steel industries. By 1953 recartelization was
well under way. The regulation of these matters had
passed from the occupation powers to the High Authority of the ECSC, and several holding companies were
formed. Because these companies did not engage in
the primary production of coal, iron, and steel and
also owned nonproducing companies, the codetermination laws seemed inapplicable. After three years of
controversy the Bundestag passed a bill supplementing the Special Codetermination Law. Holding companies are subject to special codetermination when
more than one-half of their total turnover is derived
from the primary production of iron, steel, and coal.[35]
The DGB and the SPD were overridden by the CDU since
labor preferred the application of codetermination
on the basis of personnel rather than turnover. Under the terms of this law the labor manager is chosen
in the same way as other members of the managerial
board, without any special voice for labor; and the
majority of the labor members of the supervisory
board are elected by the employees from among themselves, with only a minority to be selected by the
unions.

The extension of codetermination to all industrial enterprises has long occupied a central position in the DGB's basic program. The most recent
DGB proposal aimed at instituting codetermination in
all industrial companies with at least 2,000 employees and an annual turnover of DM 150 million. The
Budenkopf Commission, formed by Chancellor Willy
Brandt to study the question, in its 1970 report
pronounced itself against the general extension of
full codetermination. Instead, it proposed that the
supervisory boards of firms with a minimum of 2,000
employees should be composed of a ratio of seven

representatives of management to five staff members,
although both sides of industry would enjoy an equal
vote in electing management boards. The fate of
general codetermination is uncertain, for it rests
upon the assent of SPD's coalition partner, the Free
Democratic Party (FDP). The latter is generally
against the principle of worker participation in
management.

The DGB is determined to safeguard its codetermination gains under the proposed European Company
Law of the EEC. It has been successful in rallying
other European trade unions behind it and in gaining
the sympathetic ear of the European Commission. The
latter has firmly supported worker participation in
the draft statute for a European company and has en-
listed the help of the European trade union organizations in formulating the proposal.

When the ECSC was in the process of being established, the DGB expressed strong reservations.[36]
At that time its negative attitude was influenced by
the opposition of the SPD to the ECSC; however, these
reservations were dispelled over the years, largely
as a result of the participation of key union officials in the Consultative Committee, the Common Assembly, and the Committee of XXI. They saw that
this institution could be of use in achieving cherished national demands. The claims of the DGB for a
forty-hour week without reduction of pay were strongly
enhanced by the High Authority's comparative wage,
hour, and purchasing-power studies. In addition,
ECSC institutions had the power to curb the unchecked
concentration of the German steel, coal, and proces-
sing industries that labor feared. In the early
years of the ECSC, the DGB opposed European integration whenever a strong national interest was jeopardized, as in the case of cartelized coal sales or the
free movement of labor.[37]

From a lukewarm adherent of supranationalism,
the German labor movement has become a strong supporter of the economic and political unity of Europe.
The fact remains that the ECSC and the EEC have become important elements of an economic environment

with which the DGB must cope. For German labor this
means the challenge of ensuring trade union participation in the functioning of European institutions.
It is critical of the fact that no means of direct
influence on EEC organs were accorded the trade
unions, that they were granted the right of consultation only. It has frequently condemned the fact that
the Economic and Social Committee does not enjoy the
right of initiative and that it is composed on a
tripartite rather than on a parity basis. In the
DGB's opinion the Committee should perform important
economic functions, such as exercising jurisdiction
over investment policy and the European Investment
Bank.[38] In the late 1960's the DGB began to press
for revision of the Rome Treaties in order to establish a European Commission endowed with true executive powers and a financially independent, directly
elected European parliament. It is deeply concerned
that the economic groupings and mergers resulting
from economic union will elude both national and EEC
political control unless the latter's institutions
are both strengthened and democratized.

Over and above these considerations, the German
labor movement is attracted to European integration
as a logical extension of codetermination. The Rome
and Paris Treaties can be used as a basis for working
toward higher living standards through a genuine relationship between the two sides of industry. The
DGB has been in the forefront of European labor's
recent efforts to achieve Community-wide collective
bargaining, codetermination in European companies,
and in defining a social policy going beyond the
Rome Treaties.

ITALY

In Italy labor unions are ideologically oriented
and affiliated with political parties. They are controlled by the parties; and, although they participate
in intraparty debates, they are generally reliant on
the political strategy of their respective parties
rather than originators of party policy. Until recently the unions lacked the organization and social

acceptance to engage in collective bargaining from a
position of strength and preferred to meet their
counterparts in the political arena, influencing
legislative activity not so much by lobbying as by
controlling centers of power from within. In Italy
the party system is highly fragmented and faction
ridden; it is therefore possible for interest groups
to engulf party positions and to participate directly
in the exercise of power.

The largest and strongest labor organization in
Italy is the Communist-dominated General Confederation of Italian Labor (CGIL). It is the only confederation in Italy that can collect regular financial
contributions from its members. During the 1950's
the CGIL exploited its superior size, wealth, and
organizational strength to pose as the only genuine
representative of the working class and the only pro-
ponent of Socialism. However, it suffered a sharp
decline at the end of the decade, owing to abuse of
the confederation as a political weapon and to a loss
of prestige after the upheavals in Eastern Europe.
During the 1960's Communist labor attempted to forge
a new role for itself in Italian political and economic life by concentrating on trade union issues in
industry and reducing its purely political activity.
As part of its image transformation the CGIL has
sought to mitigate its subordination to the Communist
Party and to appear as the only nonideological, non-
party, and genuinely unitary labor union. This policy
was aimed particularly at placating the large Socialist minority in CGIL ranks. As a consequence, the
Socialists in CGIL have indeed acquired increased
leverage in policy making and have played a major
role in pushing the CGIL to active acceptance of the
EEC.[39] Underlying its attempts to create a more
moderate, unitary CGIL image is that organization's
long-term aim of reorganizing the entire Italian
labor movement under its own guidance.

The second largest Italian labor confederation,
the Italian Confederation of Trade Unions (CISL), is
affiliated with the Christian Democratic Party.
Most of the parliamentary deputies of the CISL were
elected on Christian Democratic lists. They are

torn by the dilemma of being true to union ideals at
the risk of causing the government to fall in a
Parliament run by a narrow majority and of exercising
political responsibility at the cost of delaying
union goals. This basic incompatibility of roles has
caused dissension within the confederation. However,
the fact that labor deputies hold the balance of
power within the party means that the latter must
make certain concessions to labor. Of course, the
Christian Democratic Party will extract quid pro quo
from CISL deputies, but there is no clearly defined
Christian Democratic policy. Torn by right, center,
and left factions, the party structure permits a
significant amount of manipulative behavior by CISL
deputies. Because it has been successful in compet-
ing with the CGIL and in the struggle for power within
the Christian Democratic Party, the CISL has managed
to stave off party members who would make it an openly
Catholic trade union.[40] Thus, while the CISL is
closely tied to the Christian Democratic Party, it
is not dominated by it.

Italian labor's tragedy has been the failure of
Socialism in Italy, which has vitiated its strength
by seeking to reconcile incompatible elements. The
Socialist Party, which is the bulwark of democratic
labor movements in other EEC countries, supports
three distinct confederations in Italy. The CGIL
enjoys the left-wing Socialist support of the center
faction, and the Italian Union of Labor (UIL) is a
Social Democratic trade union with Republican support. In the UIL leadership and following are evenly
split among Social Democrats and Republicans. Both
influences within the union tend to cancel each
other out, so that neither party can force the policy
orientation of the UIL.[41] Moreover, the UIL has
none of the interlocking directorates that are characteristic of the CISL and the CGIL.

Unlike the CISL the UIL is not averse to cooperating with the CGIL. It refuses to stay out of
specific negotiations merely because the CGIL might
also be active in them and insists that where agita-
tions are of interest to labor's goals there should
be no objection to working in unison with the CGIL.

It is between extremes in its political philosophy
and considers itself as a third force between the
CGIL and CISL. Because of this it has been frequently
attacked by both, depending upon its stand on a particular controversy. The CISL and the UIL often have
demonstrated different strategies and tactics because
of their differing political and philosophic premises.
Although their policies on European integration are
similar and although both are affiliated with the
International Confederation of Free Trade Unions
(ICFTU), the CISL tends to resent the presence of a
small, independent UIL.

In the late 1960's the Italian labor movement
embarked upon a profound and far-reaching renewal
of its objectives, organization, and tactics. At
that time all three confederations undertook organizational changes intended to decentralize policy
making. Together they developed a broad program for
social reform within the Italian political system
and sought a new role for labor within the nation by
means of unification of the confederations and their
autonomy from the political parties. These dramatic
transformations have been apparent since the period
of industrial strife referred to as the "hot autumn
of 1969" and represent a clear break with the past.
Although these changes are interrelated, they may be
examined separately for the purpose of analysis.

The renewal of grass-roots activity in the three
labor confederations has been in process within certain of their members since the early mid-1960's and
has occurred in response to demographic changes and
pressures from the rank and file. The innovators in
this process were the metalworkers' federations of
the three organizations. Because a complete renewal
of leadership and widespread debates on organization
had occurred well before the surfacing of discontent
in 1969, these federations were able to retain firm
control of their membership during the "hot autumn."

In response to pressures from its Socialist minority, the metalworkers' union (FIOM) of the CGIL
chose the path of grass-roots democracy as early as
1963, a decision that resulted in significant changes

in leadership and a wider margin of autonomy from
the CGIL in order to seek united action with its CISL
and UIL counterparts. A parallel change in leadership occurred in the metalworkers' union (FIM) of the
CISL; and with the removal of the entire leadership
of the 1950's, which was dedicated to cold war strategies, the FIM acquired freedom from the political
restraints imposed by Christian Democratic ideology.
Although a minority union, the UIL has undergone
changes comparable in scope with those of its larger
counterparts and has succeeded precisely where the
Socialist Party has failed: in recruiting young,
committed Socialists.

The demands for wage increases that were among
the precipitators of the 1969 disturbances were formulated at the base of the unions and as a result of
widespread debate. The unity displayed by the three
labor groups at the summit was paralleled at the company level and expressed in new bodies called "workers' assemblies." The latter not only generated demands but also allowed the rank and file to manage
the strategy of conflict and to monitor the progress
of negotiations until the final ratification of
agreements. Throughout 1969 and 1970 workers' assemblies were established in workshops, depots, work
teams, and assembly lines as well as at the factory
level; and all now elect their own delegates to the
various councils and committees within the enterprise, rather than their being selected from above
by trade union officials. Debate still rages within
the unions on the proper relationship between these
new forms of labor representation and the unions,
but their validity as a means of labor participation
and trade union presence within the enterprise is
generally accepted. They have played an important
role in negotiating agreements on working conditions;
and their continued existence beyond the settlements
of 1969 points to the legitimacy of concluding collective agreements at the company level, overlapping
collective agreements in national and industry-wide
contracts--a situation reminiscent of the collective
bargaining system in Britain.

However, while the unions may evidence the same
desire for equality and participation sought by the

extreme Left and the student movement in Italy, labor
has deliberately dissociated itself from the political
goals and methods of the latter groups that the more
superficial convergence of aims among them might suggest. It is more accurate to describe the unions as
leaders in the regeneration of the Left rather than
as ploys of the extreme Left.

The democratization of the unions and the new
surge for participation embodied in such organs as
the workers' assemblies cannot be viewed apart from
labor's new commitment to far-reaching social reform
within the Italian nation. The goals jointly promoted by the trade unions since 1969 overlap the
traditional subjects of contract negotiations and
are directed at reforms in housing, health, education,
and transportation. These demands are couched in
broad programs and include such proposals as rent
control, management forms for the construction of
public housing, and new policies for Italy's depressed
South and for agriculture. Previously these demands
were presented to the parties for their mediation,
but they are now the subject of direct negotiations
between labor and the national cabinet. The movement
toward the unification of the three labor groups has
enhanced labor's efforts to wrest autonomy from the
political parties and to seize political initiatives
from them. In fact, the unions' capacity to formulate programs, to generate wide consensus, and to
mobilize the membership is partly a reflection of
the decline in effectiveness demonstrated by badly
split parties unable to aggregate the interests ar-
ticulated by labor into comprehensive policy proposals.

The settlements of 1969 represent a new balance
of political forces in Italy, for they were achieved
with the benevolent intervention of the minister of
labor. Whereas in France direct negotiations between interest groups and the relevant ministries
are government sponsored and deliberately designed
to reduce the influence of parties, in Italy today
the cabinet is compelled to deal directly with the
labor unions, eschewing the mediation of the parties.
The unions wield powerful leverage, for they can
brandish the new techniques developed in 1969:   the

broad mobilization of workers and the threat of massive strikes. Italian political parties will have to make serious efforts to prevent a lapse into corporatism by redefining their relations with the unions.

Forging a new role for labor in the Italian political system will depend not only upon redefining the unions' relationship with political parties but also upon the unification of the trade union confederations into a united labor front.

During the autumn of 1969 the three confederations collaborated in formulating claims and conducting negotiations, and they submitted the results of these for approval at joint meetings.

The following fall the general councils of the three labor groups met in Florence for four days of talks that culminated in a declaration of intention to coordinate their action at all levels and to express this unity in the creation of joint executive offices, public relations services, and research facilities.

Throughout 1971 the confederations convened at regular intervals to shape plans for an eventual organizational merger. During the meeting in November a timetable of fifteen months was set for complete unification, with the official dissolution of separate organizations taking place in September 1972 and formal inauguration of the new labor front occurring in 1973.

However, agreement on organization and social policy has been more easily achieved than agreement on political and international affiliation. Important differences continue to separate the three labor unions and can hardly be masked by organizational engineering. The CISL and the UIL maintain that the unified movement must not be linked with any political party, while the CGIL does not consider trade union membership incompatible with political office. On the contrary, its leaders assert that trade unionists cannot fulfill their political duties toward the working class unless they are free to be active in the parties of their choice.

An even more serious question is that of the international affiliation of the unified movement. The CGIL is prepared to renounce its affiliation with the WFTU, an association that had proved detrimental to its goals in the nation and in Europe. However, rather than switch international affiliation, it would renounce all organized international trade union collaboration in favor of loose ad hoc links with other national trade union movements. The CISL and the UIL, however, wish to retain their membership in the ICFTU, which represents the majority of trade unions in Western Europe, and insist that the new labor front be a member. They also wish to retain their positions within the ECFTUC.

To date, the unification of Italian labor has made significant progress only among the metalworkers. While there have been substantial moves toward joint action, there is still considerable reticence toward complete organizational merger within the ranks of the CISL and the UIL. This state of affairs is reflected in labor organizations within the EEC.

The CISL and the UIL are enthusiastic supporters of the European Communities, regarding them as the first step toward their cherished goal of European integration. Both consider an integrated Europe to be capable of alleviating the difficulties of the Italian economy through the importation of foreign capital and increased migration opportunities for Italian workers.[42] Both always have favored Community-wide collective bargaining as a means of achieving harmonization of Italian wages and working conditions upward toward those in other member countries. The CISL aspires toward a common European standard for working hours, overtime, and holiday pay. Both unions wish the workers to be represented in all Community organs.

Because of their weakness Italian unions are eager for the support of the European Communities and the stronger labor unions of the northern member

countries. Their dependence upon governmental action
to achieve their basic goals has prompted them to
transfer these aims to the European forum through
their spokesman in the European Assembly. Their demands at the European level parallel their domestic
campaigns for labor participation in economic planning and the development of a full employment policy.
Italian labor has consistently campaigned for a European regional policy, investment policy, and employment policy. It has greeted the Commission's two
medium-term economic plans with enthusiasm.

The CISL and the UIL have demonstrated great interest in the European Social Fund. Although the
UIL hoped that it would include provisions for cyclical unemployment and would accord more initiative
to the European Commission, it nevertheless considers
the Fund an important element of a European social
policy. All three Italian labor confederations have
expressed the desire for extensive revisions of the
Fund in order to improve its scope and powers.

When the ECSC was established, the CGIL followed
the policies of the WFTU and opposed European integration. Its attitude toward the EEC was also unfavorable. It regarded the EEC as a potential disas-
ter for the workers, certain to strengthen the
managerial class to the detriment of labor. However,
by 1961 the CGIL had developed a view of European
integration independently of the WFTU's determined
opposition. One inspiration and justification of
CGIL's independent European policy lies in the strong
Socialist presence in its ranks. Independence is
also explicable on the basis of the irreconcilable
differences of policy and style between the CGIL and
such staunchly orthodox members of the WFTU as the
French General Confederation of Labor (CGT), which
provides its leadership. The CGT will openly attack
such threatening aspects of capitalist reality as
the EEC, whereas the Italian Communists will attempt
to moderate capitalist manifestations of reality
through cooperation. Italian Communists have come
to regard the EEC as a reality that they must confront
positively. As long as they lack the strength to
destroy it, they must seek to mitigate its worst

features by attempting to influence it from within.
Thus, in the early 1960's there appeared a deep gulf
between the CGIL's and the WFTU's strategy toward
Europe.[43] Both the Italian Communist Party and the
CGIL felt that the EEC would enable capitalism to
overcome its weakness and that it was unwise to oppose an organization that helped contribute to Italy's
growing prosperity. Abetting the WFTU's propaganda
campaign against European unity meant isolation from
the political mainstream and forestalling working
relations with the Socialists.

When the CGT opposed its Italian counterpart's
attempt to establish a joint information bureau in
Brussels, the latter formed its own European office
in 1963. The CGIL's aim was not to influence the
EEC but to facilitate contacts with the non-Communist
trade unions. This move was taken with an eye to
CGIL's domestic interests. The maintenance of Communist-Socialist collaboration in the CGIL and the
long-term aim of alliance among Italy's left-wing
forces required convincing Communist attempts to
forge unity with moderate trade unions. CGIL's European policy is intended to provide evidence that it
can cooperate with other working-class groups in order
to achieve reform.

FRANCE

The French labor movement operates in a social
environment similar to that of the Italian labor
movement and has been beset with many of the same
problems. The weakness of organized labor is a result of France's economic and political history,
characterized by a slow rate of capitalist development, a Leftist revolutionary strain inherited by
the Communists after World War I, and tradition-bound
employers suspicious of organized labor. These conditions and the syndicalist tradition in France,
which proclaimed and perpetuated the virtues of loose
organization and low dues, has retarded the growth
and strength of French unionism. There still exists
latent suspicion of efforts to create centralized
union power. A large proportion of French workers

are not organized, and among workers affiliated with
labor organizations there are many who fail to pay
their contributions regularly and who regard their
organizations with a mixture of apathy and cynicism.
This helps perpetuate a trade unionism that does not
afford its members a sense of continuing representation and integration in industrial life. The chronic
weakness of French unions has made them dependent
upon political action for social gains.

The structural forms of French trade unions
also help perpetuate an ideologically and politically
oriented unionism rather than a job-oriented unionism.
French unions were constructed on a geographic rather
than on a craft or industrial basis. All French confederations are decentralized. Their national congresses meet biannually and are dominated by local
units rather than affiliated national unions. Except
for textile, metal, and chemical workers, regional
unions grouping all local unions across industrial
lines have been the true source of power.[44] In other
European countries the growth of industrial unionism
has occurred simultaneously with a decline in the
regional organizations, whereas in France regional
bodies are still powerful.

The Communist CGT has managed to retain the
leadership of the most active and articulate industrial workers. It boasts the largest membership of
the confederations, but it has remained frozen in
its postwar mold and displays little of the initiative and flexibility of its Italian counterpart.
Its leader, Georges Seguy, justified its lack of initiative during the 1968 strikes by characterizing
the union as "la grande force tranquille." Therefore, although the CGT surpasses the moderate unions
in revolutionary slogans and ambitious programs, the
façade of militancy covers a bureaucratized organization, weak in initiative and subservient to the
French Communist Party. As does its Italian counterpart, the French Communist Party controls its labor
union by a system of interlocking directorates at
all levels and the interchangeability of activists
between the party and the union. However, in contrast with Italy, the workers to whom the French

Communist Party most appeals are not the depressed.
The CGT has had its greatest success with the younger
workers.

The French Confederation of Christian Trade
Unions (CFTC) shed its confessional character to become the French Confederation of Democratic Trade
Unions (CFDT) in 1964 and to form a rallying center
for all free French labor. It emerged as the best-
organized and most militant labor union, although
second in membership to the CGT. A small part of
the CFTC refused to accept deconfessionalization and
a change of name and formed a new rump CFTC, which
is recognized by the French government. The old
CFTC was rent by the antagonistic outlooks of two
rival social philosophies among its leadership. The
younger, more aggressive group of leaders demonstrated
a greater willingness to experiment and an orientation
toward a nondoctrinaire Socialism. This group was
behind the 1964 reorganization that divested the
union of all references to Christian institutions.

The CFDT is more explicitly committed to the
principle of a Socialist society than the avowedly
Socialist union the General Confederation of Workers'
Organizations (CGT-FO). This minority union was
formed from a dissident section of the CGT after World
War II over the issue of Marshall Plan aid. Its
greatest strength lies in the civil servants, the
textile industry, and banking. As a moderate, ostensibly Socialist union, it suffers from the effects
of a strong, well-organized Communist trade union on
the left and is reluctant to cooperate with the latter for fear of losing its identity. Therefore, the
CGT-FO's top leadership avoids cooperating with the
CGT, although unity is occasionally practiced at the
plant level. The CGT-FO is highly suspicious of
CFDT's deconfessionalization and cites the latter's
continued ties with the WCL as evidence of persistent
church ties.[45] It resents the CFDT's willingness to
engage in joint action with the CGT and their formal
pact of 1966 for unity on economic questions.

Plural unionism has weakened the influence of
organized labor in France. Competition among unions

provides the temptation to let one's rival shoulder
the constraints and to act more militantly. However,
cooperation among the CFDT and the CGT since 1966
has enhanced labor's effectiveness and has helped
mitigate the adverse effects of divisiveness. French
labor has a history of common action in times of
political crises. A common front was displayed
briefly in 1967 against de Gaulle's proposal for
emergency powers and during the disturbances of
spring 1968. Unfortunately, this bestows recurring
legitimacy on Communist labor without compromising
its traditional revolutionary appeal.

An improvement in industrial relations is apparent in the new large companies and plants in elec-
tronics, electrometals, chemicals, and petroleum.[46]
In these sectors the achievement of a higher standard
of living and relative affluence is reflected in the
fact that local union bodies are becoming integrated
in these enterprises. Here the function of unionism
seems more linked with its role in industrial relations. In other sectors, however, there is a marked
contrast between poorly developed industrial relations and advanced social legislation. In most cases
of collective bargaining the negotiating unit is the
primary employers' organization, either local or regional. The moderate unions have sought to launch
industry-wide negotiations on a national basis in
order to offset their weakness at the local level,
for only the CGT can afford local bargaining. The
employers' organizations are far superior to the
unions in discipline, resources, and solidarity.
Their staff greatly outweighs that of the unions.
Opposite the well-organized employers' associations,
the unions are divided and short of means, for, given
their differences, no consistent pooling of strength
is possible. Collective bargaining legislation does
not require a sole bargaining agent. Provision is
made for participation by "the most representative
organization" or "several most representative organizations," even though they may represent a minority
of the labor force.[47] This practice tends to insti-
tutionalize the divisions in French unionism.

Because the unions are insufficiently strong to
satisfy most of their basic demands through collective

bargaining, they have recourse to political action
to achieve their goals. The government has an extensive role in determining wages and working conditions;
and government determination of family allowances,
social insurance levels, and fringe benefits removes
at least one-third of the workers' remuneration from
the realm of private bargaining.[48] By shop steward
laws and laws ensuring union functions at the plant
level, the state sets the basic conditions for workers' representation in the shop. One of the basic
objectives of the widespread strikes of May 1968 was
to strengthen the union's role and representation
within the enterprise. The Grenelle Accord, which
was concluded among the labor unions, the employers'
associations, and the government and which restored
social peace, provided that the issue of union rights
would be the subject of legislation.[49] A statute
passed in December 1968 guaranteed the representation
of all major federations in enterprises of fifty or
more employees and some of the basic rights sought
in the strike, such as the right to hold union meetings in the plant and payment to union delegates who
lose time through handling of worker grievances.
The Grenelle Accord is in the tradition of the
Matignon Agreement of 1936, which achieved major social gains with the help of the government during a
time of social disturbance.

    The weakness of French unions has led them to
seek governmental intervention in order to obtain
bargaining rights, but they are concerned about governmental intervention in their negotiations in the
public sector. The French government employs more
than one-fourth of the civilian, nonagricultural
wage earners in the administration and the nationalized industries, and nationalized enterprises are
exempt from the laws governing collective bargaining.[50]
After reviewing the past trend of wages, the government consults the unions and fixes lump-sum increases
in wages in the light of guidelines set in the plan.
Bargaining can affect only the distribution of the
sum, and the constraints of the plan function as
those of profitability in private enterprise. The
unions are concerned with the governmental practice
of wage policies in the public sector based upon
economic policies with which they do not agree; for

although French labor participates in the national economic planning process, it plays only an advisory, consultative role and shares the desire of other European labor organizations to secure control over nonwage factors.

The original CFTC supported the European Communities in principle as a potential field for economic democracy. It believed that its social doctrine of class collaboration and harmony could be achieved by tripartite commissions at all levels of the economy, both national and international.[51]

Its successor, the CFDT, has transferred its goals of a planned economy, democratically managed, to the European setting. Its design for a workers' Europe is one of the most ambitious among those proposed by the labor unions. It includes trade union supervision of key industrial and commercial sectors of the European economy, including regional planning and a voice for labor in the entire range of decisions taken by the European institutions and industries.[52] Only in a fully united European union, not in a customs union, can labor's goals of full employment and the upward harmonization of living conditions be achieved.

The CGT-FO has been a steadfast supporter of European integration and of supranationalism in principle. This enthusiasm was initially tempered with some practical reservations concerning the free movement of labor and those aspects of labor policy in which the total cost bills of other member countries are below the French cost structure. As in Italy, the loyalty of French trade unions to the European Communities is partially inspired by their domestic weakness. Because they depend upon governmental action in the national arena, they have easily transferred their social demands to European institutions. Long-term CGT-FO aims include common policies for each sector developed by the European executives with the aid of the trade unions and social prosperity resulting from European social policies and Community-wide collective bargaining.[53] In order to achieve these ambitious goals, a European political authority is essential.

Like its Italian counterpart, the CGIL, the
CGT's initial attitude toward European integration
was one of complete opposition. It condemned the
ECSC as a conspiracy of monopolies and as part of a
NATO plot against the Soviet Union. Although this
attitude softened considerably over the years, the
CGT displayed none of the adaptability of the CGIL.
The policy of the CGT long mirrored that of the
WFTU, whose secretary-general, Louis Saillant, came
from its ranks. Like the WFTU it regarded the CGIL's
idea of a united action of Communist and non-Communist unions within the EEC as a dangerous reformist
idea, a sentimental illusion detracting from the
necessity of fierce struggle against the EEC. Until
the mid-1960's it resisted all CGIL efforts to elicit
participation in establishing a Brussels office and
in seeking genuine unity with the non-Communist
unions. The gulf between the French and Italian Communist labor unions was paralleled by a dispute between the Italian and French Communist Parties,
mainly over the issue of polycentrism. It was only
with the satisfactory resultion of this dispute at
the Geneva conference in 1965, and the San Remo conference of the following year, that the CGT would
accept coordination with the CGIL within the EEC.[54]
In the compromise effected at San Remo, the French
Communist Party adopted most of the Italian positions
on the EEC. Both the CGT and the CGIL have come to
realize that in order to remain in the forefront of
the labor movement, they have to reorient their activity with respect to the European Communities.

Although labor's support for the ECSC and the
EEC included a wide range of divergent national as-
pirations, all labor groups saw in a larger economic
space the possibility of solving economic and social
problems by more modern and rational methods. Both
the Christian and Socialist labor organizations have
internationalist traditions and are committed to
democratic economic planning over the widest area
possible. Since the neoliberal philosophy underlying
the Rome and Paris Treaties does not coincide with
this doctrine, the trade unions have sought to develop broad programs to strengthen and democratize
supranational authority and to ensure that the workers obtain their fair share of the beneifts of

TABLE 1

Trade Unions in the Six and in Britain

| | 1 | 2 | 3 | 4 | Trade Union Strength (thousands) | | | | | 10 |
	Total Population (millions)	Civil Labor Force (millions)	Wage and Salary Earners (millions)	Unemployed (per-cent of col. 2)	5 ICFTU	6 WCL	7 WFTU	8 Other	9 Total	Workers Organized (col. 9 as percent of col. 3)
Belgium	9.7	3.7	2.8	2.5	FGTB 760	CSC 878		218	1,856	66
France	50.3	20.3	15.3	1.1	CGT-FO 500	CFDT 800	CGT 1,500	300	3,050	20
Germany	60.8	26.5	21.4	0.7	DGB 6,400	CGB 200		1,300	7,900	37
Italy	54.1	19.3	12.6	3.4	UIL 500		CGIL 3,000	1,000	7,000	57
Luxembourg	.3	0.1	0.1	0.0	CGTL 30	LCGB 10		10	50	50
Netherlands	12.9	4.5	3.6	1.4	NVV 560	NKV 420 CNV 240		300	1,520	42
Community	188.1	74.4	55.8	1.7	11,250	2,548	4,500	3,128	21,466	38
Britain	55.6	25.4	23.1	2.0	TUC 9,362			1,312	10,674	46

Note: Cols. 1-4 are for 1969; cols. 5-10 are for various years from 1966 to 1969.

Source: European Communities, Press and Information Service, Trade Union News from the European Community (Summer 1971).

integration. Also, labor favors the idea of a unified, enlarged, and democratic Europe as a means to
Western European influence in world affairs.

Thus, while there may have been little unanimity
among labor organizations on a specific program or
on the scope and function of European institutions,
a sufficient basis of consensus prevailed when the
European Communities were established to form the
basis of European trade union organizations functioning as European interest groups, not as international
labor organizations.

NOTES

1. Derk Roemer, "Trade Unions in the Netherlands," Free Labor World (June 1965), p. 180. The
NVV has 526,425 members, the NKV has 420,000, and
the CNV has 230,000.

2. Everett M. Kassalow, Trade Unions and Industrial Relations: An International Comparison (New
York: Random House, 1969), p. 259.

3. John P. Windmuller, "Post-War Wage Determination in the Netherlands," Annals of the American
Academy of Political and Social Science (March 1957),
p. 116.

4. Derek Robinson, "National Wage and Incomes
Policies and the Trade Unions, Issues and Experiences,"
in Solomon Barkin et al., eds., International Labor
(New York: Harper & Row, 1967), p. 225.

5. Ibid.

6. Gordon L. Weil, The Benelux Nations: The
Politics of Small Country Democracies (New York:
Holt, Rinehart and Winston, 1970), p. 118.

7. Ibid., p. 120.

8. European Economic Community, Commission,
Exposé sur l'évolution de la situation sociale dans

la Communauté en 1967 (Brussels, February 1968), p. 111.

9.   International Confederation of Free Trade Unions, Activities Report of the Second World Congress (Brussels, 1951), appendix VIII, "Proposals Submitted by Affiliated Organizations."

10.   European Economic Community, European Parliamentary Assembly, Cahiers mensuels de documentation européenne (December 1959), p. 63.

11.   Ibid.

12.   "Le Conseil du K.A.B. et le problème de l'emploi," Labor (August 1958), p. 159.

13.   "Le Cinquantenaire du C.N.V.," Labor (October 1959), p. 227.

14.   European Communities, Press and Information Service, Trade Union News from the European Community (1967), 2, p. 16.

15.   Ibid. (1968), 1, p. 5.

16.   Weil, op. cit., p. 126.   The CSC includes 52 percent of white-collar and 51 percent of blue-collar workers.   The FGTB accounts for 41 percent of the white-collar and 54 percent of the blue-collar workers.

17.   Confederation of Belgian Christian Trade Unions, The Christian Trade Unions of Belgium (Brussels, March 1958), p. 4.

18.   Cahiers mensuels de documentation européenne (January 1961), p. 16.

19.   Marcel David, La participation des travailleurs à la gestion des entreprises privées dans les principaux pays d'Europe occidentale (Paris: Librarie Dalloz, 1959), p. 112.

20.   Joseph Fafchamps, <u>Les conventions collectives</u> <u>en Belgique</u> (Brussels: La Pensée Catholique, 1961), p. 51.

21.   <u>Ibid.</u>, p. 31.

22.   <u>Ibid.</u>

23.   <u>Ibid.</u>, p. 56.

24.   Ernst B. Haas, <u>The Uniting of Europe: Po-litical, Social, and Economic Forces</u> (Stanford, Calif.:   The University Press, 1958), p. 235.

25.   <u>Ibid.</u>, p. 237.

26.   <u>Cahiers mensuels de documentation européenne</u> (November 1961), p. 17.

27.   <u>Ibid.</u> (October 1960), p. 54.

28.   International Confederation of Free Trade Unions, <u>Information Bulletin</u>, IX, 20 (Brussels, No-vember 1, 1958), 151.

29.   Auguste Cool, "L'action de mouvement syndical chrétien," <u>Labor</u> (August 1959), p. 185.

30.   William H. McPherson, "Labor Relations in Post-War Germany," <u>Annals of the American Academy of Political and Social Science</u> (March 1957), p. 56.

31.   Walter Kendall, "Trade Unions in Germany," <u>European Community</u> (March 1970), p. 20.

32.   Herbert J. Spiro, <u>The Politics of German Codetermination</u> (Cambridge, Mass.:   Harvard Univer-sity Press, 1958), p. 154.

33.   <u>Ibid.</u>, p. 160.

34.   <u>Ibid.</u>, p. 77.

35.   <u>Ibid.</u>, p. 79.

36.   European Regional Organization of the International Confederation of Free Trade Unions, European Integration, Report of the European Trade Union Course held in London, September 2-11, 1959 (Brussels: European Regional Secretariat, 1959), p. 30.

37.   Haas, op. cit., p. 221.

38.   Cahiers mensuels de documentation européenne (August-September, 1960), p. 32.

39.   Donald L. M. Blackmer, Unity in Diversity: Italian Communism and the Communist World (Cambridge, Mass.: MIT Press, 1968), see ch. 9 on the Common Market controversy.

40.   Joseph LaPalombara, The Italian Labor Movement: Problems and Prospects (Ithaca, N.Y.: Cornell University Press, 1967), p. 56.

41.   Ibid., p. 51.

42.   Letters sent by Bruno Storti, former head of the Italian Confederation of Trade Unions, to the minister of foreign affairs concerning labor's opinions on the European Economic Community (October 1962).

43.   Blackmer, op. cit.

44.   Kassalow, op. cit., p. 114.

45.   Ibid., p. 120.

46.   Ibid., p. 121.

47.   Walter Kendall, "Trade Unions in France," European Community (April 1970), p. 17.

48.   Jean Daniel Reynaud, "The Role of Trade Unions in the National Political Economies of the Developed Countries of Europe," in Barkin, et al., eds., op. cit., p. 50.

49. Exposé sur l'évolution de la situation sociale dans la Communauté en 1969 (Brussels, February 1970), p. 113.

50. Reynaud, loc. cit.

51. "Le 40ème Anniversaire de la CFTC," Labor (September 1959), p. 223.

52. Trade Union News from the European Community (1967), 2, p. 13.

53. Ibid. (1968), 1, p. 15.

54. François Fejto, The French Communist Party and the Crisis of International Communism (Cambridge, Mass.: MIT Press, 1967), p. 196.

2

INTERNATIONAL TRADE UNION ORGANIZATIONS

National labor organizations in the member countries of the European Communities have followed diverse avenues to national policy making and social
power. How effectively has this influence been
pooled and translated into a fluid transnational setting? Has a truly European labor organization emerged
parallel with the development of European integration, or has another international labor organization
simply been added to an already long list of such organizations in Europe? This chapter will trace the
development of European labor organizations within
the European Communities, and Chapter 3 will examine
the extent of their influence in the decision-making
process of the European Communities.

Because the labor organizations in the EEC
countries are not exclusively interest groups but
also display characteristics of movements--subcul-
tures within their national society seeking extensive
democratic reforms--their goals within the European
Communities are equally broad. Also, since national
trade unions are affiliated to separate international
organizations, they are apt to reflect this allegiance in varying degrees. Therefore, trade union
plurality has persisted at the European level. Although the extent of divisiveness has diminished
over the past few years, it has prevented the formation of an organized common trade union front in the
European Communities.

INTERNATIONAL CONFEDERATION
OF TRADE UNIONS

Trade union support for European integration
was already evident when the ICFTU was founded in
1949. The principal objectives of this new organization were established at its initial congress and
included the achievement of welfare policies for its
members; representation of its affiliates in all international organizations of economic and social
relevance to workers; and the ideological aim of com-
bating the influences of Communism. The ICFTU's
general approach to the problems of economic integra-
tions is also indicated in its objectives:

> To advocate for the raising of the general
> level of prosperity, the idea of economic
> cooperation among nations according to a
> well-conceived plan, to stimulate the de-
> velopment of larger economic entities and
> the freer exchange of goods, and to seek
> the full participation of workers' repre-
> sentatives on official organs dealing with
> these questions.[1]

Having more than 2 million of its members in the
coal and steel industries, the ICFTU was bound to
express an active interest in appraising proposals
of the Schuman Plan, and it was quick to draw up a
report expressing the fears and expectations of the
labor unions concerning the proposed ECSC. The report was drawn up by the ICFTU's secretary-general,
J. H. Oldenbrock, who believed that a large-scale
market created by the economic union of Western
Europe would improve the prospects of economic and
social prosperity, provided the problems of the
transition to economic integration were satisfac-
torily solved.[2] He was deeply concerned that the
transition process might involve large-scale industrial dislocation, unemployment, and pressure on
wages and working conditions. In order to mitigate
the shock of the integration process and to compensate for any adverse effects resulting from it, he
called for social safeguards for the workers,

including a systematic policy of full employment
within an expanding production. To ensure the latter, he envisaged the establishment of a Joint European Planning Commission that would include representatives of the trade unions to supervise the expansion
of markets and investment for industrial relocation.
Special institutions should be created within the
ECSC to help finance the relocation of industries or
their rehabilitation. The free trade union movement
supported the Schuman Plan in principle, although it
expressed serious reservations about possible adverse
effects and insisted upon positive policies favoring
labor.

To ensure that its views would be accounted for,
the ICFTU participated in the preparatory stages of
the establishment of the ECSC. For this purpose it
established a Committee for the Schuman Plan composed
of delegates of the national confederations of the
Six and of the international trade secretariats of
miners and metalworkers. The main task of this committee was to coordinate the activities of the trade
union delegates with the governmental delegations
to the Schuman Plan negotiations and to develop a
policy in accordance with the objectives of the
ICFTU as well as with those of the national confederations. It was very active in proposing amendments
to the Rome Treaties' provisions, seeking to clarify
the role of the High Authority, its employment policy, and the problem of raising living standards. It
continually pressed for trade union participation
in ECSC institutions.

The efforts of the Committee for the Schuman
Plan were rewarded by treaty provisions in the field
of social policy, by the acceptance of trade union
participation in ECSC institutions, and by the fact
that the ICFTU as well as the national governments
received the right to submit lists of candidates for
the High Authority. Among its other achievements
are the creation of a single Consultative Committee
and the appointment of a trade union representative
to the Court of Justice. In short, the work of this
committee resulted in the appointment to the High
Authority of persons enjoying the confidence of the

labor unions and the adoption of specific safeguards
for the interests of the workers. On the other side
of the balance sheet, the Committee for the Schuman
Plan was disappointed with the failure of the ECSC
to eliminate cartels. It would have liked the
High Authority to enjoy far-reaching powers of control over production and investment.[3] In addition,
the powers actually granted the Common Assembly were
a shadow of the democratic control of the High Authority demanded by the Committee.

The ICFTU favors regional economic cooperation
in principle; however, since it is committed to the
welfare of all its affiliates, its ultimate goal is
the economic association of all Western European
countries. It expressed regret, therefore, that the
Rome Treaties included only the six members of the
ECSC and concern lest the EEC become a protectionist
bloc within Western Europe and the world.[4] Repeatedly it has stressed that the EEC and the European
Free Trade Association (EFTA) should seek close association and avoid hindering the trade of other
countries by their policies. On the other hand, the
ICFTU favors close economic union among EEC members
based upon common financial, agricultural, and transport policies and a general social and economic
policy. This should be achieved under the democratic
control of a European parliament elected by universal
suffrage and under European executives. Above all,
the ICFTU has insisted that the trade unions receive
adequate representation in the European Communities.

The European Regional
Organization

In 1950 the European Regional Organization (ERO)
was established within the ICFTU to handle trade
union relations with the Organization for European
Economic Cooperation (OEEC), the ECSC, and NATO.
Its membership includes the Western European affiliates of the ICFTU, all of which, with the exception
of the CISL, are essentially Socialist in tendency.
The objectives of the ICFTU are included in ERO
statutes. However, the particular tasks of the ERO
include forging agreement among its members on

regional problems, coordinating free trade union activities in the region, gathering and diffusing information on matters of concern to the trade unions
in the area, and furthering general ICFTU aims in
Western Europe.[5] As its parent organization, the
ERO is not a centralized structure enjoying power
over the policy of its affiliates; rather, it serves
principally as an international trade union forum
for the region.

The ERO has served its members principally in
the representational task of supporting a carefully
developed labor viewpoint during European integration.
From the time of its establishment it was actively
concerned with European integration and instrumental
in defining the free trade unions' program for Europe.
In order to elicit the interest and support of its
affiliates for European integration, it organized
annual trade union schools on various aspects of
European unification.

During the 1950's and early 1960's the policies
of the ERO bore the imprint of its secretary-general,
Walter Schevenels, who worked tirelessly to enlist
labor support for European integration. Schevenels
equated economic integration with the survival of
Europe and its ability to attain an important role
in world affairs and develop its technical resources.
He believed, somewhat naively, that the influence of
private capital would decrease in proportion to the
degree of integration and, conversely, that the integration of the labor force would strengthen the
power of the labor movement. As early as 1954 he
called for social integration, the progressive
adaptation of fiscal systems, and the free movement
of goods, capital, and men under the aegis of a European supranational authority vested with wide political powers.[6]

The ERO publicized its views through frequent
and wide circulation of its resolutions and through
its biennial conferences. The latter are designed
to coordinate national policy on regional issues
with ERO policy.

The first ERO conference endorsed Oldenbrock's report on the Schuman Plan. Although the trade unions supported the principle of integration, they were apprehensive of possible adverse effects.[7]

However, during the first few years of the ECSC's operation, wages and working conditions of miners and metalworkers in the Community showed a general improvement. Therefore, the 1954 ERO conference at Strasbourg expressed greater conviction that economic integration would enhance European prosperity and help create a rise in living standards.[8] By this time the trade unions' general expectations had crystallized into the specific demand for greater economic stability through European countercyclical policies. The rise in their expectations prompted them to request greater competence for the ECSC and its democratization through control by an Economic and Social Council. At that time, however, there was no agreement among ERO affiliates on a specific European social program. The CGT-FO proposed the most ambitious program, including the formation of a European Manpower Board to organize migration and collective bargaining at the European level. On the other hand, the DBG feared that such undertakings might result in a downward pressure on living standards.

When attempts were made by the foreign ministers of the ECSC to revive the European idea in 1955, the ERO lent its full support to the movement. In order to seize upon the hopes aroused by it and to help ensure practical results for European unity, the ERO called the Conference on the Revival of the European Idea, devoted to an appraisal of the Messina Resolution of June 1955. The conference produced the "Statement on the Revival of the European Idea" for the ministerial committee at Messina, in order to gain a hearing for labor's views on Europe.[9] It emphasized the basic motive for the free trade unions' support of European economic integration, the necessity of raising living standards and of securing full employment so that

> every step towards economic cooperation
> and integration should be accomplished

> within the framework of a policy of full
> employment and social progress in general,
> including an upward adjustment of social
> conditions.[10]

The statement also included demands for readaptation
measures and the coordination of national policies.
The liberalization measures involved in the creation
of a common market would have such profound repercussions on the economic structure and traditional trade
relations of the countries concerned that the harmonization of the social and economic policies of
these countries was deemed necessary. The free trade
unions were pleased that the need for a gradual harmonization of social conditions was recognized at
Messina. However, because of the difficulties encountered by the High Authority in this field owing
to vague and restrictive treaty clauses, they insisted that formal guarantees of the promised harmonization measures be included in the projected
treaty.

The following year an ERO conference discussed
the Messina projects, and in 1957 ERO submitted
"Observations Relative to the Draft Treaty for the
European Common Market" to the president of the
Ministerial Committee at Brussels.[11] Its remarks on
the institutions of the proposed European Economic
Community included suggestions for specific procedures to strengthen the positions of the Assembly
and the European Commission with respect to the Council of Ministers. It also proposed that the Economic
and Social Committee be granted the right of initiative to study any problems arising from the functioning of the Common Market and of making proposals
where necessary. All institutions should be obliged
to solicit its opinion on any important measure contemplated. In addition that body should have the
competence to designate European parity committees
to solve problems arising in a given sector. The
free trade union proposals on European institutions
were intended to render the EEC more democratic and
to give it greater independence vis-à-vis the national governments. With this end in view, they
also suggested that the budgetary resources of the

EEC be secured independently of the national budgets, either by special taxes or by a direct levy.

Because the institutional complex of the EEC did not correspond to trade union hopes for a community more independent of the national governments, the unions sought detailed provisions for policies favorable to labor. Since most of the political parties to which ERO members are affiliated were in the opposition at that time, and because of their disappointment with national reform, they seemed to believe that a truly supranational Community would increase the power of labor and would be more receptive to it. They feared that if the individual governments retained complete freedom of action within their frontiers, private capital would use the new opportunities afforded by the Common Market for its own ends.

Several themes have recurred in the discussions and declarations of the ERO on the subject of European integration, so an ERO attitude can be defined on the matter. Ever since its foundation, the ERO has been aware that European integration offered the hope of increased prosperity and has frequently stated that much can be gained from the common exploitation of resources and the extension of national markets. It has continually advocated broader economic cooperation and social harmonization. When the creation of the EEC was proposed, the ERO considered it an opportunity for modern mass production and a high level of employment--provided, of course, that the fruits of production were equitably distributed.

To ensure this, ERO feels that labor unions should participate as equal partners in all EEC institutions. Trade unions feel that they are in a position to represent not only organized labor but also a large body of consumers and that their viewpoints should be heard on all matters concerning European integration.

Another point repeatedly made by the ERO is the necessity for specific guarantees to protect labor against the disruptions of the transitional period in the integration process, whether in the form of

readaptation measures or through the harmonization
of economic and social policies.

The ERO developed a very explicit idea of a
truly supranational institutional structure, based
upon democratic principles, for the European Communities. In this complex, the European Assembly would
enjoy the attributes and powers of national parliaments and the European Executives would merit that
title by retaining powers to formulate economic and
social policy. This particular set of demands resulted from ERO experience with the ECSC and from
the fact that the provisions for the alignment of
economic policy are the weakest points of the treaty
creating the EEC.[12] There are no means for compelling
the member countries of the European Communities to
pursue a common policy based on full employment.
The solution of the trade unions lies in the transfer
of economic and political powers to European authorities in which they would enjoy an important voice.
The fact that, for the most part, these goals remain
unachieved after so many years is reflected in trade
union attempts to render their European secretariats
more effective.

With the adoption of the Rome Treaties in 1958,
the ERO relinquished many of its activities concerning the European Communities to the European Trade
Union Secretariat and the Intersyndicale. It now
serves as a forum for contact between the trade
unions of the Six and those of other Western European
countries.

The Committee of XXI

When the ECSC began to operate, the Committee
for the Schuman Plan of the ICFTU was disbanded and
replaced by a permanent organization. The ERO wished
to assume the task of coordinating trade union activity within the ECSC, but the desire of the miners
and metalworkers of the Six to form their own coordinating committee prevailed.

The result was a free trade union committee
for the ECSC consisting of two bodies: a working

committee of fifteen members representing the miners
and metalworkers of the Six, their international
trade secretariats, the ICFTU and its ERO; and the
plenary Committee of XXI to represent, in addition,
the national trade union federations.[13] The working
committee proved too unwieldly to manage the daily
tasks it was assigned and was replaced by an eight-
member executive committee.

Within the Committee of XXI each trade union
organization was represented by one delegate and
had one vote. However, I.G. Bergbau and I.G. Metall,
the German coal and steel unions, were the largest
and strongest members. They accounted for over one-
half of the affiliated rank-and-file membership and
for a proportionately large share of the financial
contribution. The split in the French and Italian
labor movements was an added source of strength for
German labor. Only non-Communist unions were represented in the ECSC. However, the CGT-FO in France
and the CISL and UIL in Italy were weaker than their
Communist rivals, particularly in the coal and steel
industries. Nevertheless, the predominant strength
of the German trade unions was not used to influence
the proceedings of the Committee.

The Committee of XXI did not function as a centralized policy-making body.[14] Rather, it acted as
a coordinating organ for its membership. Members
negotiated with each other in a formal, diplomatic
manner and plenary meetings occurred only three or
four times a year. In the interval the executive
committee managed daily activity, although policy
decisions required confirmation by the full committee.
In addition, the practice arose of convening biennial
conferences attended by three delegates from each
affiliated organization.

The liaison office of the Committee of XXI included a secretary and two assistants, a specialist
on questions connected with the coal industry, and a
specialist conversant with the problems of the steel
industry.[15] It acted as a communications channel
between the Committee of XXI and its affiliates on
all questions concerning the ECSC. In addition the

Committee of XXI established various ad hoc study
groups to reach agreement among its members on such
matters as price policies, investments, cartels, collective agreements, and social security, as well as
committees to implement the programs adopted by the
general trade union conferences.

The official functions of the Committee of XXI
were rather strictly circumscribed. They included
representational and servicing tasks: maintaining
relations with the High Authority, informing union
members of developments within the ECSC, and providing workers represented in ECSC organs with up-to-
date information and data. It established a technical section within its liaison office for this purpose, but because of its limited resources and lack
of personnel it did not engage in extensive research.[16]
Rather, it depended upon the research departments of
member unions and the national federations. The
most important function of the Committee of XXI was
to coordinate the positions of its members on various
issues in order to present a united stand within the
Consultative Committee. It met before each session
of that organ in order to achieve consensus. In addition, its secretariat served as the secretariat of
the ICFTU members of the Workers' Group of the Consultative Committee.

What were the goals sought by the Committee of
XXI within the ECSC, and through which channels did
it seek to exert its influence? It performed its
lobbying functions through regular informal consultations with the High Authority and the Socialist
Group of the Common Assembly. It frequently used
the Consultative Committee as a platform for pressing
its aims of increased influence for labor within the
ECSC, thus intertwining its official and pressure-
group activities.

From initially divergent national positions, the
Committee of XXI managed to develop a broad social
program of improved living and working conditions
for ECSC workers.[17] The program called for the attainment of social progress through European collective agreements negotiated by European parity

committees created expressly for that purpose. The
Liaison Office also prepared some practical proposals
for the reduction of the workweek to forty hours and
for an improvement of working conditions. Committee
delegates presented these proposals to the Council
of Ministers and to the Common Assembly. In line
with national trade union traditions of relying upon
governmental action to attain many of their goals,
the Committee of XXI insisted that the High Authority
find ways to further these aims.

The Committee of XXI also devoted considerable
energy to the problem of safety in the coal mines,
participating in the preparation of safety standards
for the mines formulated by ECSC organs.

The Committee's initial demands of the ECSC for
economic policies were rather loosely defined, frequently conflicting, and apt to reflect national
reservations. By its 1956 conference, however, its
demands were conciliated into a program calling for
countercyclical investments, price controls, and
production planning.[18]

At the end of the transition period the Committee published extensive proposals for revision of
the Paris Treaty and submitted them to the High
Authority, the national governments, and political
groups of the Common Assembly.[19] These proposals
were aimed at endowing the High Authority with sufficient means to pursue a vigorous social policy and
formulated with the treaties for Euratom and the EEC
in mind. The principal modifications suggested by
the proposals concerned the institutions of the ECSC
and social and economic problems.

One factor that helped produce a common policy
for the free trade unions was the overlap of persons
serving on the Common Assembly, the Consultative
Committee, and the Committee of XXI. The same trade
unionists frequently met in different places, acting
in different capacities on each occasion. Under
these conditions some assimilation of viewpoints was
bound to occur.

While the members of the Committee of XXI moved closer together in their stands on economic and social issues and even developed common policies, they did not deem it necessary to develop a more closely integrated trade union structure. The role of the Committee as a lobbying agent for labor's viewpoint was of greater value to its members than its official functions. The secretary-general and the Liaison Office maintained a continuous flow of information on trade union views to those in a position to influence Community policy and developed what the unions consider a reasonably satisfactory relationship with the High Authority. The latter consulted the unions on a regular basis and, in its turn, the Committee of XXI was able to communicate its views to the High Authority on all matters relevant to labor.[20] The Committee also acquired the active support of the Common Assembly's Socialist Group on matters of interest to labor.

Two basic motives inspired the formation of the Committee of XXI: to enable labor to participate in ECSC decision making along with management and the governments, and to promote and protect the interests of labor. A statement of Heinrich Straeter, president of the Committee, attests to the importance of ECSC organs in achieving the former:

> In the ECSC, the trade unions have to provide concrete opinions on practical questions. Their work in international organizations until now has been exclusively confined to recommendations and the expression of non-committal views. Previously, they never studied such questions as market research or systems of pricing. Now, within the Consultative Committee, unions have to give their opinions on this kind of question and to discuss economic problems jointly with the representatives of enterprises. In many countries, such practical discussion, before important decisions are taken, had hitherto not been possible.[21]

From a European Trade Union Secretariat
to a European Confederation
of Free Trade Unions

The Trade Union Secretariat for the European
Communities was established at Brussels in May 1958.
The organization of the free trade unions within the
EEC was the subject of heated controversy within the
ERO.[22] The executive of the Committee of XXI proposed that the Liaison Office in Luxembourg be expanded to deal with the ECSC, the EEC, and Euratom.
An alternative proposal, suggested by the CGT-FO,
was for the establishment of a general committee and
liaison office representing the six national trade
union federations. Subcommittees would be formed to
deal with Euratom, the ECSC, and industries warrant-
ing special attention. However, the ERO executives
were convinced that the ERO should be the official
coordinating agency for trade union activities in
the European institutions. Because of the major
role it had played in promoting the Rome Treaties
in the trade union world, it felt that it should be
closely associated with the new trade union structure.
Nevertheless, the trade unionists of the Six did not
wish to grant the ERO an important role in matters
concerning the EEC once the latter had begun to operate. They feared that the ERO would be unduly def-
erential to the views of Britain and the Scandinavian
countries, which had declined membership in the EEC.
As a result the ERO was accorded the same status as
any other participant in the Executive Committee of
the Trade Union Secretariat. The free trade unions
of the Six wished ERO representatives to serve merely
as a liaison between them and other members of the
ERO.

The structure of the Trade Union Secretariat
was more elaborate than that of its predecessor, the
Committee of XXI. However, it was of the same nature: a congress of equals possessing no federal
characteristics or central decision-making powers on
matters of importance.

The first year of the Trade Union Secretariat's
operation was devoted to obtaining agreement on its

structure.[23] The Italian CISL would have liked a
more closely integrated structure, directly elected
by member organizations in proportion to their numer-
ical importance and entrusted with decision-making
power. Its essential task would be to formulate and
promote a Community trade union action and policy on
economic affairs, labor mobility, social security,
and collective agreements, all matters of direct
concern to the Italian labor movement. Although the
German unions were disappointed that the EEC included only six members and were lukewarm about collective bargaining at the European level, they also
favored a centralized structure. L. Major of the
Belgian FGTB, stressed the necessity of a trade union
movement that would defend the interests of the workers in the member countries of the EEC on the basis
of supranational ideas. On the other hand, the NVV
believed that the situation was not yet ripe for a
European trade union organization with a strong
executive and broad powers. It claimed that a supranational trade union organization should be established only if it dealt with concrete problems that
could be solved within the national context. Having
attained its goals within the national framework,
the NVV manifested little interest in extending its
claims to the European level. Although all affiliates
of the European Trade Union Secretariat agreed upon
the necessity for increased information and communication channels to deal with European institutions,
they differed on the organization of their mutual
relations and were somewhat unwilling to cede part
of their national powers.

The Trade Union Secretariat was composed of the
General Assembly, which established the main lines
of policy; the Executive Committee; and the Secretariat. Subcommittees dealt with the ECSC, Euratom,
and the EEC; and industrial committees focused upon
various sectors of the economy.

The General Assembly held biannual meetings and
included delegations of ICFTU-affiliated unions of
the Six. These were composed of representatives of
national trade union boards and of the most important
industrial federations. The Assembly also invited

observers from the International Trade Secretariats
and from countries not included in the European Communities.

During the interval between assemblies, the Executive Committee directed the work of the organization.
It was composed of representatives of the national
confederations, each of which was a member of the
European Parliamentary Assembly, the Economic and Social Committee, or both. The principal task of this
body was to coordinate policy between its members.
Theoretically it was supposed to meet four times a
year; but because of the domestic pressures on its
members and the difficulties in finding convenient
meeting dates, it normally convened three times yearly
and at irregular intervals. The Secretariat tried to
fill the gap by convening unofficial meetings of the
Executive Committee just before sessions of the Economic and Social Committee and at the time of other
trade union meetings. However, direct and detailed
discussions between the various confederations were
necessary to develop consensus at the European level,
and relations with the Secretariat did not prove an
adequate substitute.[24] Therefore, the Executive Committee functioned more as an international organization rather than as a supranational organ. This
tended to affect the cohesion of the free trade union
structure as a whole. In addition the Committee was
enlarged in 1967 to include the British TUC and a
token presence of the Danish and Norwegian trade
unions. The enlarged Committee proved so unwieldy
that two years elapsed before its next meeting.

Reporting to the Executive Committee was the
Committee for the Management of a Common Fund, established in 1965. The Fund was established in order
to strengthen the Trade Union Secretariat's affiliates and to support trade union activities within the
EEC. France's CGT-FO has been the major recipient
of aid so far, particularly after the troublesome
events of the spring of 1968.[25] The Italian unions
have also benefited from funds in order to support
training programs for labor officials.

The Secretariat acted in this capacity for the
General Assembly, the Executive Committee, and some

of the industrial committees. Its particular task
was to coordinate trade union action and to prepare
common stands on economic and social problems within
the European Communities. It included an economic
committee, a social committee, a committee on the
democratization of the economy, a committee on collective bargaining, and one on nuclear energy to
prepare the positions of the Workers' Group of the
Economic and Social Committee and the opinions requested of the trade unions by the European Commission. The social committee has been instrumental in
preparing stands on almost all aspects of social
policy.

The industrial committees are concerned with
matters pertaining to specific sectors. The committees for agriculture, for the food industry, for
transport, and for metallurgy confided the secretariat
of their group to the Secretariat. The other committees worked in close collaboration with it.

Until 1967 coordination between the Secretariat
and the industrial committees was sporadic.[26] Since
then they have met more regularly. Frequently members of the European Commissions' General Directorate
for social affairs and for industrial policy are
present at these meetings. Annual conferences between the national confederations and the industrial
committees were instituted the same year and were
intended to publicize, to inform, and to gain support
for the Trade Union Secretariat's committee work.
Topics covered during these conferences have included
"Relations Between the Trade Unions and the Employers' Organization at the European Level" and "National
Experiences with Economic Planning."

The ERO frequently questioned whether trade
union interests would not be more effectively assured
by the traditional method of collaboration through
the International Trade Secretariats and the ERO.
However, the free trade unions of the Six were convinced that their organizational solution was effective:

We have created a functional trade union
organization because we must face new

tasks for which the organizations of the
Six are alone competent.[27]

The European Trade Union Secretariat was a medium through which the various labor confederations
could draw upon each other's experience and a permanent body for contacts with the European institutions. Like its predecessor in the ECSC, it proved
its value as a channel for the exchange of views and
information between the trade unions and Community
institutions. Its daily work consisted in maintaining contact with the European Commission and its
services. The latter regularly invited experts from
the Secretariat for consultations.

However, the influence of the Trade Union Secretariat was seriously limited by the fact that it was
not always able to formulate sufficiently detailed
stands, even for important questions. This limitation was due essentially to lack of financial means
and expert personnel.[28] As a result its initiatives
were modest and its activity limited to problems suggested by the European institutions.

One of the most thorny problems of the European
Trade Union Secretariat lay in the relationship between the industrial committees and the Executive
Committee. Since the latter met infrequently, the
industrial committees were able to function almost
independently. Consequently, the general organs of
the Trade Union Secretariat received few communications on the activities and policies of the industrial
committees, and there was some confusion over competence for representing labor at the European level.
Because of the Secretariat's loose structure, collaboration between representatives of particular interests and those representing the broader interests
of labor occurred on a pragmatic basis. The need
for a more centralized organization was apparent.

The limitations of a trade union organization
that was loosely structured and confined to cooperation on a purely pragmatic basis appeared painfully
evident to its leadership in the late 1960's. It
seemed ironic that labor leaders were confronting

the extension of European unity with demands for supranationalism while they themselves retained a structure with the characteristics of a coordinating
board. In order to cope with the problems of strengthening the structure of the European Trade Union Secretariat, endowing its Executive Committee with
greater competence, and improving its relationship
with the industrial committees, the General Assembly
of the Free Trade Unions in Europe decided to revise
its organization.

The formal decision to reorganize the European
Secretariat was taken at its Fifth General Assembly
in Rome in 1966; and in April 1969 the European Trade
Union Secretariat drew up new statutes in order to
constitute the ECFTUC.[29] The General Assembly was
transformed into a congress in which representation
is determined not only on a national basis but also
in proportion to trade union strength. The industrial
committees were granted three seats each for the
first 500,000 members and one more seat for each additional 500,000 members. Besides weighted representation the congress boasts the unique feature of
decision making by qualified majority vote rather
than by unanimity.

The Executive Committee was enlarged to include
members of the national confederations (the DGB and
CGT-FO each have two representatives), a member of
the Intersyndicale, and a member of each industrial
committee with consultative voice. The Committee on
the Management of the Common Fund continues to report
to the Executive Committee, which meets on a bimonthly
basis and reviews the trade union situation in each
country annually. As in the congress, decisions are
taken by a qualified majority of those present.

The task of ensuring regular consultations between the industrial committees and the national confederations belongs to the Secretariat.

The function of ensuring collaboration among
affiliates is shared by the annual assembly. It is
intended to maintain continuity between congresses
and is composed of the Executive Committee and five

members from each industrial committee. Its meetings will serve the purpose of eliciting interest and support for the activities of the new confederation.

Andre Kloos of the NVV was elected president of the confederation, a position long held by the DGB. Theo Rasschaert of the FGTB now serves as secretary-general.

The Industrial Committees
of the ECFTUC

The ECFTUC includes ten industrial committees and European branches of the International Trade Secretariats of the ICFTU. The latter have a tradition of considerable support for their affiliates through research, welfare work, and strike support. Therefore, it is not surprising that the industrial committees have demonstrated greater cohesion and effectiveness within the EEC and the ECSC than their corresponding European Trade Union Secretariat.

The European Federation of Agricultural Workers Unions in the Community is concerned chiefly with problems related to the application of the CAP. Federation members participate in various consultative bodies for agriculture established by the European Commission, notably the Consultative Committee for the Social Problems of Agricultural Wage Earners and of Farmers. It has maintained close relations with the Commission's Directorate of Agriculture and Directorate of Social Affairs and enjoys the confidence of Sicco Mansholt, architect of the CAP. The Federation has become a pioneer in labor's achievements in the EEC, for it was a partner in the first collective agreement negotiated at the European level. In 1968 it signed, along with the Committee of Agricultural Associations of the EEC (COPA), the "European Agreement on the Harmonization of the Length of Working Time of Full-Time Agricultural Wage Earners."[30] However, because there is no legal basis for a European collective agreement that would be directly applicable in all EEC countries, the agreement is more in the nature of a recommendation. It constitutes only one stage in harmonizing working time among EEC countries, for it covers only full-time agricultural laborers, not seasonal workers. Nevertheless, the trade unions consider the agreement a major achievement, chiefly because it and future agreements have the advantage of occurring independently of the European institutions.

It appears that the industrial committees will not only manage to develop a genuine industrial dialogue at the European level but will also be ahead of the European Secretariat in forging a common trade union front. The Federation of Agricultural Workers Unions in the Community has prepared a proposal for a statute federating agricultural laborers of the ICFTU industrial committees and the WCL industrial committees.[31]

Regular cooperation between ICFTU affiliates and its Christian and Communist counterparts is also proceeding apace within the European Metalworkers' Committee.[32] In 1968 the Federation of Metalworkers of the French Confederation of Democratic Trade Unions (CFDT-FGM) withdrew from the Christian International Federation of Metalworkers to join the ICFTU's International Trade Secretariat and its European Committee. And, since the CGT-FO and the CFDT cooperate regularly with the Communist CGT in France, there is a back-door cooperation of all French unions in the Committee. The Italian CGIL's FIOM (metalworkers' union) is also unofficially collaborating with the Committee. A statutory recognition of this cooperation is presently under review.

The Metalworkers' Committee has provided important services for its members. Since 1969 it has published an information bulletin on trends in collective bargaining, economic concentrations in the metal industry, and the industrial policy of the EEC. It also prepares positions on various EEC policies relevant to the metalworkers' unions.

The European Metalworkers' Committee has been instrumental in establishing contact between trade union representatives of various branches of the Phillips Trust in Eindhoven and the Fiat-Citroen

Trust.[33] These meetings review comparative social
and economic conditions among branches and personnel,
investment, and production policies, and assess the
scope of decision making enjoyed by the branch manager. Through these activities the Committee is aim-
ing at European collective bargaining and mutual
support in the event of strikes. In 1968 the Committee engineered its affiliates' support of its Belgian
members striking against the Ford plant at Genk. At
present, however, the divergencies among the Committee's affiliates have permitted agreement on collective bargaining only on the minimal goals of guaranteed trade union rights in the establishment and
protection against the effects of rationalization
and mergers.

When one compares the relationship between employers' organizations and labor unions within the
parity commissions set up by the European Commission's
Directorate of Social Affairs of within the Economic
and Social Committee, one is struck by the differences. Labor contacts with the Union of Industries of
the EEC (UNICE) are dependent upon sessions of the
Council of Ministers for Social Affairs. Hence,
they are sporadic, separated by long intervals, and
confined to such narrow subjects as minimal agreement
between the two groups can provide. Since they are
not dependent upon Community institutions for their
initiatives, the industrial committees have displayed
a greater vitality than the ECFTUC as a whole. They
have been able to take genuine initiatives in establishing industrial relations and enjoy a membership
more easily aware of the European dimensions of their
occupations.

The Trade Union Committee of Transports for the
European Communities includes representatives of the
International Transport Federation as well as of the
ICFTU transport unions of the Six. It is concerned
chiefly with the social aspects of a slowly emerging
European transport policy and has formulated opinions
on the proposals of the European Commission through
its representation on the committee of experts provided by article 83 of the EEC treaty and on the
specialized section for transports of the Economic

and Social Committee. Its members also participate
in the consultative parity committee for the social
problems of road transport established by the European Commission. On the basis of a proposal prepared
by the Commission with the help of the Committee of
Transports, the Council of Ministers has recently
enacted a regulation on the harmonization of certain
social provisions in road transport, such as driving
hours, daily rest periods, and other working conditions.[34]

The Trade Union Group of the Food, Tobacco, and
Hotel Industry is represented on various consultative
committees for agricultural products in the EEC. It
is concerned with the application of the CAP and the
defense of its affiliates' social interests. This
is a difficult task to accomplish in the consultative
committees; for they discuss extremely technical
problems, and are convened at irregular intervals.
Therefore, the workers have been frequently absent
from meetings and have displayed little interest in
consultative committee proceedings.[35] Moreover, this
particular industrial group has experienced great
difficulties in ensuring trade union cooperation
with the EEC. It encompasses a multiplicity of sectors and includes affiliates with a great diversity
of structures, strength, and influence in industrial
relations. The lack of a common decision-making organ within the Committee is evidence that European
problems are of secondary importance to most of the
membership.

The Joint Committee of Building and Woodworkers
of the European Communities enjoys close contacts
with the European Commission's Directorate of Social
Affairs. It has recently drawn up a European action
program for its members including, among other
things, demands for security of employment, shorter
hours, longer holidays, and wage maintenance in the
event of incapacity.[36] The Committee is interested
in developing European collective bargaining.

The ECFTUC also includes committees of chemical
workers and textile workers, the Coordinating Committee for Managerial and Supervisory Staffs and White

Collar Workers, and the Group for Postal and Telegraph Workers. All of these committees engage in
similar activities on behalf of their membership:
gathering and diffusing information and applying
pressure in EEC organs. They convene general assemblies for information purposes and maintain relations
with the ECFTUC, parallel committees in the Christian
Confederation, and employers' groups.

The Intersyndicale ECSC

With the creation of the European Trade Union
Secretariat in 1958, the Intersyndicale ECSC assumed
the functions of the Committee of XXI. It is composed
of the mining and metallurgy unions of the Six plus
representatives of the International Federation of
Miners and the International Federation of Metalworkers. For the present it is represented by a member
on the Executive Committee of the ECFTUC. However,
when the ECSC and the EEC are merged, the Intersyndicale will cease to exist.

Members of the Intersyndicale were active in
most of the former High Authority's technical committees created to study ECSC problems.[37] For example,
the High Authority regularly invited representatives
of steel consumers to Luxembourg to discuss problems
of the Common Market for steel. Twelve members of
the Intersyndicale participated in each of these
meetings so important for the establishment of general objectives for steel. At these meetings the
trade unions enjoyed the opportunity of discussing
such matters as the state of the steel market, the
long-term consumption of steel, and the development
of prices and trends in the transforming industries.
The trade unions also participated in the committee
of experts concerned with the preparation of the
general objectives for steel. These have a direct
bearing on full employment and therefore are of particular concern to the trade unions. Labor enjoys
an access to policy making in the ECSC that is denied
it within the EEC.

In order to combat the growing disaffection
with the mining occupation and the instability of

the labor force in the collieries, a working group
of the Intersyndicale formulated the European Miners'
Statute, which was adopted at a conference of ICFTU
miners in 1959.[38] The Statute included a series of
demands that would grant the mine worker a privileged
position among industrial workers with respect to
wages, working conditions, and social benefits. The
European Trade Union Secretariat published the Statute in four languages as a brochure and distributed
it to all ECSC institutions, the OECD, and the ILO.
However, the only ECSC organ that concerned itself
seriously with the Statute was the Social Affairs
Committee of the European Parliamentary Assembly.
The latter included the Statute in a report on the
social aspects of the coal problem.[39] The Assembly
voted a series of resolutions stressing the importance
and the urgency of the Statute. Although the High
Authority originally proposed such a guarantee for
European miners in 1956, a few years later it considered the time unpropitious for discussion of the
Statute. Moreover, the Consultative Committee was
formally opposed to a discussion of the matter, and
the Mixed Committee for Coal had not met for more
than a year.

In response to pressures by the Intersyndicale
to resume the session of the Mixed Committee for
Coal, the High Authority countered that circumstances
did not warrant placing the Statute on the agenda of
the next meetings. The trade unions were again referred to an enthusiastic European Assembly, which
unanimously approved a report on the Statute by the
president of the Intersyndicale. After much hesitation on the part of the employers, the Statute was
placed on the agenda for the 1961 meeting of the
Mixed Committee for Coal. However, the governments
felt that structural differences in the economic and
social conditions of the member countries justified
the existence of varying working conditions and that
the development of wages and working conditions in
the collieries could not be dissociated from those
in other economic sectors. The employers opposed
the means suggested for effecting the Statute as
well as the contents. It would mean a new legal
instrument, an international, tripartite, collective

agreement.   They pointed to article 68 of the Paris
Treaty, which stipulates that the means of fixing
wages and social allowances cannot be affected by
the ECSC.   The attempt to use the ECSC as an arena
for the extension of collective bargaining met with
the refusal of both the governments and the employers.

Since the adoption of the Miners' Statute has
not been forthcoming, the Intersyndicale drew up a
European Social Plan for the Protection of Workers
in the Event of Loss of Employment and Income in 1969
and forwarded it to the Commission.[40]   The plan is
comprehensive and provides for compensation in the
event of dismissal and of early retirement of older
workers and for wage guarantees in the event of unemployment due to production or technological and organizational changes.   Because the iron, steel, and
coal industries are undergoing far-reaching changes,
the Intersyndicale is also concerned with maintaining
employment for its members through programs for industrial modernization.   It is interested in the
creation of large-scale European redevelopment programs, including retraining and reemployment programs,
the whole financed by the European Communities.

Although the Intersyndicale has been unsuccessful in obtaining European collective agreements, it
scored a notable success in influencing ECSC organs
with respect to the revision of article 56 of the
Paris Treaty on readaptation.   It advocated extending the possibilities of applying article 56 to all
cases of structural, technological, or other unemployment threatening the living conditions of the
miners and metalworkers.   Article 56 as modified in
1960 allows the High Authority to intervene on request of the government concerned if

> . . . profound changes in the marketing
> conditions of the coal mining or the iron
> and steel industry not directly connected
> with the introduction of the common mar-
> ket, make it necessary for certain enter-
> prises permanently to discontinue, curtail,
> or change their activities.[41]

Because of the deterioration of the coal-mining
industry, the Intersyndicale has maintained constant
pressure for a European energy policy, though the
trade unions have difficulty in reconciling their
interests on energy even on the national level. The
practical proposals of the Intersyndicale for the
achievement of a common energy policy aim toward the
establishment of a single market for all sources of
energy. This would require a harmonization of price
fixing as well as the elimination of obstacles to
trade in energy within the EEC.[42] The proposals also
include provisions for establishing a system of Community-wide regulation of EEC energy imports and for
agreements on long-term investments for all forms of
energy. The Intersyndicale believes that the treaties establishing the European Communities should be
revised in order to solve the problems of the coal
industry, to account for changes in the fuel market,
and to provide for a progressive social policy. The
possibility of obtaining a European energy policy
through the cooperation of the European Authorities,
the national governments, and international companies
seems remote to them, for the attempts made by the
national governments to solve energy problems without
a European conception have proved fruitless. They
therefore demand that a public European authority
for energy be created and entrusted with the task
of developing a European policy.

Because the ECSC allows labor a greater voice
in its operations than does the EEC, the Intersyndicale is concerned about the projected merger of the
European Communities.[43] The High Authority of the
ECSC had always included one member nominated by the
labor unions and had always displayed a greater willingness to consult labor on economic issues than had
the European Commission. Unfortunately, the unions
have been unsuccessful in retaining these features.
When the executives were fused in 1967, labor lost
the right to a coopted labor member, although Wilhelm
Haferkamp of the DGB was named to the new executive.
Labor is also denied membership in the EEC Committee
for Medium-Term Economic Policy, although the trade
unions participate in drawing up the general objec-

tives for coal and steel. Finally, the Intersyndicale
wished the levy to be generalized and raised because
it has provided the financial source for the ECSC's
social policy. Again it was unsuccessful. The levy
remains confined to the coal and steel industries,
and a ceiling has been placed on it. Although it
has no basis for this belief, the Intersyndicale is
firmly convinced that the creation of a genuine political unity within the fused Communities will be necessarily favorable to labor.

The ECFTUC: An Effective
European Interest Group
for Labor?

From present indications the creation of the
ECFTUC will help improve the internal cohesion so
necessary for effectiveness in conducting lobbying
and representational activities. However, when it
comes to achieving agreement among the membership
beyond circumscribed issues pertaining to European
integration and on general matters of economic and
social policy, organizational improvements may not
effect changes in attitude. In the last resort the
viewpoints of individual members will be determined
largely by the political circumstances in their countries and by the structure and strength of their
unions. There also remain important problems of
material resources, personnel, and contacts with the
grass-roots membership in the factory.[44] These
problems are not peculiar to labor. They are shared
by other interest groups. The problem of resources
can be rapidly characterized by terming them inadequate. Dues from the affiliates provide the main
source of funds. The problem of personnel is closely
related to the matter of financial resources. The
permanent European staff of the ECFTUC is still very
limited, and the leadership of the organization is
provided by the top leadership of the national confederations. Because they are occupying two important positions and perhaps a seat on the consultative
organs as well, the union leaders must establish a
workable balance between their domestic responsibili-
ties and their activities at the European level.
Finally, union members at the grass roots must be

convinced that the activity of the European trade
union organization is relevant to them. This is no
small task, given the pressures of limited resources
and personnel.

Influence must be backed up by the possibility
of some form of coercion or power. However, the
ECFTUC's means of exerting pressure in order to influence EEC decisions are limited to lobbying and
publicity. Although there is an emerging trend toward transnational cooperation in strike action,
exemplified by the EEC unions' support of the Belgian
workers during their strike against the Ford factory
at Genk, the power of the trade unions is still operative chiefly at the national level.

"Europeanization" is a two-way process. How
have the national confederations adapted their structures to the European reality? The DGB is unique in
its establishment of a Committee on European Affairs
on its executive board. However, since the reorganization of the European Free Trade Union Secretariat
in 1969, the NVV has revised its statutes to include
a provision that ECFTUC decisions will be binding on
it. The other members of the confederation have
stated that they will respect the decisions of the
ECFTUC until they have formally followed suit.

Another indication of the impact of European
activities on national trade union affairs can be
observed in the fact that the national confederations
are taking note of their counterparts in other EEC
countries in drawing up their programs. However,
it is the industrial groups of both the ECFTUC and
of the WCL's European organization that are moving
cautiously toward European collective bargaining.

In assessing the effectiveness of European labor
organizations, a comparison with some of the European employers' groups is in order. UNICE, the
Council of Federations of Commerce (CFC), the League
for European Economic Cooperation (LECE), and the
Union of Handicrafts of the EEC (UACEE), among others,
are all loosely structured entities dependent upon
their national affiliates for support. Among their

most important functions are the gathering and diffusing of information on the EEC. Like the labor
groups they rely upon congresses, round tables, and
courses to inform and educate their members. The
organization of all these groups is weighted in favor
of the national membership. UNICE, in particular,
is patterned after the European Council of Ministers
with its Council of Presidents and its Committee of
Permanent Delegates. A permanent secretariat headed
by a rotating secretary-general serves as adminis-
trator for UNICE and coordinates the work of its
special committees and working parties.[45] It includes a secretary for the Employers' Group of the
Economic and Social Committee. Decision making within
this organization is complex, time-consuming, and
produces consensus on individual issues only. Although employers' groups within EEC reputedly enjoy
greater resources than their labor counterparts,
the latter have achieved greater organizational cohesiveness. Labor's minority status within the European Communities may provide the explanation.

In seeking to influence the fluid and complex
policy-making process within the EEC, both labor and
management groups are confronted with similar problems. Both are barred from the source of decisions
within the European Communities, the Council of Ministers, and must therefore resort to their respective
national capitals to press their positions. Hence,
the predominance of national politics in these groups.

A Trade Union Program for Europe

At the time of the establishment of the Rome
Treaties, the free trade unions had recommended a
European authority invested with broad powers and
placed under the democratic control of a European
parliament. They had also demanded that the trade
unions participate as equal partners in the operation
of the new institutions. These demands were not
satisfied. The free trade unions regard the institutional structure of the EEC as too weak to obtain
the goals fixed by the Treaties, and too exclusively
based on an unjustified confidence in the efficiency
of liberalism and the permanent goodwill of the

national interests concerned. However, the trade unions considered the establishment of the EEC as progress in itself, even if it were achieved by forces they regard as not overly progressive. They are convinced that European integration will mean new economic and social possibilities for its members.

The goals of the free trade unions--both their negative desire to prevent the development of the Common Market along purely classic economic lines and their positive demand for increased economic and social benefits, equitably distributed--require a supranational authority enjoying broad powers. The trade unions are the radical Democrats of the European Communities. They seek a broad transformation of the EEC structure and rapid progress toward European political unity in a manner reminiscent of Wilsonian schemes for harmony and peace through a democratic organization of the like-minded. They seem to feel that if the EEC is modeled on a classic parliamentary democracy, the proper structure will yield the correct policy. Regardless of the realities of national power, the interests of labor would prevail. Although these dreams of a unified Europe, granting a role to a parliament that has long disappeared on the national level, may appear unrealistic, the trade unions have defined a problem of concern to many participants in the European Communities. The central decision-making organ of the EEC, which functions as a highly efficient international organization surrounded by myths of supranationalism, remains immune from public scrutiny. Certainly one could argue that review would vitiate the possibility of achieving positive results by exposing the fragility of national negotiations and hardening national positions. However, labor wishes to participate in policy making. It enjoys representation on the consultative bodies of the EEC and good relations with the European Commission. Therefore, it wishes these organs to serve as key sources of policy. For years the trade unions have called for the creation of a directly elected European Parliament enjoying true legislative and budgetary powers, a Commission exercising supranational powers and answerable only to the Parliament, and a Council of Ministers taking

decisions by a qualified majority. A model and sub-
missive executive, the Council of Ministers would
render its decisions within a specified period and
publish the debates leading to such decisions. When
one reflects what publicity has wrought on the decision-making process of U.N. organs, one would not
request publicity for corridor conversations. Or,
where publicity is a policy, as in the Council of
Europe, one is not surprised at the meager fare for
discussion. The fact remains that the Council of
Ministers is an intergovernmental organization, subject to realities exceeding the competence of the
European Community as a whole.

The trade unions have transferred their goal of
a role for labor in managing the economy to the European Communities. They would like the Economic and
Social Committee and the Consultative Committee to
enjoy the right of initiative and parity committees
to be established for all sectors of the economy.
Because labor has not fully attained these goals in
the national setting, it is willing to contemplate
the transfer of core decisions of national sovereignty
to the European level. When one is not wielding
power, it is easy to envisage a situation in which
incumbents of power will divest themselves of key
elements of authority--for the greater good.

Labor is not interested in European unity for
economic and social reasons alone. A unified Europe
would be a force to reckon with in world affairs.
Once powerful, Europe would be wise. It would dis-
pense significant aid to developing nations and con-
ciliate a world rent by quarreling giants.

When the trade unions characterize the Rome
Treaties as inadequate, they are also voicing concern
that the institutional structure of the EEC is too
weak to provide political supervision of multinational firms and mergers. Together the strength of
multinational corporations and the inadequacy of the
EEC will allow the unchecked development of economic
interests that can affect labor's goals. Labor's
answer to this problem lies in the creation of a

supranational authority with competence to coordinate
cyclical, monetary, budgetary, and regional policies,
all based on medium-term planning and accomplished
by governmental intervention.

A trade union program for Europe has been developed from the consensus created within the ECFTUC.
Basically, it refers to the harmonization of living
and working conditions, the achievement of an employment policy guaranteeing full employment, and the
democratization of relations within the enterprise.[46]

Harmonization can be accomplished through the
traditional route of autonomous collective bargaining
and through European policies. Labor suggests a
European incomes policy to advance economic growth
and improve the distribution of revenue. It believes
that a well-conceived incomes policy can avoid the
inflationary consequences of rising demand and provide a more equitable share of revenue for weaker
income groups, if accompanied by common monetary,
budgetary, and general economic policies. Closely
tied to a European incomes policy would be a European
policy for capital-sharing and profit-retention
schemes, the union's latest social achievement on
the national level.

Another avenue to the upward harmonization of
wages and labor costs is the development of European
trade union programs to serve as guides for national
collective bargaining. The ECFTUC's Committee on
Collective Bargaining developed a common action program for ECFTUC's affiliates in 1965 and is now reviewing the follow-up.[47] The action program is being
pursued in all EEC member countries. Among its provisions are demands for the reduction of the working
week to forty hours spread over five days without
loss of pay, four weeks of annual vacation with
double wages serving as a holiday bonus for the period, and guaranteed wages in the event of disability
resulting from illness or accident. The program was
also intended as a reminder that economic growth
should be constantly gauged by the extent of social
progress.

Labor's aim of a European employment policy is
intended to ensure full employment by protecting the
individual worker against the effects of technological change. The trade unions have always laid particular stress on the need for vocational training
and retraining programs to ensure that workers will
have the possibility of constantly acquiring new
skills and on European social schemes to protect
workers against loss of employment due to technological or organizational changes in the enterprise. In
addition European modernization plans should create
new opportunities for employment in depressed regions. The labor unions have long pointed out the
necessity for revising the European Social Fund so
that it can help promote a European employment policy
and operate in close cooperation with the European
Investment Bank.

The democratization of relations within the
enterprise, and especially within multinational enterprises, has been one of labor's goals for many years.
The ECFTUC's Committee on the Democratization of the
Economy has carried out extensive studies on codetermination in the member countries of the EEC. On
the basis of its findings, it recently drew up a
position on the European corporation.[48] It would
ensure that European companies allow codetermination:
equal representation for labor and capital in management, and labor's right of inquiry and information
on the state of the enterprise. The ECFTUC's position on European corporations bears the imprint of
its main author, the DGB, which wishes to make certain that German firms will not escape codetermination obligations by closing down companies under
German law and registering them as European corporations under the European Company Statute. The trade
unions were successful in ensuring that provisions
for codetermination would be included in the European
Commission's proposal on European companies. However, it is safe to assume that the latter proposal
will lie dormant in the Council of Ministers until
the enlargement of the EEC is accomplished.

European collective bargaining is on labor's
agenda for the future. Does it constitute a genuine

path to harmonization of wages and working conditions, or is European collective bargaining just another myth pronounced in the litany of supranational pieties?

The ECFTUC's Committee for Collective Agreements has produced a series of basic principles on collective negotiations within the EEC.[49] The Committee engages in constant review of collective bargaining in each country for the information of its members and feels that common demands among different programs can serve as the basis for common bargaining positions. Precontracts could be concluded for each sector and with European trusts. These would serve as guidelines for national negotiations and would constitute a first stage in harmonizing bargaining. Presumably, this stage would be followed by a progressive coordination of bargaining policies. The basic principles for collective bargaining adopted by the ECFTUC are too broad to arouse much controversy. The goals include the improvement of wages, the elimination of inequality in wages and working conditions between men and women, reduced working hours, longer vacations with vacation bonuses, and protection against technological innovation. No mention is made of procedures except for the expression of the trade union's desire for full autonomy in conducting negotiations. The basic principles reflect the fact that, given wide divergencies in industrial relations among countries, for the present common programs will be based on a narrow range of agreement. There is indeed a consensus that there should be negotiations between the social partners at the EEC level generally and by industry. However, agreement on substance and procedure is still limited.

At present there is no suitable organ within the EEC that could provide a setting for talks between the social partners. Organized discussions between management and labor within the parity committee for harmonization established by the European Commission have been confined to studies on the situation in various countries but have yielded no further action. The trade unions would prefer regular contacts with employers' organizations in order to conclude collective agreements in the area of harmonization and to remedy gaps in the EEC; however, the few meetings that the unions have managed to engineer with UNICE have focused upon the application of Treaty provisions for the Social Fund, vocational training, and the free movement of labor. In order to make progress toward collective bargaining, the unions have requested the creation of parity committees for each industrial sector. This request was aired both in the Economic and Social Committee and in the various meetings with UNICE. The employers have consistently opposed such developments.

From present indications it appears that European collective bargaining will remain in the formative stage for some time. Progress in this field is more likely to emerge from the industrial committees than from the general organization of the free trade unions.

WORLD CONGRESS OF LABOR

The International Confederation of Christian Trade Unions (ICCTU) represents Christian labor. Although it does not confine its appeal to a specific denomination, the overwhelming majority of its affiliates and of its leadership are Roman Catholic. Almost three-fourths of its membership is concentrated in Western Europe. Within the EEC countries it includes the CFTC and the CFDT of France, the CSC of Belgium, the KAB and the CNV of Netherlands, and the German Christian Trade Union. There is no Christian labor organization in Italy, for although the CISL includes Christian Democrats in its leadership and within its ranks it is an affiliate of the ICFTU. In 1968 the ICCTU was renamed the World Congress of Labor (WCL) and its charter was revised in order to alter its confessional character and broaden its appeal.

Compared with the loosely organized ICFTU, the WCL enjoys a greater centralization of power. Its Executive Council has greater power to decide matters of program and policy than its counterpart within the

free trade union organization. This is partially
due to similarity of political tendencies among its
affiliates and to the role of ideology. However,
the tightly knit organization of the WCL has not
proved an unmixed blessing to its European Organization (EO).

Christian Social Doctrine:
Christian Labor's Ideology

The philosophy of the WCL is based upon Christian social doctrine and is characterized by the
goal of an economic and social order that avoids the
extremes of both an unfettered liberal economy and a
socialized economy. On the one hand it rejects the
unchecked individualism of neoliberalism, which permits the strong to exploit the weak, for Christian
social doctrine requires that liberty be limited by
considerations of the general welfare.[50] On the
other hand it opposes Socialism and Communism with
their concept of class struggle, because the latter
is contrary to the law of fraternity and leads to
the domination of society by a portion of its members.
Relations of collaboration based upon justice and
charity should exist between all classes and nations.
The aim of Christian doctrine is the achievement
of a harmonious social order characterized by cooperation between different sections of the population
and permitting the development of the person by
guaranteeing him his rights and the exercise of his
liberties.

The WCL believes that the weakness of the working class in relation to the forces of capital is a
salient characteristic of contemporary economic
life.[51] As long as this situation persists, governmental intervention must assure improved working
conditions. As do the free trade unions, the Christian unions look to the government to create the
conditions assuring labor of an equal voice in the
direction of the economy. However, the WCL is opposed
to the nationalization of the economy and supports
the principle of private property, provided that it
is managed with responsibility. Rather, it aspires
toward comanagement, an integral association of the

workers with all economic decisions in all branches
of production, culminating in a national economic and
social council. The latter would harmonize the interests of various occupations and determine the
goals of economic policy. The WCL considers this a
solution that would permit labor to participate in
the management of the economy without being subjected
to the state.

WCL and European Integration

Within the WCL there was no major bloc of unions
hostile or indifferent to European integration.
Partly because of their identification with Christian
political parties, Christian labor unions have always
favored European unity and sought to promote it even
before the ICFTU had clearly committed itself to
such a course. According to Catholic social thought,
human association is a natural hierarchy rising from
family unity to the universality of mankind. The
nation-state as a major focus of loyalty is regarded
as a usurper to be overcome by supranational federation. According to M. Vanestandael of the WCL Executive Council:

> Not until European solidarity has ceased
> to be a vain expression, imprisoned within
> the narrow view of national interests will
> the European countries be able to forsake
> their short-sighted policy and grotesque
> concern for balancing ill-understood in-
> terests.[52]

Unlike the ICFTU, the WCL supported the "New
Start" heralded by the Messina Conference in 1955
by insisting upon the creation of supranational institutions enjoying real power. Agreement within
the WCL also included demands for specific social
provisions. The Christian trade unions thought that
the projected European treaties placed insufficient
emphasis on the social problems of integration and
treated them in an incoherent manner. Instead, they
would have liked to have seen a European organ responsible for the study of labor problems in the Community and modifications in the social structure,

including the harmonization of living standards and
of codetermination provisions.[53] As did the free
trade unions, they constantly stressed that a social
policy for Europe must not be a function of economic
imperatives but a goal in itself. They urged that
this include the achievement of full employment, the
free mobility of labor, a European policy for social
security and for vocational training, and substantial
aid to the underdeveloped regions of the European
Communities.

The Christian trade unions demonstrated a greater
supranational zeal than the free trade unions in re-
questing European trade union representation in the
preparatory committees and conferences for the Rome
Treaties.

Despite their many requests and applications,
they had to rely on information from Christian trade
unionists included in national delegations rather
than on a separate representation for labor.

Christian labor was disappointed with the liberal orientation of the Rome Treaties. The Christian
unions argued that the elimination of customs barriers alone could not produce economic and social
achievements, but should be paralleled by provisions
for common economic and social policies.[54] They
would have liked the European Commission to enjoy
broad powers of initiative and decision on matters
of general economic and social policy, as well as a
more equitable distribution of powers between the
Commission and the Council of Ministers. They were
particularly disappointed that principal responsibility for policy rested with the Council and that the
European Parliamentary Assembly lacked true legislative competence. Finally, the Christian trade unions
had hoped for the establishment of an economic and
social council enjoying the right of initiative and
competent to render opinions to the Council of Ministers, the European Assembly, and the Commission.
Such a council would be the embodiment of Christian
social doctrine, the collaboration of all segments
of society in the management of economic and social
affairs.

Within the WCL consensus on European integration
was manifested earlier and was broader in scope than
within the ICFTU. It included the endorsement of a
federally organized Europe and the demand for a European social policy and for European trade union representation on conferences drafting European treaties.
European integration was defined by the WCL's Executive Council as

> a process of constitution of several Euro-
> pean states in a supranational community
> of economic intent and institutionally as
> the creation of a democratic supranational
> organ with its own legislative, executive
> and judiciary organs and its own consul-
> tative institutions.[55]

Federation of Christian Trade Unions for the ECSC

Originally a European Committee of the WCL was
responsible for relations with various European organizations. This body proved inadequate for the
coordination of national policies, and the unions
found that their national organizations did not suit
the wider framework of the ECSC. In March 1955 they
established the Federation of Christian Trade Unions
for the ECSC to gather and diffuse information relative to the ECSC and to study the problems of its
development, especially those concerning the situation of the workers. By creating an independent
federal structure, the Christian labor organizations
hoped to achieve the collective strength to influence
Community organs and to increase their power in Community institutions, especially the Consultative
Committee. Federation would also mean a big improvement in the quality of labor's research staff. Because the individual confederations have few experts
at their disposal, they found it hard to match the
experts staffing the governments and the producers'
organizations. By pooling the resources of individual confederations, the Federation could prepare
common policies on ECSC problems and more efficiently
pursue all other activities designed to further the
interests of Christian labor within the ECSC.

The Federation of Christian Trade Unions for
the ECSC has a much smaller affiliation than the Intersyndicale of the ICFTU, especially since the
CFDT's metallurgy union has joined the ECFTUC's Industrial Committee for Metallurgy. However, it does
not have the latter's problem of the overwhelming
influence of a single national organization, since
most of its strength stems from the trade union organizations of the Netherlands, France, and Belgium.
National federations and the individual miners' and
metalworkers' unions are represented by one delegate
and enjoy one vote. In addition, the Federation of
Christian Trade Unions for the ECSC includes representatives of white-collar workers.

The Executive Committee of the Federation of
Christian Trade Unions is responsible for formulating
the general policy of the Federation and has power
to define common positions for the collectivity.
Decisions reached by a two-thirds majority of the
Federation are binding on all affiliates, ensuring a
greater degree of unity than the free trade unions
were able to command before their 1969 reorganization. The dissident minority is bound to implement
disputed decisions and consistently complies. If
sharp disagreement should arise among delegates, the
Executive Committee of the WCL may be called upon to
arbitrate.[56]

The secretary-general of the Federation of
Christian Trade Unions enjoys broad powers of discretion.[57] Subject only to the instructions of the
Executive Committee, he has full powers to represent
the Federation within the ECSC and to bind that organization. In addition he wields patronage powers
that are effective in persuading hesitant national
organizations, such as the right to make nominations
for appointment to the numerous expert committees
fostered by the European Commission as well as nominations to the Consultative Committee. Moreover,
he enjoys the authority of bypassing the national
federations' bureaucracies and calling upon the experts of member unions to work on Community matters.
By establishing direct relations with the economic
advisers of the confederations and by coordinating

their recommendations and studies, the secretary-
general has facilitated the development of a unified
doctrine at the leadership level, an informal expert
staff with which he can successfully manipulate the
Federation. In addition he acts as single lobbyist
on behalf of the whole Federation with regular access
to the European Commission and the Secretariat of the
Christian Democratic Group of the European Assembly.
He may also represent the Federation's members on
special committees of the Consultative Committee if
the spokesmen for member unions are not available.

Like the Intersyndicale, the Federation of
Christian Trade Unions was established in order to
gain equality for labor in decision making within
the ECSC; and, although its structure differs from
that of the free trade union organization, it has
performed similar tasks. It has acted as a lobbying
agent with the former High Authority (European Commission) and the Assembly and has developed common
stands for its representatives in the Workers' Group
of the Consultative Committee. Owing to its organization, the nature of decision making, its more
homogeneous membership, and its greater commitment
to a politically federated Europe, it has had greater
success than the Intersyndicale in achieving a common policy on Europe.

Program of the Federation
of Christian Trade Unions
for the ECSC

Like the Intersyndicale the Federation of Christian Trade Unions is concerned with promoting full
employment and the improvement of living and working
conditions. However, the Christian labor movement
was particularly concerned with the development of
a substantial European social policy and as early as
1954 demanded increased power for the High Authority
in the social field.[58] To the Federation of Christian Trade Unions the social provisions of the Paris
Treaty appeared purely negative and designed to
promote economic rather than social progress. ECSC-
wide collective bargaining could restore a proper
balance between economic and social progress. There-

fore, the unions repeatedly requested the High Authority to facilitate the conclusion of collective agreements in order to fix minimum standards for the
industries of the ECSC. At this time, however, the
High Authority was cool to the idea of bringing together workers and employers at the European level.

Although the Federation of Christian Trade
Unions and the Intersyndicale met informally to discuss the promotion of a European Miners' Statute,
each organization published its own version with a
slightly different emphasis. Both labor organizations sought to promote as great a uniformity as
possible in the living and working conditions of the
European miners and to grant the latter special protection as compensation for the insalubrious aspects
of their occupation. However, the Federation of
Christian Trade Unions wished the Statute to be
adopted in the form of a collective agreement concluded on the European level between both sides of
industry and sanctioned by the High Authority.[59]
This would be the first step in a series of European
agreements and regulations concluded between free
and autonomous social partners.

The Federation of Christian Trade Unions has
also campaigned for a European energy policy including
a common policy for coal and the creation of a European occupational council for the coal industry.[60]
Although it does not espouse the free trade unions'
desire for long-range planning, it nevertheless
favors setting production goals for each basin and
each enterprise. Like the Intersyndicale, it insists upon adequate readaptation measures to safeguard the workers' interests and believes that the
workers should be consulted on all reconversion decisions. It favors the establishment of a European
occupational council for the coal industry to inte-
grate the coal industry in the framework of an energy
policy, to harmonize rules of competition between
coal and other sources of energy, and to supervise
external commerce.

The Federation of Christian Trade Unions published a series of proposals for the revision of the

Paris Treaty at the same time as the Intersyndicale
that were similar to the latter's proposals regarding the democratization of the ECSC and the extension
of its social policies.

Although the Federation of Christian Trade
Unions for the ECSC is characterized by a greater
degree of consensus and a more tightly knit organization than its free trade union counterpart, the
Christian unions are numerically weaker. The two
labor organizations have maintained the practice of
exchanging views before sessions of the Consultative
Committee in the hope of finding common ground; but
because of their differing traditions, organizations,
and policies they have not sought more formal arrangements.

European Organization
of the WCL

In 1952 the WCL created a European Organization
as part of an overall plan for giving the movement
a regional structure and to deal with the problems
of the European Community, the Organization for Economic Cooperation and Development (OECD), and the
Council of Europe. The membership of this organization has given rise to severe problems having an adverse impact on its effectiveness. Since the WCL
has only two Western European affiliates outside the
EEC, in Austria and in Switzerland, a single European
structure services WCL members in all European organizations. Members of the EEC countries in the WCL
are unhappy with this organizational solution, for
they consider themselves at a disadvantage vis-à-vis
the ICFTU's ERO and the ICFTU.[61] Also, the split
between France's CFTC and the CFDT has had unfortunate
consequences for the European Organization, for both
unions look upon themselves as heir to the original
CFTC. However, the larger and more important CFDT
will not countenance representation of both unions
within the European Organization; and since the CFTC
has maintained its representative and the CFDT did
not submit a candidate, the latter has been absent
from the European activities of the WCL. Moreover,
a decision in 1967 to accept the Italian Christian

Association of Italian Workers (ACLI) as an extraordinary member has been the source of considerable
misunderstanding with the ECFTUC.

Because the bulk of the WCL's membership is in
Western Europe and because of its centralized organization, there exists considerable rivalry between
the WCL and its European Organization. The latter
has always sought full autonomy. Before the 1969
reorganization, however, there was no clear division
of responsibility or of resources between the two
organizations and a considerable confusion and overlapping of functions ensued. The result was that
the WCL's Secretariat provided much of the servicing
for the European Organization's membership. The
European Organization's repeated complaint that it
included the WCL's strongest confederations yet endured the weakest regional organization was partially
responsible for the 1969 decision to form a European
Confederation of Christian Trade Unions.[62]

The European Organization was composed of a biennial conference, a Secretariat, and an Executive
Committee including the national confederations, the
International Trade Secretariats, and a member of the
Federation of Christian Trade Unions of the ECSC and
of the WCL's Executive Committee with observer status.
A Select Committee, an emanation of the Executive
Committee, managed the organization and established
the general lines of policy. Coordination and synthesis of trade union action and policy was sought
during sessions of this committee and its various
working groups, and its decisions were binding on
national affiliates.[63]

The fundamental aims of the European Organization included the pursuit of a supranational trade
union policy, coordinating the action of its affiliates, representing the workers' interests in European
institutions, and providing a permanent information
service for its members.[64] In order to ensure the
equal participation of the trade unions in the functioning of the EEC and to represent Christian workers
at the European level, the European Organization
maintained numerous contacts at all levels to gather

information, prepare meetings, define its point of
view, and defend its position. These efforts included official encounters at the ministerial level
with the European Commission and the European Assembly and unofficial contacts with the European administration and various European personalities representing political, social, and economic sectors. In
order to achieve a coordinated action for the defense
of Christian positions within the Community, the
European Organization established cooperation with
the Christian employers' organizations and the
Christian Democratic Parties. Although this cooperation bore certain fruitful results, it involved difficulties for the trade unionists. On the European
level Christian Democratic Parties lack coordination
and a common policy. Also, the socially heterogeneous
composition of Christian Democratic Parties and their
split into right and left factions mean that the
party often defends interests opposed to those of the
workers. However, cooperation with Christian Democratic Parties is necessary to ensure a balance in
nomination for the administration of the Community.[65]
This balance is very unfavorable for Christian labor
at all levels. Cooperation with the ICFTU in this
domain is not possible because of the latter's
reserve.

The Decision to Establish a
European Confederation of
Christian Trade Unions

In 1968 the Executive Committee established a
special subcommittee to revise the constitution of
the European Organization in order to improve its
functioning. Friction with the WCL was not the only
factor causing the European Organization to transform
its structure. For a number of years certain glaring
weaknesses had been the subject of vigorous debate.
In 1965 and 1966 the unions ruefully admitted that
they were unable to influence the governments, the
European Commission, or the employers to develop
European social policies, not because of the EEC's
structure but because they had not exhibited sufficient initiative and vigor in drawing up common programs. They concluded that they constituted a passive

presence in European institutions and exerted minimal
influence because of the ineffectiveness of their
organization.[66]

The European Organization did not forge close
ties with the International Trade Secretariats.
While the ICFTU acknowledges the autonomy of its
strong International Trade Secretariats, the WCL's
international secretariats are of secondary importance, limited in scope and confined to France and
the Benelux countries. They are highly jealous of
their autonomy at the European level.[67] Hence, the
European Organization lacked a strong vertical structure; its contacts with the International Trade
Secretariats were limited and sporadic, and it was
unable to provide sufficient servicing for them.
The new European Confederation of Christian Trade
Unions is attempting to establish close links with
the ECFTUC's industrial committees in order to compensate for the limited resources of its own industrial groups. Joint trade union action at the level
of large enterprises and sectors, implemented in a
coordinated manner, would enable the trade unions
to persuade employers to negotiate at the European
level and to exert effective pressure on the governments. The transformation of the European Organization into a confederation was necessary to begin
the difficult task of fusing notably unenthusiastic
International Trade Secretariats with a European
labor group.

The most important objective of the European
Organization, developing common action programs for
the concerted efforts of its affiliates, was hampered
by the diversity of its membership. European Organization affiliates vary greatly in strength and employ
diverse methods of action and strategy in broadly
heterogeneous social and economic environments.
Among the rank and file of these confederations there
is little awareness of, and interest in, European
problems. In an impassioned plea for reform Auguste
Cool, president of the European Organization, said:

We must ask ourselves whether we are guilty
of undue conservatism in our structure and

our organization and of nationalism in our
thinking. We must ask ourselves if we are
not trying too much to protect ourselves
within our own country, thus compromising
the long-term future.[68]

Aside from the lack of internal cohesion, the
European Organization suffered from the familiar
hardship of inadequate resources. Its Secretariat
operates with a very small staff and has no research
service able to assemble and analyze national and
European data, although it is able to entrust national
secretariats with European problems. Moreover, the
European Organization's impact on the national scene
has also been compromised by lack of funds and personnel, for the grass-roots membership still needs
to be convinced of the necessity of European trade
union action. The road from resolutions on European
unity to committee reports, to reamendment and final
acceptance by national affiliates is one strewn with
peril for European labor policies. There are wide
differences between assenting to general resolutions
in Brussels and incorporating European action programs
in national programs.

Because of widespread desire to create a genuine
European trade union movement within the EEC and to
help ensure that European integration would be a
major concern of the national confederations, the
European Organization revised its statutes to create
a European Confederation of Christian Trade Unions
in 1969.[69] The main organizational changes consisted
of converting the biennial conference, a deliberative
assembly, into a congress with the power to take decisions and determine guidelines for coordinated
action. All organs of the new confederation will
take decisions by majority vote, rather than by
unanimity, and annual conferences of the national
confederations and the International Trade Secretariats will help achieve coordinated policies and adopt
measures for improving the financing of the organization.

The fusion of the International Trade Secretariats with the new confederation was not achieved at

the time of reorganization, but was relegated to a
list of medium-term goals to be achieved in three
years.   The industrial groups associated with the
European Confederation include committees for transport; food and agriculture; textiles; metals; public
service; postal, telephone, and telegraph workers;
and a European Council of the International Federation of Christian Unions of White Collar Workers,
Technicians, Managerial and Supervisory Personnel,
and Traveling Salesmen.

The effectiveness of reorganization will be subject to the same constraints as those operative on
the ECFTUC: the overriding importance of national
politics and the continuing shortages of personnel
and resources.   The creation of a genuine European
labor organization will be a lengthy process, for
although reorganization will enhance internal cohesion and promote unity of action the material, psychological, and political factors necessary for
integration are not present.   The power of the European Confederation is operative mainly at the national level, where crucial decisions on social
policy are taken.

Two decades of trade union participation in the
process of European integration has resulted in the
development of a common labor program for the European Communities.   From initially divergent stands
on Europe, the Christian trade unions and their free
trade union counterparts have developed common policies on the institutional configuration for an enlarged Europe, on social affairs, and on the need
to instill a greater degree of democracy at all
levels of the economy.   Both European labor groups
are convinced that social programs can occur only
within the context of European planning and European
policies for each sector of the economy.   They are
deeply concerned with what they regard as their
waning influence in Europe: In the process of European integration, key national decisions are taken
in Brussels, where labor has minimal influence.
Therefore, they have instituted the practice of close
collaboration in developing and promoting European
platforms favorable to labor.

WORLD FEDERATION OF TRADE UNIONS

While ostensibly concerned with labor problems, the WFTU's true function is to marshal and control its affiliates in support of Soviet foreign policy. Therefore, it has consistently mirrored Soviet hostility to European unity and has waged a protracted propaganda campaign against the European Communities.

WFTU affiliates were staunchly opposed to the ECSC and sought to blame it for all the unemployment and other difficulties suffered by their members. On occasion they attempted to impede Community activities, as in the case of the High Authority's readaptation scheme for the transfer of miners from the Centre-Midi to Lorraine. A WFTU pamphlet on the subject, entitled "Mineworkers United Against the Schuman Plan," was typical of Communist labor's attitude toward the ECSC:

> The putting into effect of the Schuman Plan
> is a step toward the realization of a po-
> litical and military union. Its essential
> purpose is the rearmament of West Germany
> and the utilization to the utmost of the
> Ruhr arsenal for a war against the U.S.S.R.
> and the Peoples' Democracies.[70]

Three main themes appeared consistently in the WFTU's attacks on the ECSC: that European integration is designed to benefit American military and capitalist policies and German monopoly interests; that it would mean a lowering of economic standards and political effectiveness for Western European workers; and that it splits the geographic unity of Europe.

However, the main course of action of WFTU affiliates in Western Europe was to ignore the ECSC. They did not establish their own bureau in Luxembourg to maintain contact with the High Authority or ask for representation in the Workers' Group of the Consultative Committee.

When the EEC was established, the CGIL displayed a change in attitude and revealed irreconcilable differences with the WFTU over European unity.[71] For the CGIL, the EEC represented a golden opportunity to work toward one of its major long-term goals, the achievement of labor unity in Europe. Lending credibility to its efforts for labor unity entailed either influencing the WFTU's international line or dissociating itself in a convincing manner from the latter's official policy. But the WFTU maintained a rigidly sectarian view of labor unity and would never seriously countenance cooperation with labor organizations that would not accept either the ideology or the foreign policy premises of the Communist movement. The idea that Communist unions might effectively counter the EEC by boring from within seemed illusory to its leadership, who preferred to wage a protracted campaign from without in order to destroy the EEC. Since it was unsuccessful in its attempts to gain an influential voice in formulating the WFTU's international line, the CGIL has concentrated on creating an image of independence for Italian Communist labor in domestic politics and in European affairs.

The CGIL wished to establish an effective official presence in Brussels. This meant persuading the orthodox CGT to accept its Italian counterpart's polycentric views and healing the considerable rift that separated them. One of the numerous attempts at reconciling these two trade unions resulted in the creation in 1958 of a Trade Union Committee for Coordination and Action with the Common Market. It included the CGT and the CGIL, as well as the diminutive Communist labor unions of the Netherlands, Luxembourg, Equatorial Africa, Cameroun, and Madagascar. It was intended to represent member organizations vis-à-vis other trade unions and the authorities of the EEC and to seek the entry of its members into the consultative organs of the Community. However, it did not produce converging attitudes between its chief members, the CGT and the CGIL. After convening three or four times, it quietly expired with the sole achievement of a series of policy statements

on the EEC neutralizing CGT-CGIL divergencies: The
CGIL could prevent the inclusion of denunciations
of EEC's purposes and ensure a prominent place to
the theme of united action with non-WFTU unions in
its declarations, and the CGT could block references
to participation in EEC organs and any genuine attempts at labor unity.[72]

Aside from its polycentric views the CGIL had
more to gain from the EEC than did other WFTU members,
for the EEC had a beneficial impact on the Italian
economy. If the CGIL adhered to the strict opposition of the WFTU toward the Common Market, it would
lose considerable following and risk isolation both
domestically and in Europe. Hence, in 1962 it re-
newed its efforts to create a coordinating bureau in
Brussels and to achieve contact with the moderate
European labor groups. The CGT refused to take part
and, rather than oppose WFTU policies, suggested as
counterproposal a world trade union conference on
trade relations. Undaunted by this failure, the
CGIL established its own information office in Brussels, staffed by three members and limited essentially
to observing the activities of the EEC and the moderate trade unions and sending reports to the CGIL's
international office. Apparently this move was not
convincing proof of the purity of CGIL aims, for
both the ICFTU and the WCL's European Organization
refused to cooperate with it, on the ground of its
affiliation with an organization consistently de-
nouncing the EEC. Alone the CGIL could not develop
full fledged polycentrism within the Communist labor
movement or create a European branch of the WFTU enjoying the prestige and support of the world organization, yet exercising sufficient autonomy to pursue
action tailored to its regional situation.

The CGT's success in achieving unity with moderate labor groups on the domestic scene in 1965 also
marked the end of its isolation in Europe and resulted
in the establishment of a joint CGT-CGIL standing
committee in Brussels.[73] It was staffed by Augostino
Novella and by the CGT's Benoit Frachon, one of the
most vociferous critics of cooperation with European
labor organizations within the EEC. The Geneva and

San Remo conferences of the French and Italian Communist leadership had produced a reversal in attitude and tactics in the French Communist movement.[74] As a result, the French Communist Party accepted polycentrism, most of the Italian positions on Europe, and coordination of trade union activity on a European scale. Once the Communist parties officially claimed their right to full representation in the European Parliamentary Assembly, the trade unions followed suit and initiated serious attempts to achieve representation on the consultative organs of the European Communities. With polycentrism formalized in a regional organization of Western European Communist Parties and in a trade union bureau in Brussels, the labor unions could, with some reason, protest as discrimination their exclusion from EEC institutions.

Two years later, in 1967, the Standing and Action Committee was transformed into a permanent liaison bureau with an enlarged staff.[75] Since then the main activities of the bureau have focused upon producing broad policy statements on European integration that would appeal to all labor groups and thus help create a common trade union front in Europe. The pragmatism of these European labor programs and their lack of propaganda embellishments are evidence of the CGIL's policy triumph over the CGT. For the proposals that the liaison bureau regularly circulates to its WCL and ICFTU counterparts are intended not so much to influence policy within the EEC as to forge unity among all labor unions preparatory to unity among all left-wing forces in Western Europe and as a prop for Communist-Socialist collaboration in Italy.

The CGIL has been successful in its European mission, for it has obtained official recognition from the European Commission and therefore participates, along with its Socialist and Christian Democratic counterparts, in all Community activities relevant to labor. Initially member governments of the European Communities refrained from nominating members of the WFTU to positions in the EEC as a matter of principle. The Italian government was the first to break this tacit agreement by appointing two

members of the CGIL to the Economic and Social Committee in 1966. The CGIL triumph was dimmed by the
selection of Socialist rather than Communist members
from its ranks and their placement on the Consumers'
Group rather than the Workers' Group of the Economic
and Social Committee; nevertheless, it set a precedent. In 1969 formal relations were established between the CGT-CGIL liaison bureau and the European
Commission. Since then the liaison bureau has participated in a variety of meetings and conferences
organized by the Commission with the employers' organizations and the governments. However, it is not
so much the equal participation of WFTU affiliates in
European activities that represents the major break-
through for Communist labor, but the significant fact
that both the ICFTU and the WCL affiliates have accepted this participation, however grudgingly.
Prior to 1969 the ECFTUC scrupulously avoided any
contact with the liaison bureau as a matter of principle and refused to participate in any activity of
the European Communities that included WFTU affiliates. The cooperation of all labor groups in European
endeavors can be considered a milestone on the road
to the CGIL's goal of labor unity, domestically and
in Europe. Polycentrism and the more flexible CGIL
approach to European unity have prevailed despite
the staunch opposition of the WFTU leadership and
the initial hostility of the CGT.

A COMMON TRADE UNION FRONT
FOR EUROPE?

    Differences in ideology, programs, and tactics
separate the ICFTU, the WCL, and the WFTU at the international level. Has their participation in the
European Communities enabled them to bridge these
differences and to develop practical cooperation?
If so, what factors have favored united trade union
action and to what degree has collaboration been
achieved?

    Efforts toward joint action are motivated both
by the unions' lack of success in influencing policy

within Europe and by changes of attitude toward cooperation within the ranks of each European Organization.   Goals shared by the ECFTUC and the Confederation of Christian Trade Unions have been the achievement of an increased voice for labor in the operations and decisions of the Community and the development of an industrial dialogue at the European level for general and sectoral matters.   However, labor is excluded from key EEC institutions and has failed to gain access to the Council of Ministers. It has fared slightly better in the area of industrial relations because the unions are strong in the industrial committees and because the Commission's General Directorate of Social Affairs has actively supported joint meetings between UNICE and the employers' organizations.   The trade unions wish to improve their marginal role in the European decision-making process and therefore have cooperated in developing policy and have issued joint statements on key European issues.   Since lobbying and publicity remain the chief means by which labor can exert its influence on the EEC, the unions have sought to increase their strength by coordinating their attempts to gain access to the Council of Ministers and by defining common programs.

Although the leaders of the ECFTUC and the European Confederation of Christian Trade Unions are officially enthusiastic on the matter of developing close working relationships, no institutionalized or regular form of cooperation has emerged.   Joint consultations are sporadic and ad hoc and rarely occur at the level of the executive committees.   Contacts occur only in order to develop policy on impending major European decisions, such as the geographic extension of the Community, the merger of the treaties, or the creation of a European company.   Also, the trade union groups meet for coordination purposes before participating in meetings with employers' organizations or in conferences and round tables sponsored by the European Commission.   Working relations are dependent upon the activities of the European institutions and are limited to matters suggested by the Rome Treaties.

The divisiveness of labor is most apparent in
the functioning of the main institution on which labor is represented. Friction among the world organizations and national misunderstandings have prevented
the ECFTUC and the European Confederation of Christian
Trade Unions from collaborating in preparing sessions
of the Economic and Social Committee. The appointment of the small German Christian Trade Union (CGB)
to the Economic and Social Committee in 1966 halted
the close working relations between the ICFTU and
the WCL on the Workers' Group.[76] Two years elapsed
before regular consultations could be established between the trade unions groups preparatory to committee sessions because the DGB did not wish to have
contacts with its lesser rival. In the interval a
highly formal arrangement was developed in order to
coordinate trade union positions before Committee
sessions.

Because the ICFTU and the WCL adhere to differing philosophies, the very definition of unity is an
issue. The ECFTUC favors an organized relationship
in which its majority position would be recognized.[77]
If only the European Confederation of Christian
Trade Unions would frankly accept its lack of strength
in Italy and Germany, cooperation would be assured.
However, a minority position does not necessarily
imply willingness to cede organizational identity in
the interest of increased effectiveness. Because
the Christian trade unions are determined to preserve
their identity and because this identity includes
the goal of transforming the capitalist system, they
have opted for unity through pluralism.[78] The practical implications of this form of unity consist in
the developing and establishing of joint programs
with the support of organized contacts between the
executive boards of the European labor organizations.
Because of its overwhelming strength relative to the
Confederation of Christian Trade Unions, the ECFTUC
has not responded favorably to the establishment of
regular contacts on the former's terms. One can only
conclude that despite assertions on the necessity
for labor unity, relations between the two organizations are still in a diplomatic stage, although discussions aimed at establishing more structured
relations are in progress.

With the official recognition of the CGT-CGIL liaison bureau, the European labor organizations have been confronted with a thorny problem. Because the Christian trade unions do not espouse a Socialist philosophy and because they cooperate regularly with WFTU affiliates on the national level, they are not so wary of cooperation with the WFTU in the European Communities as are their ICFTU counterparts. The latter organization originated in a split from the WFTU in 1949 and embodies militant anti-Communist aims. Hence, the ECFTUC has rejected contact with the liaison bureau and protested the Commission's official recognition of it on the grounds that the latter is not an autonomous organization.[79] Until 1970 it flatly refused to participate in any Commission-sponsored activities that included representatives of the liaison bureau. The European Confederation of Christian Trade Unions has generally deferred to the ECFTUC on this matter, although it is interested in normalized relations with the liaison bureau.

While hostility toward the WFTU is official on the international and European levels of the WCL and the ICFTU, it is not uniformly pervasive within the ranks of each organization. Generally, the members of each European labor group will seek to extend their national attitudes toward the WFTU affiliates, favorable or unfavorable, to the European level. Thus, the CGT-FO adamantly opposed access by the CGT to European institutions, while the Italian UIL and CISL have not opposed cooperation with the CGIL in Europe. The FGTB of Belgium is unique in consistently supporting close practical cooperation with the Communist unions as a matter of principle.

The debilitating consequences of trade union divisiveness in Europe have been officially acknowledged by the various labor groups. However, because this division is anchored in mutually exclusive ideologies and reflected in national and international friction, labor unity within the European Communities does not represent a short-term goal. When and if it occurs, it will be through the industrial committees rather than among the general organizations of the European labor groups.

In assessing the effectiveness of European labor organizations, one must consider the nature of the decision-making process in the European Communities, for interest groups will generally attempt to tailor their activities to the characteristics of the system they seek to influence. Chapter 3 will consider the channels of access available to labor. However, the style of European decision making merits brief attention here, since it affects the internal features of European interest groups.

The major constituency for the highly technical decisions of the EEC is the economic and administrative elites of the member countries. General public awareness of European activities is low, for EEC decisions do not impinge upon the daily welfare of the European population in a continuous, intense manner; hence, the low level of awareness and interest in European Community affairs evident among the grassroots membership of European labor organizations. There is no such phenomenon as European public opinion, only a vague and uninformed support of "European unity."

For the economic and administrative elites in Europe, the legitimacy of the EEC is based upon its concrete achievements, not upon the general procedures and purposes emerging from the Community. Business groups support the European Community for its economic results. Labor supports the EEC for ideological as well as economic reasons, but it does not identify with either the decision-making procedures or the policies of the EEC and has acted as champion of the democratization of the entire European structure. Legitimacy does not accrue from the manner in which results are achieved within the EEC, for these are focused upon national unanimity and achieved by diplomacy in the Committee of Permanent Representatives. While a complex procedural consensus has painfully emerged over a period of time, it has proved highly vulnerable to wrecking tactics periodically indulged in by individual governments. This intermittent disruption radiates from the Council of Ministers to other EEC organs and acts as a damper on their activity and on the activity of

European interest groups. The multiple centers of
European decision, from the Commission to the lesser
consultative organs, are bounded by the will of the
governments to proceed with integration. In times
of crisis, interest groups realize that the actual
decision-making power on which they must exert their
pressure remains the national one. The European
bureaucracy headed by the Council of Ministers is
highly vulnerable to national pressures and is protected from the general control of the public by
the secrecy of its proceedings and the technical nature of its decisions.

Hence, the power of labor groups is exerted
chiefly on the national level, and the European pressure groups operate in the rarefied atmosphere of
support from national elites and the European Commission. Because the latter does not enjoy power, it
has directly stimulated a vigorous consultative activity with specialized interest groups in order to
help the latter act as political mediators with member states. In turn labor groups have lent the Commission their staunch support in the hope that it
would eventually acquire power. The dialogue between
the Commission and the interest groups is like a
two-way process of artificial resuscitation. The
Committee has favored the development of professional
associations through personal contacts, participation
in their meetings, round tables, and study groups.
Thus, it helps to stimulate a group of functionaries
in the interest groups who are well versed on European
problems and the importance of European activities
to their membership. The Commission also wishes to
promote favorable attitudes toward the EEC among the
interest groups so that their national affiliates
can assist the Commission by lobbying for its policies in the national capitals. A characteristic
interest group-Commission interaction is the exchange
of information: Interest associations track down
studies and proposals of the Commission in order to
learn its intentions and in turn communicate their
own wishes and needs to the Commission. In addition
there is a special affinity between the labor organizations and the Commission that abets their symbiotic
relationship: Labor groups are generally dedicated

to the goal of European unification and provide ample
publicity for this aim at their periodic congresses.

The chief functions of the European labor organizations consist of representation and lobbying. Their
effectiveness can be gauged by their internal cohesion and by the ability of their leadership to mobilize the energy, support, and resources of their
members. Labor groups in Europe enjoy a highly effective leadership; and, although those in top positions must divide their energy and attention between
national and European tasks, they manage to maintain
effective communication with the membership.

One of the most serious problems assailing the
internal cohesion of trade union associations, the
relationship between the industrial groupings and
the horizontal structure, is being gradually eliminated as a result of their recent reorganization.
Within a more centralized structure the secretariats
can perform their functions of communication and information in a more effective manner, and the executive boards have found their task of interest articu-
lation easier to accomplish. Although the attitudes
of the broad membership will still be determined by
national political circumstances, the upgrading of
the general assemblies of the ECFTUC and the European
Confederation of Christian Trade Unions into congresses with weighted membership and majority vote
will undoubtedly help form an interested and aware
rank and file. One measure of the degree of European
awareness among national confederations is not so
much the number of pious speeches praising European
integration as the number of national trade union
platforms inspired by European activities. There is
ample evidence that national confederations have
benefited greatly in pressing their claims at the
national level from contact with their colleagues
in their European organizations.

While the labor organizations in the EEC have
managed to keep abreast of European integration by
strengthening their structure, their resources remain
insufficient for their tasks. Their funds and their
European staffs are not adequate for servicing their

memberships, and the Christian trade union organization is heavily dependent on the WCL (and on the national services) for this function. Both European
trade union associations rely upon the services of
the European Commission for the statistical studies
and the comparative information that their own secretariats are unable to provide. As a result, their
initiatives have been limited.

The ECFTUC and the Confederation of Christian
Trade Unions wield no political sanctions in the EEC.
The chief source of labor's power, the strike, is
operative only at the national level and will not be
applicable within the EEC in the near future. Labor's
chief means of exerting pressure on the European
level is confined to publicity and to lobbying, and
just as there is no constituency on behalf of foreign
aid that sends members of parliament to the national
capitals, there is no administrative constituency in
the EEC on behalf of increased European expenditures
for improved living and working conditions. The
trade unions have sought to obtain a progressive
European social policy from the minister of social
affairs in Brussels and a genuine industrial dialogue
with the employers. They have been unsuccessful in
their attempts because they have no means of political coercion at their disposal in the EEC. Although
there have been examples of transnational cooperation
in strike action within the European Community, relations between multinational companies and the
unions are still in the formative stage. Collective
bargaining contracts are still drawn up at the national level and ministers of social affairs remain
responsible to their respective national parliaments.

The trade unions have managed to create effective European organizations to represent labor's
interests within the EEC. These organizations have
exhibited a more advanced structure and a greater
degree of internal cohesion than their industrial
counterparts, perhaps because of their minority
status within the European Community. Although
significant problems persist in labor's European organizations, they are shared by all European interest groups and can be traced to the decision-making

procedure of the EEC, which is highly dependent upon
national politics and shrouded in secrecy.

NOTES

1. Confédération Internationale des Syndicats
Libres, <u>Procès-verbal officiel de la conférence mon-
diale du travail et du premier congrès de la Confédération internationale des syndicats libres</u> (London,
1949), pp. 283-85.

2. International Confederation of Free Trade
Unions, <u>Report of the Second World Congress, Held
at Milan, Italy, 4-12 July, 1951</u> (Brussels, 1951),
pp. 59-62.

3. International Confederation of Free Trade
Unions, <u>Information Bulletin</u>, II, 20 (Brussels, November 1950), 7.

4. International Confederation of Free Trade
Unions, <u>Report of the Sixth World Congress, Held in
Brussels, 3-11 December, 1959, Including the Report
on Activities and the Financial Report for 1957-1958</u>
(Brussels, 1960), p. 236.

5. European Regional Organization of the International Confederation of Free Trade Unions, <u>European
Regional Conference, Held at Brussels, 1-4 November,
1950</u> (Brussels: European Regional Secretariat, 1950),
p. 5.

6. Walter Schevenels, "The I.C.F.T.U.'s European Regional Organization," <u>Free Labor World</u> (January 1954), p. 8.

7. <u>European Regional Conference, Held at Brussels, 1-4 November, 1950</u>, p. 4.

8. European Regional Organization of the International Confederation of Free Trade Unions, <u>European
Regional Conference, Held at Strasbourg, 3-5 November, 1954</u> (Brussels: European Regional Secretariat,
1954), p. 8.

9. European Regional Organization of the International Confederation of Free Trade Unions, Report
on the European Trade Union Conference for the Revival of the European Idea, Held at Brussels, 25-27
August, 1955 (Brussels: European Regional Secretariat, 1955).

10. Ibid., appendix IV, "Statement on the Revival of the European Idea."

11. "Observations Relative to the Draft European
Common Market Treaty Submitted to the President of
the Ministerial Committee by the Free Trade Union
Organizations of the Community" (Brussels, January
30, 1957). (Mimeographed.) In the files of the
New York office of the International Confederation
of Free Trade Unions.

12. Ibid.

13. International Confederation of Free Trade
Unions, Report of the Third World Congress Held at
Stockholm (Brussels, 1953).

14. Ernst B. Haas, The Uniting of Europe: Political, Social, and Economic Forces (Stanford,
Calif.: The University Press, 1958), p. 363.

15. Information Bulletin, V, 10 (May 1954), 63.

16. William Diebold, Jr., The Schuman Plan: A
Study in Economic Cooperation, 1950-1959 (New York:
Frederick A. Praeger, 1959), p. 462.

17. Information Bulletin, VII, 4 (February 15,
1956), 26.

18. International Confederation of Free Trade
Unions, Report of the Fifth World Congress, Held in
Tunis, 5-13 July, 1957 (Brussels, 1958), p. 164.

19. Communauté Européenne du Charbon et de
l'Acier, Actes officiels du Congrès international
d'études sur la Communauté européenne du charbon et
de l'acier, Milan-Stresa, 31 Mai-9 Juin, 1957, III,

L'orientation sociale de la Communauté (Milan: Dott.
A. Giuffre, 1958), pp. 365-69.

20. Alfred Braunthal, "The Free Trade Unions'
Role in the Process of European Integration," Free
Labor World (July 1954), p. 8.

21. European Coal and Steel Community, Bulletin
from the European Coal and Steel Community (November
1954), p. 5.

22. Information Bulletin, VIII, 14 and 15 (July
15-August 1, 1957), 107.

23. Secrétariat Syndical Européen, Deuxième Assemblée générale des syndicats libres des états-membres des Communautés européennes (Luxembourg, November 1959).

24. Secrétariat Syndical Européen, Rapport du
secrétariat à la Deuxième assemblée générale des
syndicats libres des états-membres des Communautés
européennes (Luxembourg, November 10, 1959), p. 20.

25. Secrétariat Syndical Européen, Sixième assemblée générale: Rapport d'activité 1966-1968
(Brussels, April 1969).

26. Ibid., ch. 1, p. 5.

27. Rapport du secrétariat à la Deuxième assemblée générale des syndicats libres des états-membres
des Communautés européennes, p. 26.

28. Secrétariat Syndical Européen, Rapport
d'activité du Secrétariat syndical européen à la
Troisième assemblée générale des syndicats libres
des états-membres des Communautés européennes (Brussels, January 1960), p. 21.

29. Confédération Européenne des Syndicats
Libres dans la Communauté, Premier congrès: Discours,
décisions, résolutions (Brussels, April 1969), pp.
77-83.

30. Sixième assemblée générale: Rapport d'activité 1966-1968, ch. 5, pp. 10-13.

31. Ibid.

32. Ibid., ch. 1, pp. 14-18.

33. Ibid.

34. European Communities, Commission, Deuxième rapport général sur l'activité des Communautés en 1968 (Brussels, 1969).

35. Sixième assemblée générale: Rapport d'activité 1966-1968, ch. 5, p. 32.

36. Ibid., p. 46.

37. Intersyndicale CECA, Rapport d'activité de l'Intersyndicale CECA (Luxembourg, December 1961), p. 12.

38. Ibid.

39. M. G. M. Nederhorst, for Assemblée Parlementaire Européenne, "Rapport fait au nom de la Commission des affaires sociales sur les aspects sociaux du problème charbonnier qui se pose actuellement," doc. no. 16 (Brussels, March 1959).

40. International Confederation of Free Trade Unions, Economic and Social Bulletin, XVIII, 1-6 (Brussels, January-February 1959), 10.

41. European Economic Community, European Parliamentary Assembly, Débats de l'Assemblée parlementaire européenne, Compte-rendu in-extenso des séances (session of January 1960), no. 23, p. 80.

42. European Economic Community, European Parliamentary Assembly, Cahiers mensuels de documentation européenne (March 1960), p. 17.

43. European Communities, Press and Information Service, Trade Union News from the European Community (1967), no. 3, p. 10.

44.   Harm Buiter, "Labor Speaks on the Community
Level," Labor in the European Community (July 1964),
no. 4.

45.   Carl J. Friedrich, Europe: An Emergent Nation (New York: Harper & Row, 1969), see ch. 4.

46.   Premier congrès: Discours, décisions, résolutions, pp. 62-70.

47.   Trade Union News from the European Community
(1965), no. 1, p. 11.

48.   European Parliament, European Documentation
(April-June 1969), no. 2, p. 34.

49.   Premier congrès: Discours, décisions, résolutions, pp. 62-70.

50.   "Quarante ans de la Confédération internationale des syndicats chrétiens," Labor (March 1960),
p. 105.

51.   Robert Vautherin, "Un programme constructif
et audacieu," Labor (March 1960), p. 117.

52.   M. Vanestandael, "Le Marché commun et Euratom, notre position," Labor (February 1957), p. 46.

53.   "Résolution concernant l'intégration européenne," Labor (February 1955), p. 129.

54.   Auguste Cool, "Les travailleurs devant le
Marché commun européen," Labor (December 1956), pp.
243-46.

55.   "La 25ème réunion du conseil de la C.I.S.C.,"
Labor (December 1957), p. 230.

56.   "Réalisation syndicale chrétienne," Labor
(April-May 1955), p. 199.

57.   Haas, op. cit., pp. 385-86.

58. "Les syndicats chrétiens des pays de la C.E.C.A. adoptent une nouvelle structure," _Labor_ (September-October 1954), p. 43.

59. "Vers une convention européenne de travail pour les mineurs," _Labor_ (February 1960), p. 87.

60. _Cahiers mensuels de documentation européenne_ (November 1960), p. 15.

61. Organization Européenne de la C.I.S.C.-C.M.T., _Premier congrès: Vème rapport d'activité_ (Brussels, May 1969), p. 32.

62. _Ibid._

63. "L'Organisation Européenne de la C.I.S.C.," _Labor_ (September-October 1959), p. 211.

64. Auguste Cool, "Pour une Europe au service de la paix," _Labor_ (March 1960), pp. 133-36.

65. "Marché commun et Euratom," _Labor_ (July-August 1958), pp. 115-18.

66. _Premier congrès: Vème rapport d'activité._

67. _Ibid._

68. Auguste Cool, _L'orientation des structures et de l'action du mouvement syndical dans une dimension européenne_, report to IVème Conférence Européenne des Syndicats Chrétiens, Amsterdam, 6-8 October 1966 (Brussels: Organisation Europeen de la C.I.S.C., October 1966).

69. Organisation Européenne de la C.M.T., _Résolution générale_ (Brussels, May 1969).

70. Communauté Européenne du Charbon et de l'Acier, _Obstacles a la mobilité des travailleurs et problèmes sociaux de réadaptation_, 1809/2/56 (Luxembourg: Service des Publications Européennes, 1956), p. 47.

71. Donald L. M. Blackmer, <u>Unity in Diversity:</u> <u>Italian Communism and the Communist World</u> (Cambridge, Mass.: MIT Press, 1968), see ch. 9.

72. <u>Ibid</u>.

73. <u>Trade Union News from the European Community</u> (1965), no. 8, p. 7.

74. François Fejto, <u>The French Communist Party</u> <u>and the Crisis of International Communism</u> (Cambridge, Mass.: MIT Press, 1967), pp. 174-82.

75. <u>Trade Union News from the European Community</u> (1967), no. 4, p. 6.

76. <u>Premier congrès: Vème rapport d'activité</u>, p. 23.

77. <u>Sixième assemblée générale: Rapport d'ac-</u> <u>tivité 1966-1968</u>, ch. 1, p. 7.

78. <u>Résolution générale</u>.

79. <u>Sixième assemblée générale: Rapport d'ac-</u> <u>tivité 1966-1968</u>, ch. 1, pp. 7-8.

3

EUROPEAN
PRESSURE
GROUPS

European labor groups owe their existence to a combination of internationalist sentiment, national support, and the considerable interest of the European Commission in surrounding itself with an economic and social consensus in support of its dialogue with the Council of Ministers. These interest groups display a unique blend of national and international characteristics and constitute loose confederations of national groups heavily dependent upon the support of the national organizations for their very existence. Their main activity occurs at the national level and predominates over an emerging European activity, for both their power and their influence are operative chiefly in the national arena. Within the EEC their main functions include representation, lobbying, and gathering and transmitting information about European developments. Their effectiveness in pursuing these tasks and in participating in EEC activities has been considerably enhanced by their recent reorganization. European sentiment and activity is slowly growing in proportion to national concerns within European labor groups, and the latter are becoming increasingly effective in mobilizing the energy and resources of their members. They have increased their budgets, their staffs, and the frequency of their meetings and have developed effective communication networks to articulate interests and common strategies to realize them.

Ultimately, the activity of European interest groups depends upon the rule-making procedures within the EEC, a fluid blend of national and supranational elements. Labor has intertwined its official and lobbying activities through its participation in the EEC's consultative organs and has also pressed its claims through the institutional channels of political parties, bureaucracies, and the cabinet. The latter are available at the national level only, for the European cabinet--the Council of Ministers--is not accessible to labor; and the political parties participate in the Assembly, which has consultative status only. Labor groups must approach the European gatherings of relevant ministries through national routes. Therefore, they have often complained, and with ample causes, that they have been denied an influence in the EEC that they have won in national affairs. Hence, a radical transformation of the EEC's institutional structure is a necessary condition for an increased labor role in European decisions. The workers have insisted upon the need for procedures guaranteeing democratic policy formation, because they have been unable to exercise their influence in policy areas where political considerations are paramount and have been successful in influencing technical matters only.

Publicity and the mass media remain the chief formal channels for promoting labor's political demands. Labor's periodic conferences in Brussels attract a large press corps and the participation of the highest EEC officials. Nevertheless, the salient indicator of labor's influence in European matters is a negative one: Labor is denied representation on the chief rule-making organ and must react to the Council of Ministers' decisions after the fact, despite its close relations with the European Commission, for the latter's proposals are often changed by the Council of Ministers. Thus, labor groups resort to national capitals and parliaments to press their position.

Elite representation, the presence of a member of European labor groups or of a sympathetic and interested individual in the rule-making structure, constitutes another channel of access to European decisions. What is the extent of labor's direct involvement in the EEC's and the ECSC's decision-making structures? Although the Paris Treaty restricts the formal participation of labor in the administration of the ECSC to membership in the Consultative Committee, two or three of the High Authority's members were always trade unionists and the ICFTU and the SCL together nominated a member of the High Authority. Paul Finet, former president of the ICFTU and secretary-general of the Belgian FGTB, was the first coopted member of the High Authority and served until 1965 along with Heinz Potthof of the DGB. Roger Reynaud of the CFTC and Jean Fohrman of Lexembourg's CGT remained on the High Authority until it was replaced by a Joint Commission in 1967.

The trade unions did not succeed in having a representative of the labor movement admitted to the original European Commission. However, Commission members Robert Marjolin, Sicco Mansholt, and A. Levi-Sandri are sympathetic to labor and maintain a fairly regular dialogue with the trade unions on many economic and social issues. The trade union concept of collaboration with the Commission's work has been largely accounted for in the social field by Sandri and in agricultural affairs by Mansholt, both of whom have sought to ensure close relations with labor in formulating their programs. The Commission's consultation of the trade unions at various stages in drawing up proposals is more important to them as a means of exerting their influence than is their representation on consultative organs. In addition to consulting the trade unions on specific projects, the European Commission has engaged them in discussions on current problems at round table meetings on all aspects of economic affairs.

The unions were unsuccessful in obtaining a coopted representative of labor on the unified Commission. However, Wilheim Haferkamp, a member of the DGB's executive board, was named to the Commission when it was established in 1967.

The numerous services of the European Commission
have maintained an active dialogue with the representatives of labor groups. Cooperation between interest groups and the directorates of the Commission
is closest in agricultural and social affairs, perhaps because the minority status of the interests
represented by the pressure groups and European
officials leads to mutual identification. European
labor confederations participate in numerous bipartite, tripartite, regular, and ad hoc committees that
function in the General Directorate for Social Affairs, including the Central Committee for Social
Harmonization. While these working groups offer the
trade unions an opportunity to state their demands
and defend their interests, the Commission's activity
in the area of social affairs is dependent upon the
goodwill of the Council of Ministers and the political climate in the Community. Therefore, while
working groups within the Commission may formulate
guidelines and proposals for the latter's activity
in social affairs, they cannot compel the Council of
Ministers to act upon them or prevent it from filing
them under the heading of oblivion. Moreover, in the
past few years the Council of Ministers has sought to
restrict the Commission's activity in the field of
harmonization. This has acted as a damper on the
Commission's relations with the trade unions, and
certain bipartite or tripartite working groups created
for areas covered under the Paris Treaty's provisions
for social harmonization are dormant.

The trade unions have indeed become the spokesmen for social policy within Commission-sponsored
working groups. However, they complain that in other
policy areas they cannot bring their opinions and
suggestions to bear before proposals are completed
and that they lack adequate documentation.[1] On the
other hand, the influence of labor's representatives
on ad hoc working groups, technical committees, and
institutionalized arrangements for the consultation
of experts is more limited than that of business
organizations, because labor groups have more limited
funds and therefore experience greater difficulty in
securing the services of technical experts.

The trade unions are represented in most of the
advisory or consultative bodies of the EEC and the
ECSC. Of the 101 members of the Economic and Social
Committee (ESC), 34 are representatives of the trade
union movement, 10 from the WCL, and 23 from the
ICFTU. The ESC offers the trade unions the possibility of expressing the stands formulated by their
European organizations for European institutions and
for public opinion. In addition, members of the
European labor confederations often sit as experts
in the numerous working groups of this committee.
However, the specialized sections of the committee
meet so frequently that the trade union representatives, already overburdened at the national level,
are hard pressed to meet the requirements of European
affairs. The ESC has not proved a satisfactory source
of participation in the European political process
for labor, because most opinions put forth by the
Committee are technical in nature and only a few are
concerned with general policy. Moreover, because the
ESC exercises only a marginal influence within the
EEC, the opinions presented are the result of deliberate compromise among the Committee's constituent
groups and therefore represent the lowest common
denominator. The ESC does not have the means of making a systematic study of the impact of its decisions
on either the Council of Ministers or the European
Commission. Even without such an inquiry its members
are well aware that many of its opinions have been
disregarded.

Labor representatives participate in the consultative committees for implementing the mobility
of labor and for vocational training and in the tripartite committee on the European Social Fund. The
trade unions would like to see the activities of
these three committees more closely coordinated, but
their efforts toward this end have borne little fruit
so far. Compared with the broad goal of developing
a European employment policy, the functions of the
consultative bodies are largely routine and hence
disappointing to the trade unions.

Labor has pressed for, but has not gained, admission to the Administrative Committee for the Social

Security of Migrant Workers. As a result, European
labor organizations must work through the national
ministries of labor. Labor has also been denied
membership on the Board of Directors of the European
Investment Bank. Out of twelve directors and twelve
alternates only one of the alternates has been supported by the trade unions. The trade unions were
also unsuccessful in gaining access to the Committee
on Economic Trends and the Monetary Committee, which
are composed of civil servants and representatives
of the national banks. One of the aims of the European labor confederations is to gain access to all
EEC organs concerned with policy making; therefore,
they have often warned against the creation of a
European technocracy, which would isolate the decision-making process from political contention.

The European trade union secretariats maintain
regular contacts with the political groups of the
European Parliamentary Assembly (EPA) and are careful
to submit detailed stands to them before debates on
matters concerning labor. The political groups, in
turn, regularly seek the opinions of the trade unions.
Close collaboration is facilitated by the fact that
a large number of deputies are either sympathizers
of the labor movement or trade union members. In
1967 the EPA instituted a system of yearly hearings
on the broad lines of social policy. These have
added still another dimension to labor's attempts to
gain a platform for its demands.

Labor's relations with the European Commission
and its services have proved satisfactory to the
European labor confederations, despite the numerous
obstacles encountered by the trade unions in establishing working relations with the Council of Ministers. Ministers appear only at meetings and frequently in unpublicized ad hoc sessions. Access is
rendered even more difficult for the trade unions by
the manner in which the governments have interpreted
article 151 of the EEC Treaty and article 121 of the
ECSC Treaty, which provide for the possibility of
constituting a committee composed of representatives
of member states. The result has been the establishment of permanent delegations in which each government

has an ambassador to prepare the sessions of the
Council of Ministers. Although the trade unions have
been able to establish regular or ad hoc contacts with
several permanent national representatives to the Community, these relations have not always proved satisfactory to the European labor confederations. Therefore, the latter usually transmit their position to
Council members through the national trade union confederations; and, when a question is due to come before the Council of Ministers, trade union pressure
is exerted in all countries through the traditional
national channels. However, trade unions frequently
complain that the Council tends to consult workers
and employers at the national level, then later ad-
justs problems in Brussels. Furthermore, within the
EEC the Council of Ministers is not responsible to
the EPA, the Consultative Committee, or the ESC, where
trade union opinion might indirectly have an impact.

Prior to 1966 trade union contact with the
Council as a whole was sporadic and punctuated by a
two-year interval of complete boycott by the Ministers of Social Affairs. Since then trade union meetings with the ministers have occurred on a yearly
basis and often include representatives of UNICE.[2]
However, the European labor confederations are alone
in their desire for frequent and wide-ranging ex-
changes of views among the governments, the European
Commission, and the social partners on the broad lines
of a Community social policy. UNICE does not regard
the development of a European social policy with favor
and opposes any supranational competence in this
field. This attitude is shared by the Ministers of
Social Affairs, especially the French, who insist
that social policies and social harmonization in
particular are purely matters for intergovernmental
consultations. The rule-making procedures employed
by the Council of Ministers tend to reinforce the
predominance of national politics within European
interest groups and to deny European pressure groups
the opportunity to participate in Community building
at the European level.

European labor groups have scored a recent success in their efforts to gain a larger voice in

Community affairs. Following the suggestions offered
by the Employment Conference held in Luxembourg in
April 1970, the Council of Ministers instituted a
Standing Committee on Employment. The Committee is
intended to serve as a framework for continuous consultation between both sides of industry and the
government in order to secure the coordination of
national employment policies according to jointly
agreed-upon objectives. Its special function will
be to lay the grounwork for future decisions in this
area, an important concession to labor organizations,
for they have frequently complained that their opinion
is sought when it is too late to influence decisions
significantly. The labor members of the Committee
also enjoy an important voice in determining the
agenda for its meetings. Among the matters selected
for future consideration during the Committee's initial meeting in March 1971 are a number of subjects
of major importance to labor: the consequences of
economic and technical changes on employment, the
relation between the Community's employment policies
and its policies in other fields, regional imbalances,
and women at work. If the Committee's actual achievements correspond to its ambitious goals, its establishment will represent a milestone for labor in its
continuing efforts to achieve equal participation in
the European policy process and a social policy con-
comitant with economic growth.

RULE MAKING WITHIN THE
EUROPEAN COMMUNITIES

     Although the European summit at The Hague in
December 1969 displayed a new preoccupation with reform of the internal structure of the EEC through
its plans for expanding the budgetary authority of
the European Parliament and its proposals for European policies in technology and other fields, rule
making by the EEC occurs within an intergovernmental
body, the Council of Ministers and its permanent representatives, in collaboration with the European Commission. The decision-making process within the EEC
acquires its distinctive nature from the dialogue
between the Council of Ministers and the European

Commission, which includes a multiplicity of consultations among the cabinet members of the Six, their
bureaucracies, the collegiate Commission, and its
European administration.

The very survival of the European Commission
depends upon its ability to generate proposals that
will emerge as European decisions from the Council
of Ministers and consolidate the integration process,
and upon its skill in maintaining good relations with
the national governments and their administrations.
Since power is still firmly anchored within the nation-
states, Commission members acquire little prestige
from their office; and because they are relatively
isolated from national politics once in Brussels, they
must rely upon the prestige acquired in national service if they are to maintain contact with the broad
public outside the EEC. In order to avoid political
isolation and to gain leverage in its dealings with
the powerful Council of Ministers, the European Commission engages in continuous consultations with the
Permanent Representatives, interest groups, and political parties. This close collaboration serves both
to infuse the national administrations with a sense
of the European mission and to help the Commission
fulfill its primary function of identifying goals and
problems for EEC action.

The Commission's links with the national bureaucracies are facilitated by the fact that most Commission members have administrative backgrounds or have
served as ministers in technical fields and by the
fact that the Commission's bureaucracy is largely only
temporarily detached from the national administrations.[3] Moreover, the Commission voluntarily solicits
the approval of each government for the appointment
of Eurocrats to top policy-making offices.[4] Ultimately, all members of the Commission's directorates
must keep a wary eye on their own governments as a
source of future employment, for European service is
temporary and affords little vertical mobility for
those aspiring to higher political posts.

In preparing its proposals for presentation to
the Council of Ministers, the Commission has become

heavily dependent upon the national experts within
the Permanent Representatives. The Commission often
invites members suggested by the Permanent Representatives to participate in its working groups, and
frequently the same national experts who took part
in a Commission ad hoc working group to draw up a
proposal will also sit in on a working group of the
Permanent Representatives to consider the same proposal.[5] Thus, members of the Council of Ministers'
own staff participate in the Commission's preparatory
function; and because they have participated in preparing the Commission's proposals, they are apt to
defend them before their own governments. However,
in the last resort, although most governments will
choose representatives with enthusiasm for European
integration, the latter are responsible primarily to
the national governments, which they must obey in
case of a conflict between European and national requirements and which can replace them if the need
arises.

The European Commission articulates goals for
the EEC and prepares policy proposals in close collaboration with interest groups and the national
administrations in order to establish a policy consensus and a solid basis of national support for
integration. The manner in which it recruits its
own staff and selects members to serve on working
groups in order to develop proposals is intended to
further consensus and render the proposals acceptable.
Once the proposals are completed, the Commission takes
part in a lengthy series of intergovernmental negotiations, defending its proposals and modifying them to
accommodate specific national requirements.[6] The influence of the Commission depends upon its agility
in conducting this complex and protracted series of
consultations and its skill in dealing with the national governments within the Council of Ministers.

Although the Commission is commonly regarded as
the organ with supranational powers, the Council of
Ministers alone enjoys the legislative power to issue
decisions, regulations, and directives binding on the
member governments. There are no established procedures for decision making within the Council of

Ministers. Rather, intergovernmental bargaining ✓
among the Six is based upon the tacit agreement that
only unanimity can terminate negotiations resulting
in decisions, and that bargaining must continue until
gains and losses are counterbalanced and each government has obtained satisfaction. In order to ensure
the complementarity of national goals through European
decisions. log-rolling can occur across a wide range
of policy areas and marathon negotiations frequently
result in "package deals."[7] To these complex proceedings the Commission brings an objective point of
view, independent of any particular national interest
yet concerned with all of them.

   Each member of the Council of Ministers is sup- *COREPER*
ported by a permanent representative with ambassa-
dorial status and from thirty to sixty bureaucrats
from the relevant ministries. This permanent delegation prepares the dossier of its minister before
Council meetings and maintains a two-way channel of
communication with the home agencies and the Commission. Since it participates in formulating the Commission's proposals by transmitting the requirements
of their government to the Commission, by following
the development of the Commission's proposals step
by step, and even by participating in the Commission's
working parties, it has assumed an important role in
formulating proposals. It has also arrogated part
of the Council of Ministers' decision-making power
in technical matters by deliberating in committee in
order to prepare Council meetings and by reaching
minimum agreements on nonpolitical matters.[8]

   Rule making within the EEC is the result of the
close collaboration of the Council of Ministers, the
national bureaucracies, and the European Commission
and the initiative and drive of the latter. The
resultant decisions do not require the ratification
of the European Parliament, and control by the national parliaments is rendered difficult by the
technical nature of EEC decisions and by the fact
that decisions are the result of carefully wrought
compromises among the various national interests and
European goals. The consultative bodies of the European Communities are unable to exercise control over

this rule-making procedure, for they do not participate in decision making but function virtually on the
fringes of power, more as conscientious observers
than as instruments of domocratic control. This
policy process constitutes a novel challenge for
national and European pressure groups.

THE CONSULTATIVE ORGANS OF
THE EUROPEAN COMMUNITIES

The Consultative Committee

Development

The Consultative Committee was originally established to provide the High Authority with the
technical advice of independent experts, but it soon
developed into an organ seeking to influence the decisions of the High Authority. When it began to
operate in 1953, the producers' representatives considered it as an economic parliament destined to
guide the High Authority's policy and debated policy
issues within the Committee as if it were a veritable
economic and social council.[9] Its president, Pierre
Wigny, could comment that the Consultative Committee
took its task seriously and that it was not content
to render only requested opinions.[10] Even the High
Authority claimed that relations with the Committee
had developed beyond the consultations specifically
prescribed by the Paris Treaty.

By 1955 this pattern of behavior had changed.
Interest lagged as the producers' representatives
realized that they could gain access to the High
Authority through orthodox lobbying channels and
that the High Authority was not lending careful attention to its deliberations.[11] In contrast with
its approach to the Common Assembly, the High Authority did not encourage the development of the Consultative Committee; rather, it stressed the purely advisory capacity of the Committee and even attempted
to divert attention from its deliberations. It merely
submitted questions to the Committee, encouraging no

initiative, and even discouraged voting, stressing
that it was interested in the opinions expressed by
the different groups. From 1956, and until its replacement by a unified commission, the High Authority
has presented the Consultative Committee with a
quarterly report on developments in the general economic situation, its provisional forecasts for coal
and steel production and needs, and exports and imports. It also submitted long-term policy statements
from time to time.

The Trade Unions and the Consultative Committee

The range of subjects on which the High Authority
was obliged to consult the Committee was broad.
Through this organ the trade unions have the opportunity to acquire detailed knowledge of practically
any aspect of ECSC affairs and actively participate
in its sections for dealing with special problems,
general objectives, markets, prices, research, and
labor problems. Thus, the Committee serves as a forum
for expressing trade union views on all aspects of
economic and social policy.

Of the 17 seats allotted the Workers' Group of
the Consultative Committee, the ICFTU representatives
have normally filled 11 or 12 seats and members of
WCL have occupied 4 or 5 seats, following a division
worked out by the 2 groups. The trade unions are
generally unhappy about the existence of the Consumers' Group, wishing either to gain representation
on it or, preferably, to eliminate it altogether.
They argue:

It is an artificial unity created by certain interest groups, who due to their
social origin, their mentality, and their
professional activity, do not defend the
interests of the Community.[12]

Within the Consultative Committee opinions are
usually divided along group rather than national
lines, and the Workers' Group has demonstrated greater

cohesion than the other two groups.* This fact,
coupled with the relative indifference to the Committee shown by the Producers' Group, has lent it
more influence than its numbers would warrant. However, there have been many instances in which consumers' and producers' representatives united to form
a majority against labor; hence the latter's insistence on a bipartite committee.

The Renard Resolution

If the Consultative Committee has been ignored
by the producers, labor considers it an arena for
gaining equality with management and a means of
achieving its European program. The harmonization
of working conditions is central to the demands of
both labor groups; but the desire for harmonization
was particularly marked on the part of the Belgian
trade unions, which had already obtained the best
working conditions in the Community. They realized
that they could not persuade their employers to agree
to further improvements unless there was a leveling
up of conditions throughout the Community, and they
soon convinced the other unions of the need for uniform conditions as an argument to collective bargaining.

It was André Renard, deputy secretary of the
FGTB, who took the initiative of using the Consultative Committee in an effort to reduce the workweek
and to harmonize all benefits other than wages.
Supported by the entire Workers' Group, including
the Christian unions, he introduced a resolution in
the 1954 session of the Consultative Committee, calling upon the High Authority to take the first steps
toward the harmonization of labor standards in member
countries.[13] In particular the resolution requested
the High Authority to undertake comparative statistical studies preparatory to convening supranational

------

*The Workers' Group has presented united stands
on investment policy, price policies, and social
problems.

bipartite committees of employers and workers. These
would be assigned the task of harmonizing the work
week, vacations, overtime, and holiday pay. Renard
hoped that international conventions would result
from the work of these committees. By "convention"
he meant framework agreements establishing minimum
standards and leaving each country a certain freedom
of action in applying its provisions. This would be
the beginning of harmonization.

The lack of enthusiasm and cooperation of the
High Authority in this venture, and the evasion of
the Council of Ministers, among other grievances, led
to a joint ICFTU-WCL threat to boycott the Consultative Committee in the autumn of 1955. After a virtual
showdown debate in that body, in which the Workers'
Group claimed that the High Authority had fallen behind its treaty obligations to the Community's workers
and had delayed the implementation of the Renard
Resolution, the unions threatened withdrawal. Renard
claimed that rising living standards would not automatically result from an expanding single market, that
workers must fight for better conditions in order to
obtain them, and that too little had been done to work
toward the goal of harmonizing standards of living in
an upward direction.[14] The labor representatives demanded the establishment of Community-wide collective
bargaining codes and complained that when the unions
negotiated for better conditions the employers referred them to the governments, the governments referred them to the High Authority, and the latter sent
them back to their governments. They insisted that
the High Authority had political jurisdiction over
labor problems and translated the problem of legal
competence into one of initiative and responsibility.
In particular they wished the High Authority to
undertake studies comparing real wages among the Six,
to set targets for social policy as it did in the
economic field, and to provide new possibilities for
negotiations on the Community level by bringing employers and workers together to discuss specific
questions.[15]

The trade unions were successful in obtaining
the first and third of these requests. The studies

of the High Authority and the mixed committees will
be discussed in Chapter 4. Suffice it to say that,
as a result of the furor, the Common Assembly passed
a resolution strongly backing the requests to create
bipartite commissions for collective bargaining. The
High Authority speeded up the completion of comparative statistics on labor conditions and declared itself willing to call bipartite committees to discuss
the findings.

If the three groups of the Consultative Committee
have tended to regard this institution as an economic
parliament at times, individually Committee members
have used their relationship with the High Authority
for direct lobbying purposes. The Consultative Committee is only one among many more powerful influences
affecting the High Authority's and the Commission's
decisions. It is accurate to say that, while the High
Authority has never taken a decision against the
opinions of the Committee, it has not acted upon all
the proposals of the latter.[16] As far as the Workers'
Group is concerned, the Consultative Committee has
been a more effective medium for their demands when
supported by another Community organ, such as the
Assembly; and one of the characteristics of trade
union attempts to influence decisions is the application of pressure simultaneously at various quarters
throughout the Community.

The Economic and Social Committee

At the conferences preparatory to the Rome
Treaties there were wide differences of opinion concerning the competence of the Economic and Social
Committee; and perhaps if the example of analogous
institutions had not existed on the national level
and if the Consultative Committee had not existed the
Economic and Social Committee might not have been
created. The contention concerning this institution
is manifest in the way its tasks and powers are attributed by the Treaty. The Treaty accords it obligatory consultation for only a limited number of problems, and for a large number of important questions
consultation is only voluntary. Moreover, the Economic and Social Committee possesses no right of
initiative or of publicity.

Regulations of the ESC

The first few months of the Committee's existence were devoted to the establishment of its internal organization, a slow and difficult task. A working group discussed a project for months. The project was approved by the Council of Ministers only after new negotiations and important modifications, which lent the already limited provisions a strict inter- pretation. The regulations of the Economic and So- cial Committee, which came into effect in January 1959, were a disappointment to the trade unions.[17] They had hoped that the Council of Ministers would agree to a proposal permitting Committee members to be substituted or assisted by experts. Financing the trips of their experts to Brussels involves heavy expenditure for the labor unions; and, since the labor representatives of the Economic and Social Committee are already overburdened with activity on the national level, they find it difficult to participate in every committee meeting. Therefore, they have urged that Committee members have the possibility of being sub- stituted or accompanied by technical advisers working under the same conditions as themselves.

The Council of Ministers also refused the pro- posal of the Economic and Social Committee to have its own financial resources, and, instead, includes it in its own. The labor members argue that unless the Committee has its own budget,

> The Community will be a pseudo-democracy,
> leading to the dangerous path of technoc-
> racy...a broad interpretation of the budget
> is possible and a broad interpretation of
> the Treaty should be pursued.[18]

The most heated controversy during the formula- tion of the regulation focused upon the question of whether the Committee should enjoy the right of initi- ative. Whereas the Consultative Committee can be convened by its president on request of a majority of its members, the president of the Economic and Social Committee may convene a plenary session only at the request of the Council of Ministers or the

European Commission. Nor can the Committee commence
work on a topic that is the object of obligatory consultation without prior approval.[19] The trade unions
think that collaboration is not valid unless the consulted as well as the consulting organ have the right
to decide when consultation is necessary, and they
believe that the opinions of the Committee would acquire more value if it were granted this right.

Development of the ESC

The practice was established at the rendering
of the first opinion of having a representative of
the European Commission present at all levels of the
Economic and Social Committee: at working groups,
specialized sections, and plenary sessions. This
direct contact affords the Committee members immediate information and gives the Commission an opportunity to defend its position. Close contacts have
also been maintained between the Committee and the
European Commission outside the framework of opinion
formation, and Commission members regularly address
the Committee on various aspects of European policy.[20]
Moreover, if ESC members feel they should voice their
opinions on a particular question, they may ask their
president to request a consultation with the Commission or new consultations with the Commission member
present at plenary sessions. Thus, the scope of
problems discussed by the ESC has been broader than
originally intended, and it has been consulted on
practically every important regulation or directive
on agriculture, transport, and social policy.[21] The
ESC has also insisted that it be consulted on all
subjects that have been studied by the EPA and has
been largely successful in this endeavor.

Despite the strictly limited role that the
governments cautiously assigned the ESC, the efforts
made during the first few years of its existence to
lend it publicity and increase its influence bore
fruit. The ESC's president and members of its bureau
represent it at all important conferences organized
by the Commission; and, although the Rome Treaties
and the initial conceptions of the European Commission
and the Council of Ministers did not permit the ESC

to maintain relations with other institutions and circles of public life, the president of the ESC and the president of the Assembly agreed to form close relations and to exchange work calendars and documents.[22] The Assembly also adopted the practice of waiting for the opinions of the ESC before taking a stand on questions discussed by the Commission; and in addition some collaboration with the Consultative Committee has proved necessary, although the ESC is not authorized to have official relations with the latter.[23]

Trade Unions and the ESC

Plenary sessions of the ESC are convened eight times yearly by its chairman, at the request of either the Council of Ministers or the Commission and in order to deliberate reports from one of the specialized sections. A resulting ESC report or opinion contains a general analysis of the problem discussed, an account of the debates, and a catalogue of opinions expressed by the members. Both reports and opinions afford a complete picture of the original views of the different economic and social groups and the extent to which they are able to make mutual concessions.[24] As in the case of the EPA, the opinions of the ESC are usually unanimous and favorable to integration. However, unanimity is not always the result of the active support of a majority but the absence of vigorous debate. The opinions adopted by the ESC on the measures before it tend to reflect the various interests of its members rather than a clear synthesis, for it is essentially a corporative body and therefore has great difficulty in achieving viable compromises among its membership.

As a corporative body the ESC's membership is supposed to reflect the economic and social structure of member states; and the governments have generally followed equitable procedures in appointing members, save in their exclusion of Communist labor unions. Although each state follows its own procedures in drawing up lists of candidates, the governments usually select names suggested by the professional associations.[25] The Workers' Group of the ESC

includes 34 members, the Employers' Group numbers 27,
and a third group is composed of craftsmen, business-
men, journalists, and members of the liberal profes-
sions. As in the case of the Consultative Committee,
the trade unions resent the presence of the latter
group and would prefer a bipartite organ.[26] Since
the ESC is mainly a forum for the official representation of professional associations, there are rarely
divisions along national lines in debates or in voting; and delegates have not organized themselves
formally into national groups. However, national
alignments are more frequent among delegates representing employers' organizations than among those of
the trade unions; the former are answerable to their
associates, whereas trade union committee members are
also leaders of their associations and hence enjoy
greater freedom of maneuver. Most professional associations represented in the ESC mingle their official
and their lobbying activities by continually submitting memoranda to the ESC and furnishing it with personnel for groups of experts.

The Workers' Group has had some success in influencing opinion on important economic and social
problems, for the trade union point of view mustered
a majority in the discussions and votes on a CAP and
on opinions rendered concerning social policy.[27] As
in the case of the Consultative Committee, the Workers'
Group of the ESC has demonstrated a cohesiveness un-
attained by the other groups. During the numerous
preliminary meetings of the Workers' Group, its members have succeeded in developing common platforms
and have usually, though not always, defended European points of view in plenary sessions.

The ECFTUC and the European Confederation of
Christian Trade Unions have formed a committee to
coordinate their stands within the ESC, and plenary
sessions of the Workers' Group generally meet on the
day of the full session of the ESC.[28] In the interval
there are frequent meetings of specialized sections
and working groups. Important problems that arise
in the course of these meetings and whose solution
does not seem desirable in their framework are discussed during the plenary session of the Workers'

Group or in the Coordinating Committee. One of the
most important tasks of the European labor organizations is to formulate detailed and common stands for
their groups to defend within the ESC, and they have
sought to maintain close collaboration in this endeavor.

The secretariats of the European labor groups
also ensure the technical preparation of preliminary
meetings of representatives in specialized sections
and working groups. These efforts are somewhat
limited by the insufficiency of technical means at
the disposal of the secretariats. The trade unions
have emphasized the need for a considerable increase
in the budget of the ESC to remedy the insufficient
facilities of its worker members for translation,
interpretation, and technical consultation. Without
a considerable increase in funds, they fear that it
will soon be impossible to eliminate the dispropor-
tion between the increasing number of tasks they must
confront and their limited resources.[29]

The value of the ESC for its worker members lies
in their access to information on all matters concerning the Community and the possibility of being
heard on all economic and social questions of concern
to them. Although the ESC is useful as an opinion
forum, it has a very limited influence on the process
of policy formation. The trade unions wish to be
associated as much as possible and at all levels in
the formulation of not only social but also economic
measures affecting their situation. Consultation of
the ESC, despite its visibility, does not guarantee
sufficient trade union influence. Most items placed
on the ESC's agenda are more technical than political,
and its labor members have often proposed that the
ESC should not be consulted merely on drafts for regulations and directives but should also discuss broad
policy.[30] Moreover, in most cases, the ESC is presented with fully developed and detailed proposals,
with the task of adding slight changes by technical
amendments. Proposals are transmitted to the ESC
only after long preparatory work between the European
Commission and the national governments and their experts, and the Commission is careful to ensure that

the compromises achieved with such difficulty are not
significantly modified by opinions emanating from the
ESC.

But it is not only the judgment of definitive
proposals that interests the trade unions. They also
would like the right to participate actively in the
formulation of these proposals and feel that only when
the Commission consults the ESC at the time of formulating documents will they really collaborate in the
establishment of European economic and social policy.[31] The trade unions have also campaigned for a
revision of the ESC's statutes in order to grant it
the right of initiative to commence preparatory
studies on important questions. Increasing the ESC's
role in the European policy process would also involve the establishment of communication links with
the Council of Ministers. ESC contact with this organ
is virtually nonexistent, and it is doubtful whether
the Council of Ministers would ever agree to submit
itself to the same pressure-group activity within the
EEC that it must withstand in national politics.
Until then, the ESC will occupy only a marginal position in the EEC rule-making procedures.

THE EUROPEAN PARLIAMENTARY ASSEMBLY

The Assembly and the
Executive Organs

The resolutions of the EPA indicate the lines
of policy which that organ wishes the European executives to pursue. They also function as a support for
the actions of the executives, to strengthen their
position in their dialogue with the national governments in the Council of Ministers.

The Common Assembly and the High Authority

The evolution of the Assembly has been characterized by the struggle to achieve parliamentary
control and to promote a broader European integration. Since the Common Assembly was not granted
legislative or budgetary powers, and since the Paris

Treaty provides only for annual discussion of the
general report of the High Authority, parliamentary
control has been equated with criticism and orientation of High Authority policy. A persistent theme
of the Common Assembly's first year of operation was
the call for more and prompt information on which to
base its judgments.[32] It sought to ensure a continuous dialogue with the High Authority by the mul-
tiplication of sessions, the creation of permanent
committees, and the use of written questions. All
aspects of European policy are examined in the committees. They gather documentation independently,
invite specialists, and hold on-the-spot inquiries.
The presence of the High Authority at many committee
meetings affords the Assembly an opportunity to inform the High Authority of its opinion and to force
the latter to justify its policy.

The Assembly has not been content to wait for
consultation. Often it has taken the initiative to
suggest new policy measures. It has operated according to the formula defined by one of its deputies,
that it would

> fully avail itself of all rights expressly
> accorded it and in case of doubt will seek
> a solution in common parliamentary law and
> not in an unjustified comparison with non-
> sovereign international assemblies.[33]

Thus, it sought to extend its influence to budgetary
matters as well as to Community policy. According
to article 78 of the Paris Treaty, budgetary control
is vested in a Committee of the Four Presidents and
an independent auditor. In 1953 the Assembly requested the High Authority to present all budget
estimates for discussion before final allocation.
The following year this demand was repeated and extended to discussion on budgets of all ECSC institutions. In 1956 Pierre Wigny could conclude:

> The actions of the Auditing and Adminis-
> trative Commission, particularly in re-
> lation to the Committee of the Four Presi-
> dents, has proved the jurisdiction and the

power of the Assembly and has permitted
it thus to exercise a much more real
power, if not in law, then in fact. The
other institutions have accepted this
gracefully.[34]

The Common Assembly applied constant pressure
for a broad interpretation of the Paris Treaty. It
repeatedly expressed impatience with the High Authority's action in formulating general objectives and
in determining long-term policy for coal and steel,
and it reproached that organ with hesitation on the
subject of cartels and mergers. Characteristically,
Assembly resolutions criticized the High Authority
for not doing enough rather than for exceeding its
bounds, and some deputies consistently called for a
stronger line toward the governments. In the 1956
session of the Assembly the Socialist group made a
heated declaration to the effect that the passivity
of the High Authority had permitted the national
governments and producers' groups to exercise functions belonging to the Community in the field of
prices and cartels.[35] When it had succeeded in its
drive for a liberal interpretation of the Paris
Treaty, and when it was clear that the High Authority
had reached the limits of its authority, particularly
in social policy, the Assembly recommended broader
integration.[36]

What has been the result of the pro-European
orientation of the Common Assembly? The emphasis
of the Assembly on a greater degree of integration
and the strengthening of the ECSC has created both
pressure and support for High Authority action. In
his study of the political influence of the Assembly,
Alain Poher concluded that in the fields of transports, cartels, mergers, and social affairs the
Assembly had exercised an important but not decisive
influence.[37]

On the other hand, the High Authority has sought
the support of the Common Assembly and has encouraged
its development, supplying it with information and
calling extraordinary sessions to explain its problems and policies. Since the Paris Treaty already

states the general lines of economic policy, so that
the High Authority is rarely confronted by a political
choice, and since the Assembly plays no role in the
choice of the High Authority, the control of the High
Authority depends upon its desire to strengthen its
position vis-à-vis the Council of Ministers.

The Assembly and the European Commission

Although the Paris Treaty accorded considerable
importance to the Assembly as a control mechanism
over the High Authority, the Rome Treaties diminished
the consultative role of the EPA. The meager leverage
it enjoys over the European Commission lies in the
latter's desire to enlist the Assembly's influence in
the national arena in order to facilitate its dealings
with the Council of Ministers.

It is more accurate to speak of the EPA's dependence upon the European Commission rather than
its control over it. Since the Commission symbolizes
the force for European integration within the EEC,
and since most Assembly members are enthusiastically
committed to integration, the EPA generally supports
the Commission's proposals. The only way for the EPA
to increase its influence within the EEC is by supporting integration measures and the organ that in-
itiates proposals and provides it with the sole
channel for bringing its views to the Council of
Ministers. The committees of the EPA are in daily
contact with the Commission, a useful link for both
organs, since the Commission's testimony yields important technical information on the background of
issues; and continual contacts make it difficult for
the Commission to ignore committee reports.[38] However, the Commission rarely alters its carefully conceived and negotiated proposals in order to accommodate the EPA and allows it only a minor role in the
decision-making process. Moreover, the EPA's activities enjoy little publicity, owing to the technical nature of EEC issues and to the fact that the
national parliamentary systems enjoy a monopoly of
attention in the national media.

Ideally the EPA would like to see a classical
nineteenth-century parliamentary system operative

within the EEC, with a clear distinction between
Council and Commission in preparing policy, diminish-
ing the Council's role in favor of the Assembly and
rendering the Commission responsible to the Assembly.
However, if the Assembly realized this aim, the Commission would lose both its independence and its
freedom of maneuver, the basis of its influence in
dealing with the Council of Ministers.

The Assembly and the Council of Ministers

If the Assembly has achieved successful collaboration with the High Authority and its successor, the
unified Commission, it has experienced great difficulty in dealing with the Council of Ministers as an
institution. According to the Paris Treaty, the
Council has no organic relation with the Assembly.
It cannot be called into session by the Assembly,
nor is it obliged to answer the requests of the
Assembly. Herein lies the essential obstacle to full
parliamentary participation in policy formation at
the European level.

In 1955 the Assembly's Committee on Social Affairs established a new precedent by inviting the
Council of Ministers to participate in its discussions and to hear its opinions on the free movement
of labor.[39] The Council replied by inviting the
Committee to meet with the six Ministers of Social
Affairs. Since then individual Council members have
participated in Assembly sessions, appeared at committee meetings, and received delegations of deputies.
However, despite the repeated invitations of the Assembly, the Council as a whole did not attend a parliamentary session until 1956. Until the establishment of the Rome Treaties, contacts continued in an
ad hoc manner. Of greater significance is the fact
that these isolated instances of cooperation did not
mean that the Council deferred to the wishes of the
Assembly. It did not agree to consult the Assembly
on a regular basis and resisted all requests of the
Assembly for publication of the minutes of its deliberations and the bases of its decisions.[40] The
sole exception to this pattern of behavior on the
part of the Council of Ministers has been the appeal

of Jean Rey before the Assembly in an effort to gain support for ECSC-wide harmonization of working-time rules.[41]

Official relations were established between these two institutions by the Rome Treaties. They provide for eighteen cases in which the consultation of the Assembly by the Council of Ministers is obligatory. Moreover, the EPA has been more successful than its predecessor in eliciting a meaningful response from the Council to its requests for fruitful collaboration. It has been consulted by the Council on matters not stipulated as objects of obligatory consultation, i.e., on the free migration of labor and on the European Social Fund. In both cases the Assembly pressed for a more European solution than that proposed by the European Commission, and the Council of Ministers incorporated several amendments voted by the Assembly in its final decision on the Social Fund.[42] In this instance the Assembly's possibilities of control and consultation were exercised simultaneously. In such cases the Assembly can compel the Commission to modify its proposal through its opinion to the Council. Thus, the influence of the Assembly's opinion is more substantial then suggested by the text of the Rome Treaties.

Aside from the consultations provided for by the Rome Treaties, yearly colloquies between the Council of Ministers and the Assembly on current problems of the European Communities have become an established practice. However, a colloquy is not a true debate but simply an exchange of views; and no real dialogue is possible, because there is no Council policy except when a decision is taken. Then the Council of Ministers presents the Assembly with a fait accompli. The Assembly has continued to insist that these sessions assume the character of a veritable confrontation of ideas, that important EEC issues be regularly discussed, and that the Council participate in its debates by precise answers to parliamentary questions and broad information on its activities. Aside from presenting periodic reports on its activities, the Council will make no formal commitments to the Assembly, reminding it of its function as a consultative and not as a control organ.[43]

Although the relations between these two institutions have undergone a marked improvement throughout
the EEC's existence, the Assembly remains powerless
before the Council of Ministers. It has no direct
leverage over the Council and can only transmit a
barrage of resolutions and questions out of proportion
to the interest and attention of the Council. At
times the Assembly's lack of influence over the key
decision-making organ in the EEC has led it to support
action that the Council does not have the power to
carry out and to vote resolutions with an aura of
unreality. Because of this and the EPA's insensitiv-
ity to the limitations of the Council, the ministers
themselves sometimes insist upon a preliminary exchange of views with the Assembly in order to keep
the latter within bounds.[44] So long as the Assembly
does not have a grip on EEC policy and so long as it
is not supported by a powerful and organized European
public opinion, its influence on the Council of
Ministers can be only indirect, either through the
European Commission or as a supranational pressure
group in the national parliaments.

The Assembly and the
National Parliaments

Because of its desire to enhance its status
within the EEC and because of the manner in which it
has championed European integration, the EPA has remained aloof from the national parliaments. Instead
of seeking to develop communications with its national
counterparts in order to facilitate legislative control and supervision of the Council of Ministers, the
EPA has consistently requested an increase in its
formal powers in order to assume a role comparable
with that of national parliaments and has even proposed direct election of its membership. These attempts to replace the role of the national assemblies
in EEC affairs have only weakened the tenuous links
between the EPA and the national parliaments. The
latter have exerted themselves to protect their
political power, however insubstantial it may be regarding European questions. Aside from routine
cooperation concerning the timing of sessions, links
between the national and European parliaments have

remained fragile, and periodic proposals for strengthening these ties have inspired only increasing vigilance for the preservation of national interests.[45]

Members of the EPA occupy two time-consuming
positions, at the national and at the European level,
and must travel constantly between their national
capitals and Brussels. The national delegations to
the EPA are selected to reflect the strengths of the
various parties at home; and it is the accuracy with
which the EPA delegations reflect national party
lineups in parliaments that favors good relations
between the two organs rather than the procedures
for selecting delegates, which vary with each country.
Once in Brussels, a member of Parliament acquires no
prestige from his post but continues to reflect the
influence achieved in his national constituency and
his own position within the national party. Personalities who are prominent in Europe are not necessarily influential members of their national parties.
In fact, national party members with a penchant for
foreign policy may deliberately avoid the EPA in
favor of more vital arenas for European politics, such
as Jean Monnet's Action Committee.[46]

In important national debates on European issues
and at official party gatherings, the leading spokesmen are generally not members of the EPA, and political parties do not take their cues from the views
of their delegation within the European Assembly. The
EPA has not wielded a major influence in the national
parliaments with respect to European matters because
liaison between the two organs has been ineffective.
Although each parliament has developed a different
method for scrutinizing EEC affairs, and with varying
degrees of success, all of the Six have well-estab-
lished procedures for deliberation and resolution,
which cannot be bypassed by the EPA, and long-estab-
lished committees and ministerial departments jealous
of their prerogatives. Special committees or councils for examining European questions have proved
superfluous and unpalatable to national assemblies.

The EPA's detachment from the national parliaments has not encouraged either the Commission or

the Council of Ministers to consider it as closely
related to opinion within the Six.[47] However, the
problem of political control of the Council of Ministers remains to be solved, for national parliamentary activities are not designed to cope with the
decision-making process in the EEC; and the Rome
Treaties have reduced the scope of legislative competence of the national parliaments in favor of the
governments and their bureaucracies without a compensating strengthening of the EPA's powers. Under
the present political conditions, unfavorable to
supranational solutions, an effective means of control over the Council will not be obtained through
direct elections or by extending the powers of the
EPA but, rather, through a more efficient cooperation
of the EPA with the national assemblies. This can
be achieved not by a proliferation of committees but
through contacts between the secretariats of national
and European political groups and through the exchange of documentation services.[48] The national
institutions must be infused with a European spirit
rather than supplanted by the European institutions.

The vicissitudes of the EPA are part of the
ubiquitous decline in the role of parliament in an
age characterized by growing executive power and the
politics of technical expertise. Neither the national
parliaments nor the EPA is able to exercise sufficient
political surveillance over the increasing role of
national civil servants in determining stands on EEC
issues.

The EPA has twice adopted proposals for the
direct election of its membership. Its first attempt,
in 1960, incurred the profound displeasure of the
Franch government and almost jeopardized the progress
of integration. The matter lay dormant until 1969,
when the EPA again invited the Council of Ministers
to consider the matter. However, enhancing the EPA's
role cannot be accomplished by a mere feat of engineering an electoral system. If the EPA enjoys a
little power, deals with mainly technical issues, and
arouses little popular interest, the direct elections
of its members will not improve its effectiveness.

A recent decision of the Council of Ministers,
applicable in 1971, will expand the budgetary authority of the EPA to the administrative and information
expenses of the EEC. Each year the European Commission will work out a composite rate of increase
of these expenses based upon increases in gross
national products, budgetary expenditures, and the
cost of living over the previous year.[49] If the
Council of Ministers decides on a budget increase
of less than one-half this rate, the EPA will have
the right to bring the increase up to the full rate.
However, these expenditures account for only 3 percent of the total EEC expenses. The EPA has no power
over expenditures for financing the EEC's CAP and the
European Social Fund, the major portion of EEC spend-
ing; and the Council predicts that by 1978 the Community will cover its costs by its own resources
stemming from agricultural import levies, customs
duties, and part of the value added tax.[50] However,
the Council of Ministers declared that the Commission
must henceforth send the EPA an estimate of expenses
with every proposal and that it would be represented
at debates on the budget in order to explain its decisions. The practical effect of this decision is
small indeed, but at the very least the EPA will be
more closely associated with drawing up the budget;
and the Council has pledged an explanation of its
budgetary policies to the European Assembly.

The Political Groups of
the Assembly

How does the EPA operate? Does it function as
a congress of national delegations, or are issues
discussed according to party program? No important
decision is taken by the Assembly without the presentation of the opinions of its political groups.
These groups were formed in 1954, according to the
Assembly's regulations, and meet regularly during
the year to analyze and discuss Community problems
and to develop positions for presentation in plenary
sessions.[51]

Party membership rather than nationality de-
termines the allocation of committee posts in the

EPA: The Liberal Group enjoys a strong position on the Committee for Investments, the Christian Democratic Group has the largest representation on the Committee for Political Affairs, and the Socialist Group has a near monopoly of the Committee on Social Affairs.[52]   In addition there is a European Democratic Union, which consists of eighteen members of the Gaullist Party and functions as a political group. Political tendencies are also expressed in the presidencies of the committees.   Two Christian Democrats, two Socialists, and one Liberal have always divided the presidencies of the large committees; and the president of the Assembly has generally been Christian Democrat.   However, compared with their national counterparts, political groups have no spoils to distribute in order to keep their members in line; and important positions in the group or the prestigious role of rapporteur are distributed to achieve national parity rather than as political rewards.[53]

Until recently the large French and Italian Communist parties were excluded from the EPA by tacit agreement among the Six.   There exists no uniform procedure for selecting national delegations to the EPA precisely in order to allow the governments to devise their own methods of excluding Communists. Since 1963 the Communist Parties have been clamoring for the right to be fully represented within the EPA. However, at that time de Gaulle's exclusion of Britain from the EEC boded ill for the Community, and therefore the Italian Communist Party and the French Communist Party did not wage an intensive campaign for parliamentary seats.   More vigorous drives for representation were pursued in 1966 as a result of the San Remo Conference of Western European Communist Parties, which came to grips with the fact of the economic vitality of the EEC.   That year was also an opportune period for the Italian Communist Party to demand its rightful place within the EPA, for an investigating commission of the latter was inquiring into the credentials of the Italian delegates, some of whom had long ceased to be members of their national parliaments.   However, the decision to renew the Italian delegation to the EPA was postponed until March 1969, when the Italian House and Senate

appointed seven Communists to their thirty-six-member
delegation to the European Assembly.[54] The Communists
are not numerous enough to form an official group
within the EPA. They sit with two other left-wing
members of parliaments from the Italian Socialist
Party of Proletarian Unity and one French independent.

The French Communist Party received an opportunity to be represented in the EPA after the French
parliamentary elections in 1967, when the Gaullists
and the Federation of the Left tacitly agreed to
allow it some seats on France's delegation.[55] Consequently, it put up candidates for election, but it
failed to obtain the necessary votes. It was not
more successful in the 1968 elections, although it
received 20 percent of the votes.

The European program of these two Communist
Parties is inspired largely by the Italian party and
aims at the elimination of all supranational features
of the European Community in order to prevent integration from reducing the political power enjoyed by
the Communists in their own countries.[56] Therefore,
they insist that the control over EEC institutions
must remain in the national parliaments, where no
discrimination exists against the Italian or the
French party and where the latter are in a better
position to achieve their objectives. These two
parties have sought representation on the EPA chiefly
in order to buttress their positions in national politics.

The lack of direct ties between the High Authority, the Commission, and a parliamentary majority has
meant that each political group functions as both
support and opposition and has created a tendency to
compromise among political groups. The great majority
of committee reports are unanimously adopted, and
floor votes on committee resolutions are often unanimous. Although committee reports sometimes contain
minority opinions, members always try to reach compromises acceptable to all and consensus on an inter-
party common denominator. Members of the EPA feel
that the closer to unanimity resolutions are, the
more they can influence the Commission and, conversely,

that lack of unanimity can weaken a resolution in the
eyes of the Commission and the general public.[57]

The Socialist Group

Among the political groups the Socialists possess
the greatest amount of functional and ideological cohesion. The Group includes 8 Socialist parties and
38 members and is directed by a bureau of 6 members
for administrative affairs in addition to working
groups and subcommittees on various aspects of European policy.[58] Political decisions are taken at the
plenary sessions. In 1955 regular contacts were
established between the Group, the Committee of XXI,
and members of the ICFTU in the Consultative Committee; and when the Rome Treaties came into effect,
these contacts were extended to the European Trade
Union Secretariat and ICFTU members of the ESC. A
liaison bureau was also created among Socialist
Parties and the Socialist Group, partly to organize
biennial conferences of the national parties.[59]

The Socialist Group has been careful to show
flexibility in formulating reports and proposals for
resolutions so that the acts of the EPA will bear its
mark. They can always have recourse to plenary sessions to air their unsatisfied wishes. On many aspects of Community policy, especially social affairs,
the reports and resolutions of the Assembly reflect
the aims of its most cohesive group.

From initially divergent national positions this
group has been able to achieve consensus on most aspects of European integration. However, divergencies
on the form and content of European integration were
initially apparent. During the first years of integration the German SPD manifested a separatist tendency, because the ECSC was limited to six members
and because it feared that partial integration would
menace its national policy of full employment with
the production and sale of coal no longer in the hands
of the German government.[60] In the following years,
however, the SPD adopted a constructive point of view
with respect to High Authority policy, the extension
of the latter's competence, and new integration

projects. The Socialist Group was able to develop
a unanimous stand on the EEC and Euratom, calling
for a long-term structural policy, a countercyclical
policy, and the harmonization of financial policies.[61]
On the social aspects of integration, the Group has
stressed its concern with the adequacy of readaptation
measures to absorb structural and cyclical unemployment and with the harmonization of living and working
conditions and social changes.

One of the main elements of Socialist consensus
has been the demand for a supranational welfare
policy. The Socialists have consistently supported
the demands of the trade unions for harmonization
measures, energetic readaptation and housing policies,
a guaranteed annual wage, and the reduction of working time.

There is no European Socialist program, although
there is an outline of goals to be achieved in the
European framework. Most Socialist members of the
Assembly favor direct and universal election of its
deputies. The SPD and a fraction of the Belgian
Socialists have expressed reservations and are of the
opinion that before the Assembly can be directly
elected its powers should be increased; but the majority favor the extension of the EPA's powers. In
a meeting on the problems of the European Communities,
the Socialist Group adopted a program for strengthening the democratic parliamentary control of the
Communities and ensuring a more effective participation of the EPA in the legislative activities of the
EEC.[62] It included procedures to ensure that the
proposals of the European Commission and the major
decisions of the Council of Ministers account for the
opinions of the EPA.

The most far-reaching goal of the Socialist
Parties of the Six is the replacement of the Rome and
Paris Treaties with a single treaty providing for
common institutions for the whole Community.[63] Foreign policy and defense policy, as well as economic
policies, would be progressively integrated within
the competence of Community institutions. This conception is not far from the Christian Democratic

espousal of a United States of Europe. Here the
similarity ends, for the Socialists wish to nation-
alize key industrial sectors and submit them to the
control of public powers, which would regulate all
sectors dominated by agreements and mergers. In
addition the Socialists would like to achieve a
European revenue policy guaranteeing a more just
distribution of wealth and a European monetary policy.
Although the institutional demands of the Socialist
Group are more far-reaching than those of the ECFTUC,
their economic and social policies are similar. This
similarity is not surprising, given the close tie
between the Group and the ECFTUC and the fact that
most of the Socialist Parties of the Six have labor
constituencies.

The Christian Democratic Group

The Christian Democratic Group is organized in
a manner similar to its Socialist counterpart. It
is directed by a bureau with various committees dealing with particular aspects of European integration
and ad hoc working groups for meetings during EPA
sessions.[64] It maintains regular contacts with the
Confederation of Christian Trade Unions in the Community and extends frequent invitations to labor's
representatives in the consultative bodies to attend
its meetings.

Since there are as many as ten Christian Democratic Parties within the Six and since these are
heterogeneous, there exists considerable divergencies
on economic and social questions within the Group.
Unlike the Socialist Group, individual speakers do
not often make declarations in the name of the whole
party.[65] The Group has not achieved consensus on
many economic issues, and on social questions consensus is confined to such noncontentious matters as
housing, industrial safety, and human relations. The
trade union leaders in the parties' left wings are
alone in favoring supranational welfare policies.

Despite its lack of ideological cohesion the
Christian Democratic Group has demonstrated a functional cooperation based on its commitment to a

united Europe and has frequently managed to present a united stand on proposals favoring European integration.

The Committee on Social Affairs

By means of hundreds of debates and innumerable reports and resolutions, the European Assembly has consistently urged the High Authority and European Commission to adopt a more liberal interpretation of the Rome and Paris treaties in social affairs. The original spark for a broad social policy came from the trade unions, supported by the Socialist Group and a series of resolutions emanating from the reports of the Committee on Social Affairs.

The Committee on Social Affairs has played a leading role in formulating the social policy urged upon the European executives by the Assembly. What is the content of this policy, and how has the demand for an ambitious policy developed?

From its first contacts with the High Authority in 1953, the Committee on Social Affairs sought to encourage that organ to make maximum use of the powers conferred on it and to affirm its own role in the formulation of policy. At that time it was especially anxious to promote the general goals set forth in articles 2 and 3, and it reproached the High Authority for excessive timidity in interpreting them.[66] It argued that although the competence of the High Authority in the social field is limited and although the governments might frown on intervention this does not imply that it should refuse to deal with social problems or fail to indicate ways of improving the social situation. Without intervening directly the High Authority could stimulate the achievement of the goals stipulated in articles 2 and 3 by publicizing the social situation within the Community, making proposals, convening conferences, obtaining information from various governments and trade union organizations, and enlarging its Division of Labor Problems.[67] The Committee also expressed its desire to be kept constantly informed of ECSC activity in the social field and to be consulted on

the possible social repercussions of any economic or
financial measures envisaged by the High Authority.

The following year the Committee on Social
Affairs and the Assembly were already urging the
High Authority to go beyond the letter of its authority and to develop, along with the governments, a
procedure for establishing readaptation measures that
would circumvent the High Authority's lack of legal
initiative. In addition the Assembly requested the
High Authority to gather documentation facilitating
the conclusion of model collective agreements.[68]
From the beginning the Assembly has been concerned
with the problem of social harmonization and has regarded it as an essential element of European social
policy. The Socialist Group in particular asked the
High Authority to convene mixed commissions of employers and workers to formulate collective agreements on working conditions and to convene a general
conference of the Six to eliminate divergencies in
social legislation not covered by the collective
agreements.[69]

The Assembly repeatedly suggested modifications
of article 56, on readaptation, and article 69, on
the free movement of labor.[70] It was unhappy with
the slow development of readaptation policy and
attributed this state of affairs to the prudent use
of the provisions by the High Authority and the
reserve of the governments and enterprises, fearful
of creating privileged positions for certain workers.
In the opinion of the Committee on Social Affairs,
the authors of the Rome Treaties had intended not
only to compensate only temporary setbacks in employment that might result from technical progress but
also to ensure the continuity of employment generally.
Therefore, it argued, the means to ensure reemployment should not be considered only palliatives against
the repercussions of the establishment of the Common
Market but should also be used to develop employment
and to prevent disturbances of the labor market. The
Committee proposed that the High Authority formulate
an employment policy and that article 56 be revised
to cover all cases of unemployment, both structural
and cyclical.[71]

Article 69 leaves the member states full responsibility and initiative for effecting the free movement of labor. The Committee on Social Affairs
suggested revising that article by granting the High
Authority the right to convey precise proposals to
the member states in order to facilitate and orient
their action in applying these measures. It complained that the agreement on labor mobility was
overly restrictive, did not correspond to the spirit
of the treaty, and presented a serious handicap to
the attainment of the goals set forth in articles 2
and 3. In order to lend the agreement a supranational
character, it suggested the creation of a central organ for contacts of offers and requests for employment in the Community labor market and a number of
other modifications.[72]

The efforts of the Committee on Social Affairs
began to bear fruit in the late 1950's; and the influence of the Assembly was evident in the High Authority's policy of readaptation, its housing policy,
its studies, and its generally more active labor
policy. In its debate on the High Authority's sixth
general report, the Assembly expressed satisfaction
with the work of the High Authority. Speaking for
the Committee on Social Affairs, A. Bertrand ex-
claimed:

> In no other domain has the ECSC made so
> much progress as in the social. The
> majority of problems simply sketched in
> the First General Report are today either
> solved, or in the process of being solved.[73]

The Committee considered its task to be that of stimulating the action of the European executives and
formulating the lines of broad policy, working in
close relation with the trade unions, employers' organizations, and governmental representatives.

The clearest evidence of labor's influence on
the Assembly's social policy has appeared on the subjects of readaptation, the European Miners' Statute,
and harmonization, especially the reduction of working time. The Assembly included the trade union draft

for a Miners' Statute in its resolutions and nominated Arthur Gailly, a direct spokesman of the trade unions, as rapporteur.[74] Since 1957 it has seconded this appeal of the workers. As a result of its continued pressure the High Authority reconvened the Mixed Committee for Coal in the early 1960's, preparatory to discussion of the matter.

The Assembly has been actively concerned with the reduction of working time since 1955, when Jean Rey addressed it on the problem in Belgium and when the trade union activities toward this goal assumed Community-wide proportions. The Committee on Social Affairs pursued periodic studies of working hours in close collaboration with the trade unions and summarized its findings in a series of reports generally favorable to the claims of the workers for a forty-hour, five-day week.[75] The EPA has maintained up-to-date studies on wage trends and working conditions in the Community.

At times, however, the Committee on Social Affairs has pushed its demands for a European social policy further than the trade unions would admit. The latter oppose an extension of European power to the field of wage policy. The Assembly, however, considered that harmonization of wage policy in the Six would contribute to raising the standard of living; and in the early 1960's the Committee on Social Affairs suggested that the High Authority convene a tripartite conference to discuss wages and the cost of living and their relationship to production.[76] Significantly this is one instance in which a committee report included a dissident opinion. The Assembly has had less success in dealing with sensitive national issues and with matters that labor considers within its sole jurisdiction.

SUMMARY

The EPA, which assumed the functions of the Common Assembly for all three communities, retained the characteristics of its predecessor, especially its seemingly boundless optimism concerning the

possibility of achieving a European welfare policy.
Its Committee on Social Affairs thinks that the gap
between the social goals included in the Rome and
Paris Treaties and the strictly limited powers of
the European Commission in social affairs can be
compensated for by a firm political will; and the
Socialist Group bravely argues that even if the Rome
Treaties are incomplete in the social domain the Commission can act effectively in this field if it considers that what is not forbidden by the Treaties is
permitted.[77]

If the EPA has expressed doubts about the competence of the European Commission, it nevertheless has
pleaded for an active social policy that would include
a European right to work and a harmonization of collective agreements.[78] It has proposed numerous amendments to the European Social Fund and has suggested
that it work in close conjunction with the European
Investment Bank in order to lay the foundations for
a European employment policy. In its resolutions and
debates on the general reports of the Commission, the
EPA has emphasized its opinion that welfare policies
must be achieved along with common economic policies
and the extension of integration. In addition the
EPA and its Committee on Social Affairs have fostered
the trade union goal of establishing mixed committees
for all sectors of the economy as a framework within
which the social partners can freely negotiate matters
concerning harmonization.

The social policy proposed by the EPA includes
two broad goals: the raising of the standard of
living and full employment. Social harmonization
within an expanding economy, including Community-wide
collective bargaining, has been the means suggested
by the Assembly for achieving higher living standards.
In order to attain full employment the Assembly has
called for a comprehensive manpower policy dealing
with problems of both cyclical and structural unemployment and including free migration of labor, vocational training, regional policies, and broad readaptation measures. The EPA has sought to substantiate its claims for such an ambitious policy on the
basis of the intentions of the authors of the Rome

and Paris Treaties, the general goals of the European
Communities as stated within the Treaties. It has
also acted upon the rather tenuous claim that whatever
is not forbidden by the Treaties is permitted and thus
has promoted a very liberal interpretation of the
Treaties. Underlying the Assembly's efforts have been
its commitment to Europe and the realization that
European integration must have social content in order
to take root among the European populace.

How successful have the efforts of the Assembly
been? In order for an active welfare policy to be
achieved on the European level, it must be accompanied
by a full integration of the national economies and,
hence, by political fusion. A comprehensive European
social policy is not possible within the embryonic
state of integration in effect at present. However,
the ambitious program of the Assembly has had the
virtue of stimulating the solution of less controversial, though important, problems. The EPA has
given a strong impetus and support to the action of
the High Authority and the European Commission in the
fields of housing, health and safety, readaptation,
and studies and research. In the social domain the
EPA's role in the policy-making process can best be
depicted as one of orienting and supporting such action as the Rome and Paris Treaties and the Council
of Ministers will allow the Commission to pursue.

NOTES

1. Secrétariat Syndical Européen, Sixième assemblée générale: Rapport d'activité, 1966-1968
(Brussels, April 1969), see ch. IV.

2. Ibid.

3. W. Hartley Clark, The Politics of the Common
Market (Englewood Cliffs, N.J.: Prentice-Hall, 1967),
p. 66.

4. Ibid.

5. Altiero Spinelli, The Eurocrats: Conflict and Crisis in the European Community (Baltimore: The Johns Hopkins Press, 1966), p. 72.

6. Leon N. Lindberg and Stuart A. Schiengold, Europe's Would-Be Polity: Patterns of Change in the European Community (Englewood Cliffs, N.J.: Prentice-Hall, 1970), pp. 87-100.

7. Ibid.

8. Spinelli, op. cit., pp. 70-80.

9. Ernst B. Haas, The Uniting of Europe: Political, Social, and Economic Forces (Stanford, Calif.: The University Press, 1958), p. 475.

10. Pierre Wigny, Un témoignage sur la Communauté des Six (Luxembourg: Economic Coal and Steel Community, Common Assembly, 1957), p. 23.

11. Haas, op. cit., p. 476.

12. Secrétariat Syndical Européen, Deuxième assemblée générale des syndicats libres des états-membres des Communautés européennes (Luxembourg, November 1959), p. 15.

13. International Confederation of Free Trade Unions, Information Bulletin, IV, 3 (February 1955), 36.

14. "The Trade Unions Demand a More Active Social Policy," Bulletin from the European Coal and Steel Community (January 1956), pp. 3-6.

15. Ibid.

16. Intersyndicale CECA, Rapport d'activité de l'Intersyndicale CECA (Luxembourg, December 1961), p. 11.

17. Agence Internationale de Documentation, Pharos, Le Marché commun européen, no. 12 (June 1959), A-IV-53, doc. 62.

18. Deuxiéme assemblée générale des Syndicats libres, p. 37.

19. Le Marché commun européen, no. 11 (May 1959), A-IV-52, doc. 56.

20. European Economic Community, Economic and Social Committee, Bulletin d'information, no. 1 (Brussels, January-March 1962).

21. Ibid., no. 2 (April-June 1962).

22. Ibid., p. 12.

23. Ibid., p. 13.

24. European Economic Community, Economic and Social Committee, "Ten Years of Activity of the Economic and Social Committee of the European Communities," speech delivered by Louis Major, chairman of the Economic and Social Committee of the European Economic Community, at the Committee's tenth anniversary celebration (Brussels, 1968).

25. Spinelli, op. cit., pp. 122-23.

26. Sixième assemblée générale: Rapport d'activité, 1966-1968, ch. IV.

27. Ibid.

28. Ibid.

29. Ibid.

30. Ibid.

31. Ibid.

32. Pierre Wigny, L'Assemblée parlementaire dans l'Europe des Six (Brussels: European Economic Community, European Parliamentary Assembly, 1958), p. 32.

33. European Coal and Steel Community, Common Assembly, Débats de l'Assemblée commune, Compte-rendu

in-extenso des séances, no. 2 (Luxembourg, March 11, 1953), 16.

34. Wigny, L'Assemblée parlementaire dans l'Europe des Six, p. 43.

35. Débats de l'Assemblée commune, Compte-rendu in-extenso des séances, no. 13 (June 22, 1956), 690-92 and 768-69.

36. Ibid., no. 14 (November 29, 1956), 105-10.

37. Assemblée Commune, Poher Report, doc. no. 2 (November 1955).

38. Clark, op. cit., see ch. V.

39. Débats de l'Assemblée commune, Compte-rendu in-extenso des séances, no. 9 (May 10, 1955), 279.

40. Ibid., no. 13 (June 19, 1956) 562-76.

41. Ibid., no. 11 (November 30, 1955), 43-46.

42. Mme. de Riemacher-Legot, "Rapport sur les dispositions reglémentaires nécessaires à l'execution des articles 124 à 126 inclus du Traité, concernant le Fonds social européen," Assemblée Parlementaire Européenne, doc. no. 18 (Brussels, December 1959).

43. European Economic Community, Parliamentary Assembly, Débats de l'Assemblée parlemantaire européenne, Compte-rendu in-extenso des séances, no. 11 (April 10, 1959), 91-96.

44. Clark, op. cit., p. 94.

45. Karl-Heinz Neunreither, "Les rapports entre le Parlement européen et les parlements nationaux," Annuaire Européen, XV (The Hague: Martinus Syhoff, 1969), 51-75.

46. Ibid.

47. Michael Neblock, "Is the European Parliament Too Aloof?" European Community (April 1969), p. 17.

48. Neunreither, loc. cit.

49. European Communities, European Community (March 1970), p. 22.

50. Pierre Henri Laurent, "A Milestone for the European Community," Current History (May 1970), pp. 258-59.

51. Antoine Boisson, "Les partis politiques à l'Assemblée commune de la Communauté européenne du charbon et de l'acier," Annuaire Européen, V (The Hague: Martinus Syhoff, 1959), 80.

52. P. J. G. Kapteyn, L'Assemblée commune de la Communauté européenne du charbon et de l'acier: Un essai de parlementarisme européen (Leyden: A. W. Sythoff, 1962), p. 224.

53. Neunreither, loc. cit.

54. Walter Kendall, "The Communist Parties and the European Community," European Community (February 1969), p. 9.

55. Werner J. Feld, "National International Linkage Theory: The East European Communist System and the EEC," Journal of International Affairs, XXII, 1 (1968), 113.

56. European Economic Community, Parliamentary Assembly, European Documentation (June 1955), p. 5.

57. Kapteyn, op. cit., p. 224.

58. Boisson, loc. cit.

59. Kapteyn, op. cit., p. 73.

60. Haas, op. cit., pp. 422-33.

61. <u>Débats de l'Assemblée commune, Compte-rendu in-extenso des séances</u>, no. 9 (June 24, 1955), 609-12.

62. European Economic Community, Parliamentary Assembly, <u>Cahiers mensuels de documentation euro-péenne</u> (October 1963), p. 21.

63. <u>Ibid</u>. (October 1960), p. 23.

64. Kapteyn, <u>op. cit.</u>, p. 72.

65. Haas, <u>loc. cit.</u>

66. <u>Débats de l'Assemblée commune, Compte-rendu in-extenso des séances</u>, no. 4 (June 1953), 21.

67. A. Bertrand, "Rapport de la Commission des affaires sociales dur le chapitre V traitant des problemes du travail du Rapport général sur l'activité de la Communauté," Assemblée Commune, doc. no. 3 (June 1953).

68. <u>Débats de l'Assemblée commune, Compte-rendu in-extenso des séances</u>, no. 7 (May 13, 1954) 67-70.

69. <u>Ibid</u>. (May 14, 1954), p. 125.

70. A. Bertrand, "Rapport de la Commission des affaires sociales sur l'application des dispositions de l'article 69 du Traité concernant les mouvements de la main l'oeuvre, les mesures relatives à la ré-adaptation, la formation professionelle, la situation actuelle et le développment futur de l'emploi dans la Communauté," Assemblée Commune, doc. no. 14 (Lux-embourg, March 1955).

71. <u>Ibid</u>.

72. <u>Ibid</u>.

73. A. Bertrand, "Rapport fait au nom de la Commission des affaires sociales sur la Partie Sociale du Sixième rapport général sur l'activité de la

Communauté européenne du charbon et de l'acier," Assemblée Parlementaire Européenne, doc. no. 21 (Brussels, June 1958).

74. *Débats de l'Assemblée parlementaire européenne, Compte-rendu in-extenso des séances,* no. 26 (June 26, 1957), 587-88.

75. C. P. Hazenbosch, "Rapport fait au nom de la Commission des affaires sociales sur la réduction de la durée du travail dans l'industrie charbonnière et l'industrie sidérurgique," Assemblée Parlementaire Européenne, doc. no. 64 (Brussels, December 1958).

76. *Débats de l'Assemblée parlementaire européenne, Compte-rendu in-extenso des séances,* no. 9 (January 10, 1969), 144.

77. *Ibid.* (January 9, 1959), 105.

78. *Ibid.,* no. 32 (October 13, 1960), 117-26.

4

THE SOCIAL POLICIES
OF THE EUROPEAN
COMMUNITIES

THE TREATIES ON SOCIAL MATTERS

The Paris Treaty

The Paris Treaty accords the High Authority only limited powers over labor policy. At the time the Treaty was formulated, there was uncertainty about what kind of institution the ECSC would prove to be and doubts about the wisdom of granting the High Authority significant powers in such a sensitive field. The employers, many of whom had misgivings about the ECSC, would probably have resisted any important grant of authority in labor matters. The governments as well were reluctant to yield substantial powers, because they would be held politically responsible for the actions of others; and, furthermore, any distinction between wages in the coal and steel industries and wages in the nonintegrated parts of the economy might prove embarrassing.[1] The unions were divided, with the French and Belgian labor groups pressing for some coordination of social policy and the German and Dutch unions opposing social integration. Also, the supporters of the Treaty feared that too large an assignment in social matters would prove difficult to carry out and might hinder the success of the Community by arousing expectations it could not fulfill.

The social provisions contained in the Paris Treaty are of four types: general aims, specific rules covering wages and competition, provisions for the free movement of labor, and articles pertaining to the readaptation of workers affected by the development of the Common Market.

The general aims of the Paris Treaty, as contained in articles 2 and 3, are broad. They include the development of employment, the improvement of the standard of living, and the equalization of the living and working conditions of the labor force in an upward direction. However, the High Authority was granted no power over wages, working conditions, or employment policy and was concerned with these problems only insofar as the development of the Common Market affected them and they therefore required supplementary attention.

The High Authority could exercise positive power in social affairs only in marginal situations involving a falsification of competitive conditions. Specific rules concerning wages and competition appear in article 68 of the Treaty, which was included at the request of the trade unions who wished to preserve their complete freedom of action with respect to wages and to protect their hard-won social achievements. The article ensures that

> The methods of fixing wages and social
> benefits in force in the various Member
> States shall not be affected, as regards
> the coal and steel industries, by the
> application of the . . . Treaty.

That the reservations of the trade unions were ultimately dispelled is proved by the demand for revision of this article by the European labor secretariats and the Socialist Group of the Common Assembly.[2]

Although the High Authority was empowered to facilitate the free movement of workers in the coal and steel industries, the provision covering free movement is strictly circumscribed; and final responsibility for this matter rests with the national governments.

The High Authority was able to grant special aid to workers laid off as the result of the adaptation of enterprises to the conditions of the Common Market. However, the initiative in readaptation measures belongs to the governments.

The powers of the High Authority in the social domain are strictly limited to competencies that the authors of the Paris Treaty considered essential for the functioning of the Common Market. Social provisions indicate in a detailed manner the extent of powers conferred, the circumstances in which they can be exercised, and the rules governing their exercise. The Paris Treaty offers no basis for a comprehensive social program.

However, the combined pressure of the trade unions and the Common Assembly for an active social policy and for a broad interpretation of all Treaty provisions, according to the aims expressed in articles 2 and 3, permitted the emergence of a more ambitious policy than was warranted by the intention of the parties to the Treaty. The housing program of the High Authority and its impressive achievements in studies and research are evidence of its initiative and of its response to these demands.

The Rome Treaties

Because of the sensitivity of the national governments on the subject, the Rome Treaties include no provisions for a European social policy. Aside from provisions on the free movement of labor, a European Social Fund for readaptation purposes, specific measures concerning equality of wages between men and women, and vocational training, social policy remains within national competence. The European Commission is charged only with studying the social situation in the Community and generally promoting cooperation among the member states, rather than fixing goals to be reached by regulations, directives, and decisions by Community organs. Instead of the right to exercise delegated powers, the Commission was granted the right to recommend, to propose, to render opinions, and to promote close collaboration among the member states. The trade unions' wish for an independent European executive, wielding extensive social powers within the EEC, was not fulfilled. Hence, they considered the Rome Treaties a step backward on the road to European unity.

The European Commission enjoys the power of decision in social affairs in the single instance of line 3, article 48, on the free movement of labor. The latter stipulates that the Commission regulate the conditions in which the workers of one member state can remain in the territory of another after having been employed there. However, the provisions of the Rome Treaties for the free migration of labor are more far-reaching than their counterparts in the ECSC, which are limited to workers of "recognized qualification."

The Rome Treaties contain general obligations to promote close collaboration among member states in such matters as employment, labor legislation and working conditions, vocational training, and industrial hygience. Both European labor secretariats were disappointed with this provision. They would have liked specific obligations for the Commission in these matters and wider powers, including the financing of studies and the publication of results.[3]

More specific provisions cover equal pay for equal work between men and women and the equivalence of paid holidays. The trade unions were generally pleased with these articles, although the latter were motivated as much by France's concern for costs as by the desire for social improvement.[4]

The Treaties are responsive to the interests of the European Assembly and to the labor groups in its provision that the Commission must include a special chapter on the development of the social situation in the Community in its annual report to the Assembly. The latter may also request the Commission to report on special problems concerning the social situation.

The trade unions were disappointed that none of the extensions of readaptation proposed for the ECSC were adopted for the EEC. There is a provision for a European Social Fund to assist in the retraining of workers during the transition period. However, the European Commission has less power to act on its own initiative than the High Authority, and the procedure for granting assistance is elaborate and hedged with many restrictions.

Although the Rome Treaties cover more areas in the social domain than the Paris Treaty, the procedures for achieving social measures are vague; and the emphasis is on coordination between national social policies rather than on provision for a European social policy. However, as in the case of the ECSC, the initiative of the European Commission and its ability to elicit support from the member governments, Community organs, and the various sectors of economic life have also influenced the scope and nature of social policy pursued by the Community.

THE HIGH AUTHORITY'S POLICY
ON SOCIAL MATTERS

Prior to 1955 the social policy of the High Authority remained rigorously within the limits of the Paris Treaty. In its first general report the High Authority proposed to follow three lines of activity: aid to housing, the publication of data on wages and working conditions, and research in health and safety. The potential benefits of these courses of action were clear and the propriety of Community action noncontroversial. The High Authority argued that the Treaty did not grant it the right of initiative in social affairs and that it could not pursue activities in the social field that were not expressly provided for by the Treaty. At that time it regarded its principal task as one of recording the progress made within the Community in wages and working conditions, and it frequently cited articles 68 and 5 as reasons for its inability to pursue direct action.[5]

Except in the case of housing, the High Authority ignored all requests for a liberal interpretation of the Treaty. On the subject of free migration it reminded the Common Assembly that it was limited not only by the Treaty but also by the reticence of certain employers' and workers' groups.[6] In answer to the Assembly's request to seek greater initiative in readaptation, the High Authority replied that it was not its duty to request an extension of its activities; and, despite the protests of the Assembly and the labor groups, it reduced the percentage of the levy in 1955, even though a larger readaptation fund would have facilitated a more active policy in this area. To the condemnation of the Socialist Group of the Assembly, the High Authority replied:

> It is not our task to raise the levy. . . . It is the task of the governments to foresee new possibilities of expense favoring the workers. . . . The development of readaptation and the creation of new activities to absorb unemployment is a matter for the governments.[7]

The High Authority also declined action on the Renard Resolution, arguing that social harmonization must be preceded by the harmonization of all elements constituting the totality of economic and social life. Its inactivity in this area was a result of its wish to interpret the Treaty strictly and of its refusal to commit itself to the definition of a labor policy. The High Authority retreated behind the argument that an independent social policy could not be pursued at the ECSC level and that social improvements would accrue automatically from economic expansion.[8] It was the growing trade union pressure for action and the insistence of the Belgian government on harmonizing the workweek that finally compelled the High Authority to convene mixed committees in 1956.

What were the factors limiting the action of the High Authority in the social domain? The fact of partial integration, the limitations of the Paris Treaty, and, more significantly, the opposition of

certain governments, employers, and even labor groups
to High Authority activity in the social field acted
as a brake on the development of a European social
policy. Through the Council of Ministers the governments applied pressure on the High Authority to stay
within the bounds of the Treaty. When the High
Authority fostered the Assembly's proposal for the
establishment of an international labor exchange under article 69, the governments replied that employment policy was their own affair.[9] Moreover, the
Council of Ministers refused to associate itself with
the studies of the High Authority on the forty-five-
hour week, because it did not wish to give the trade
unions the impression that it favored the reduction
of working time. The governments showed particular
reserve toward anything that smacked of collective
bargaining. On the other hand, certain labor groups
also demonstrated reticence to High Authority action,
especially in the fields of wages and free migration.
Fritz Dahlman, president of I.G. Bergbau, claimed:

> It is the task of the national trade union
> organizations, using the effects produced
> by the common market and observing the pos-
> sibilities of comparison offered by the
> High Authority, to promote harmonization
> upward. . . . Trade union organizations
> should not regard the ECSC as a substitute
> for national regulations concerning wages
> and work.[10]

An equally important limitation on the High Authority's social policy was its own cautious attitude,
its refusal to act in the absence of unanimous agreement on broad interpretation of the Treaty, and its
practice of consulting the governments, producers,
labor, and consumer groups even when not required by
the Treaty.

During the late 1950's the High Authority demonstrated a notable change in attitude, the conviction
that a social policy could be defined for the ECSC.
For the first time the High Authority devoted a section of its general report to its projected policy
in the social field and proposed to focus its studies

on more specific and significant problems. Thus, it
gave new accent to its apparently innocuous research
endeavors in the field of wages and working conditions, stressing that it was

> able and anxious to turn studies and dis-
> cussions that could be of purely academic
> interest into a basis for concerted action
> by all those concerned in order to invest
> the Community with its full social value.[11]

However, the High Authority still insisted that it
had neither the will nor the competence to foster
collective agreements for an industry, thus indirectly
answering employers who protested that mixed committees would create a privileged group of workers.
But, while it had previously refused to even consider
mixed meetings, it now agreed not only to support
them but also to see that their activity was not
limited to fact-finding. Instead of retreating behind a treaty that made no reference to social policy,
the High Authority now committed itself to the improvement of the social situation, not only by recording the facts of that situation but also by
indicating what could be done to improve matters
through sponsoring joint discussions--in effect, just
what the first report of the Assembly's Committee on
Social Affairs had pleaded for.

One of the first indications of the High Authority's new approach to social problems was its efforts
to improve the working conditions of miners. In
its "Report on General Objectives for Coal," the
High Authority emphasized manpower problems and suggested improvements in working conditions to lend
coal mining more appeal. At that time the High Authority also offered its support for a European
Miners' Statute, and a joint committee of the High
Authority and the Council of Ministers drew up similar proposals on ways of facilitating the recruitment
of mine workers, advocating regularity of employment,
wage advantages, and the provision of housing facilities within easy reach.[12] The High Authority also
began a study of the possibilities of stockpiling in

order to ensure continuity of employment, a foretaste
of its efforts to deal with the coal crisis two years
later.

Another step taken by the High Authority toward
a more active social policy included efforts to persuade the national governments to relax their immigration laws and compensate for manpower shortages
in the mines with liberalized rules for the recruitment of Italian workers. It appealed to the governments of Luxembourg, the Netherlands, Germany, and
to the Charbonnages de France to bring in more labor
from Italy, to make efforts to help overcome language
difficulties, and to deal with technical and safety
problems as quickly as possible by setting up special
vocational training centers for foreign workers.[13]
It also acted as an intermediary between the Belgian
and Italian governments when immigration from Italy
came practically to a standstill.

However, the High Authority was caught between
the cross pressures of workers' groups seeking broad
action and producers' groups seeking to curb its
activity. As a result, the policy of the High Authority wavered. On the one hand, it exerted itself on
the controversial matter of mixed committees and
safety in the coal mines, and it sought to update
the schedule of occupations eligible for free migration. It also made wide use of readaptation measures
so that the Committee on Social Affairs of the Assembly could claim that the High Authority had made a
serious effort to follow its suggestions.[14] Ultimately, it took up Assembly proposals for a minor
revision of readaptation provisions and sought to
cushion the effects of the coal crisis on the standard of living by helping to finance the holding of
stocks in order to contain unemployment and by making
an allowance available to Belgian miners put on
short time. On the other hand, the High Authority
twice reduced the levy, against the wishes of the
Assembly, and also relaxed its efforts to achieve a
European Miners' Charter, citing governmental opposition and the difficulty of achieving a coordination
of the various legislative provisions on the matter.[15]

Starting from the rather limited position as stated in its first general report, the High Authority sought to influence the labor situation in the Community, as is evidenced by its social research, which focused on the controversial issues of wages and fringe benefits. It made a considerable effort in the field of industrial health and safety, in its housing program, and in the use of readaptation measures. However, although the High Authority acted upon the majority of the Assembly's requests, and although it abandoned its initial noncommittal attitude, it did not pursue a vigorous supranational social policy. It was unwilling to go beyond the limits of prudence and to risk unpopularity with the governments and the producers' groups in an area in which it had no political authority. Because it was politically dependent upon the national governments, the High Authority chose an indirect role in the social field, supplementing and inspiring national efforts.

THE EUROPEAN COMMISSION'S
SOCIAL POLICY

Although the European Commission is keenly aware that a European welfare policy cannot be achieved within the EEC, it has nevertheless promoted far-reaching social goals: the harmonization of national social policies, the development of a European employment policy, and the harmonization of living and working conditions--"equalization in an upward direction." However, the Rome Treaties indicate no clear course of action for the achievement of social measures.

What has been the Commission's method of operation? From the definition of its social goals the Commission has proceeded pragmatically, preceding action by studies and achieving social policies gradually by a series of measures. The Commission regards its role as one of bringing social problems to the attention of the governments and the social partners and exercising its influence so that adequate solutions will be found. It has defined its task as

coordinating initiatives, interpreting nec-
essities common to various sectors, and
harmonizing them as a catalytic agent.[16]

Undaunted by its lack of supranational powers, it has
emphasized its function as an instrument of coordination, organizing meetings between those responsible
for economic and social affairs in the Six and drawing relevant conclusions.

The Commission has operated in a threefold manner: gathering information to become acquainted with
a particular situation, disseminating its findings
to national administrations directly responsible for
social policy, and organizing meetings and conferences. Both the European Parliamentary Assembly and
the Economic and Social Committee are implicated in
this process as a measure of support. The Commission
has established direct contacts with the national administrations by sending representatives to the six
capitals and by presiding over committees of national
experts in Brussels. Frequently these experts are
the same who advise ministers in Council discussions.
For example, in seeking the application of article
119 of the Rome Treaties, it invited representatives
of the Ministries of Labor and Social Security to
Brussels for discussion.[17] It subsequently brought
together representatives of employers' and workers'
organizations to outline an inquiry on the ratio of
men to women in collective bargaining agreements.
Only after extensive study and discussion by responsible parties at the national level did the Commission
send the Conference of Permanent Representatives a
recommendation on the interpretation and application
of article 119. It has acted more prudently than
the High Authority in submitting only those proposals
it has judged acceptable, thus avoiding the risk of
refusal and a consequent loss of prestige.

The statements of the European Commission on
Social Affairs have focused upon important matters.
What has been its course of action? Despite its
declarations the Commission was slow in initiating
the application of the Rome Treaties' social measures.
Its first achievement was to win the approval of the

Council of Ministers for conventions 3 and 4 on social security for migrant workers.[18] However, the
early efforts of the Commission were devoted to compiling a general picture of the situation in the
labor market throughout the Community and to making
comparative studies on labor legislation, collective
bargaining, wage structures, and the workweek. Many
of the activities proposed by the Commission in its
first general report were carried out only at the
end of the first stage of the transition period.
This is true with respect to its proposals for vocational training, for applying free migration, for a
recommendation on social services, and for measures
concerning health and safety.

The optimum employment of human resources, a
European manpower policy, has figured prominently in
the Commission's social program. As a first step
toward this goal the Commission sent the Council of
Ministers a set of proposals in the framework of a
coordination of cyclical policies and based upon an
analysis of the employment situation in the Six between 1954 and 1958.[19] Since then the Commission has
presented annual reports to the Council of Ministers
on manpower problems, along with recommendations for
remedying them. It has supplemented these by continuing research on structural unemployment and by
studies preparatory to long-term employment measures,
including surveys on the labor services of the Six
and on national vocational orientation programs.

With the attainment of virtually full employment, most EEC members have developed sophisticated
manpower policies. The Commission has sought to
capitalize on national experience in this field and
has published reports on manpower problems in conjunction with its first and its second medium-term
economic policy programs. The second program concentrated on structural programs, outlining the role of
vocational guidance, training, retraining, readaptation, and the creation of new jobs through the establishment of new industries.[20] In drawing up these
programs the Commission gathers information on national social goals through conversations with governmental officials, management, and labor and by

periodic discussions at the Community level with governmental representatives and the social partners.
Through its studies and forecasts on industries in
expansion and contraction, the Commission can help
identify and anticipate sources of structural unemployment. Through such corrective measures as readaptation, vocational training, the European Social
Fund, and the mobility of labor the Commission can
work toward a higher level of employment within the
Community. Since these measures are currently rather
circumscribed and have a minimal impact on national
problems, the Commission has proposed a series of
extensive improvements. However, until the development of European fiscal and monetary policies, a
high level of demand and other major determinants of
expanding employment will continue to be achieved by
national measures. In the long interval the Commission can serve as coordinator of national efforts
and can seek to supplement national activity.

The Commission also has been active in dealing
with the social problems of sectors that are the
objects of common policies: agriculture, transports,
the fishing industry, and energy.[21] Its proposals
for European policies in these areas have been accompanied by measures covering the improvement of
social conditions in the relevant occupations and
for the harmonization of living and working conditions in each sector. It has instituted parity committees composed of labor and management for each
policy area in order to help develop proposals for
social measures and to design surveys on wages, working conditions, and trends in employment.

The limitations on the achievement of a European
social policy are important. The Rome Treaties do
not accord the European Commission supranational
power, and they are vague on the procedures for
achieving social measures. Moreover, the Commission
is dependent on the goodwill of the governments to a
greater extent than was its predecessor, the High
Authority, for it lacks an independent source of
funds. The absence of a levy or a similar source of
finance for its social projects has proved a stumbling
block to the efforts of the Commission. Regardless

of its initiative the fundamental obstacles to a vigorous European social policy remain the embryonic state of integration, the inability of the Commission to bind the governments, and the reticence of the governments.

THE SOCIAL POLICIES OF THE EUROPEAN COMMUNITIES

Readaptation: An Innovation

The ECSC is unique in its provision for the readaptation of workers unemployed because of technological innovation, for when the Paris Treaty was signed, none of the member governments acknowledged this right to job security in their own laws. Readaptation was designed to alleviate the impact of transition from protected national markets to a competitive single market, to avoid dislocation, and to protect the labor force. The provisions on readaptation are partially a result of trade union efforts during the negotiations preparatory to the Paris Treaty and of the hope of the Treaty authors that opposition to the removal of trade barriers would be reduced if firms unable to meet increased competition were given aid to modernize or to pursue other lines of activity.

The provisions for readaptation originally included article 56 of the Paris Treaty and section 23 of the convention containing the transitional provisions. The latter, which is more flexible than article 56, states:

> In case the consequences of the establishment of the common market oblige certain enterprises to cease or change their activities in the course of the transitional period, the High Authority, on request of the interested governments . . . should lend its aid to protect labor from the burdens of re-adaptation and assure it a productive employment, and can accord non-reimbursable aid to certain enterprises.

In 1960 article 56 was revised in order to eliminate its restrictions in scope and the time limit on section 23. The former provided for aid only if the introduction of technical processes or new equipment resulted in an exceptionally important reduction in need for labor. Section 23, which is broader in scope, was effective during the transition period only. However, the development of the Common Market had shown that the process of adjustment to its structural development would continue to create problems after the expiration of the transition period. Therefore, article 56 was revised in order to allow the High Authority to assist workers discharged as a result of alterations in the marketing conditions of coal and steel. Revision has facilitated the decisions of the High Authority and its successor, the Unified Commission, by eliminating the difficulty of differentiating between structural, cyclical, and technological causes of employment.

As amended, article 56 now states:

> Should profound changes in the marketing conditions of the coal-mining and of the iron and steel industry not directly connected with the introduction of the common market make it necessary for certain enterprises permanently to discontinue, curtail, or change their activities . . . the High Authority may grant assistance for the purposes mentioned in Section 23.

ECSC aid to readaptation is conditional on the application of the member government concerned. It may take various forms. To help workers at a lower rate of pay, the ECSC may do either of the following:

1. Guarantee for a limited period a specific percentage of the wages received by the workers affected before being discharged (90 percent to 100 percent for the first 4 months). The length of this period is generally 12 months in Germany, Belgium, France, and Luxembourg; 15 months in Italy; and between 12 and 30 months, according to age and length of service, in the Netherlands.

2. Establish the wage guarantee at between 90 percent and 100 percent of the previous net wage.

To help workers find employment in a different occupation the ECSC does four things:

1. Contributes to the cost of vocational re-training (operating costs of training centers and part of the wage for the new job during the period of adaptation).

2. Guarantees a specific percentage of the previous wage during retraining courses (between 85 percent and 100 percent of the previous wage, according to country).

3. Awards bonuses when the retraining course is successful.

4. Contributes to wages and social security payments in the new job for elderly and physically handicapped workers in Belgium.

To help workers find a job in a different region the ECSC does the following:

1. Makes a lump sum resettlement grant and refunds travel and moving expenses for workers and their families.

2. Refunds, in certain cases, additional daily travel expenses and payment of a severance allowance when the worker cannot bring his family to the new region (Germany, Lorraine, the Netherlands).

To help workers while they are awaiting new employment, the ECSC does the following:

1. Guarantees for a limited period a specific percentage of the wage received prior to redundancy. This figure is generally around 70 percent or 80 percent.

2. Grants a standard allowance for workers aged forty and over and for physically handicapped workers.

Pays wages and corresponding social security contributions when a mining or steel concern lays its workers off temporarily during a period of internal conversion.[22]

How has readaptation worked? The failure of one of the first major cases of readaptation seemed to substantiate the trade unions' criticism that the Paris Treaty authors had taken an overly theoretical view of the problems likely to arise in the application of readaptation. However, there were also notable instances of success in aiding workers affected by reconversion projects.

Charbonnages de France

Beginning in 1950 a crisis was looming in the basins of Aquitaine, Cévennes, and Provence, creating progressive unemployment. Productivity was rising and the possibility of sales was decreasing because of increasing hydroelectric competition and the importation of foreign coal along the coast. In 1953 the French government requested the aid of the High Authority under section 23.[23] Mines in Cévennes, Aquitaine, and Provence would have to discharge 5,000 workers over a period of three years. With the aid of the High Authority the Charbonnages de France planned to reemploy the discharged miners of the Centre-Midi basins in the Lorraine mines.

The French government and the High Authority reached an accord the following year by which freely accepted transfer was organized in agreement with the democratic trade unions. Those volunteering for transfer would receive a special indemnity of 200,000 francs for heads of families and 75,000 francs for bachelors, plus traveling and moving expenses and an extra day of vacation to make up for lost working time.[24] Housing was promised, as was the maintenance of the workers' job classifications and pension rights. Since the pay scale in Lorraine was higher, it was suggested that most of the transferred miners eventually would be better paid than if they had stayed in the South. Workers' delegations from the Centre-Midi visited Lorraine to examine working conditions, and trade union officials participated in the transfer arrangements.

The agreements were signed in April 1954. At the beginning of 1955 only 145 volunteers went to Lorraine. Difficulties were traced primarily to housing problems.[25] Consequently, the Lorraine mines constructed a project to house 1,200 bachelors. However, by December 1956 the number of volunteers for transfer had risen to only 560.[26] The transfer stopped at that point, and the whole project was shelved at the end of the year.

The Assembly's Committee on Social Affairs studied the organization of the transfer and the causes of its failure. It attributed the failure of the transfer to insufficient psychological preparation, insufficient collaboration between the trade unions and employers' organizations, insufficient preparations for housing, and the large scale of the project.[27]

The attachment of men to their milieu was underestimated:

Certain men are profoundly rooted, attached to their family, to the village steeple, their music society, the corner cafe where they meet their friends.[28]

All the ties to home operated along with the fear and uncertainty deterring people from radical change.

In the case of the Centre-Midi, the pressure of authorities and social groups encouraged this reluctance to leave.[29] Store owners protested the prospects of a reduction in local activity and formed defense organizations to persuade the miners not to move. Political authorities joined in the defense of the region; and officials of municipalities, deputies, and senators protested to the national government. Even the trade unions emphasized the risks of mobility. Although the CGT-FO and the CFTC cooperated with the government and the High Authority in arrangements for the transfer, local union officials were

anxious to keep their members. The strongest union,
the CGT, had refused to cooperate with the transfer
from the beginning and denounced it as a capitalist
conspiracy for the benefit of the Ruhr. It circulated
a number of tracts and newspaper articles, which
bore such titles as "We Will Not Be the Deportees of
the Schuman Plan" and "Bruay Will Not Be a Dead
City."[30]

Some of the first men to move under the plan
were dissatisfied with the change. The Committee on
Social Affairs reported:

> The transferred workers assimilate them-
> selves to the local population only with
> great difficulty. . . . In practice, there
> has been no or hardly any assimilation up
> to the present.[31]

The various reasons for this phenomenon were cited
as differences in the way of life between the Centre-
Midi and Lorraine, the differences in climate, language difficulties, and the more rigorous discipline
resulting from the complete mechanization of the Lorraine mines.

The workers interviewed by the Committee on
Social Affairs stressed the lack of logic characterizing the operation and the resulting difficulties.[32]
The unions played less of a part than they had expected and felt that the reception in the new basin
was disorganized. Social services were lacking at
various times, and the reception committee functioned
poorly. The workers also complained that the distribution of housing was arbitrary. Some of them were
installed in new one-family houses, some in tiny
lodgings, others in apartment buildings, and bachelors
in abandoned barracks. Not all of the expectations
that had been created could be satisfied; and, although matters eventually improved, the disappointments were already conveyed to the Midi.

In 1956 the High Authority declared that the
scheme for transferring miners from the Centre-Midi
to Lorraine had been discontinued because of boom

conditions that had eliminated unemployment in the
Centre-Midi.[33] Between the spring of 1954, when the
transfer scheme was introduced, and the fall of 1956
employment fell by 5,000. Meanwhile, productivity
continued to rise, but there was no unemployment in
1956 and little emigration from the area. The adjustment was made by holding down the hiring of new
workers so that those originally slated to go could
be kept on or reemployed.[34] Readjustment occurred
without the benefit of aid from the ECSC.

This experience demonstrated that although
transfer may be a necessity for the coal industry,
which is conditioned by the situation of seams,
large-scale transfer is a most inefficient palliative
for unemployment. The High Authority concluded that
workers should be allowed to choose from among a number of alternatives for employment equally suited to
their abilities, either in their old occupation or
in a new one, and preferably in the same region.[35]

Compagnie des Ateliers et Forges de la Loire

The establishment of the Common Market for coal
and steel led four small enterprises to undertake a
program of rationalization and modernization. In
1953 Saint-Chamond, Mermeny, Saint-Étienne, and Jacob
Holtzer combined to form the Compagnie des Ateliers
et Forges de la Loire.[36] About 1,500 workers were
affected by the reconversion. The High Authority
agreed to share the cost of occupational retraining
and readaptation of the workers involved, so that
reconversion could be accomplished without recourse
to dismissal.

The workers were divided into three categories
for the readaptation program. For those undergoing
occupational retraining the aid of the French government and the High Authority corresponded to one-half
of their former wage. For workers who continued to
work, although at a reduced output, readaptation aid
equaled the difference between their actual wage and
the wage paid by the enterprise as a function of
their reduced output. This rate was fixed for each

worker by agreement between the High Authority and the director of the enterprise.[37]

The Assembly's Committee on Social Affairs conducted an on-the-spot study of the program and compiled a long list of criticisms, many of which concerned the arrangements for administering and supervising the process.[38] The French Ministry of Labor had created committees to control the readaptation programs; they were capped by a group representing the High Authority; the ministries of labor, industry, and commerce; the mining and metallurgy unions; the directors of the enterprises involved; and trade union delegations in Luxembourg. It had not yet convened at the time the study was conducted, nor had a similarly composed regional committee met. A local committee composed of representatives of the employers and the enterprises and of the CGT-FO and CFTC was to meet on a monthly basis. However, it met only once in 1955 and once the following year. The workers protested that instead of consulting the local committees on which the unions were represented the firms proceeded in a unilateral fashion and the local committees did not discuss the granting of financial aid or cooperate in the process of readaptation. In their opinion the fear of seeing an overly rapid readaptation create discrimination among steelworkers and workers in other industries made the government hesitate to take the necessary administrative measures.

The main criticism of the Committee on Social Affairs was aimed at the supposed passivity of the High Authority. The Committee accused the latter of doing little but paying out funds against vouchers and of neglecting to supervise the manner in which the readaptation program functioned.[39]

Despite these criticisms the program can be considered a success. The workers involved fared better than their comrades in nonintegrated industries, for the latter receive an unemployment compensation of 30 percent of the average wage in their category; and in communes, where there are no unemployment funds, they receive no compensation. The

employers concerned were satisfied that aid from the
ECSC enabled them to achieve their reconversion
projects without reducing their labor force, and,
as a direct result of this experience, the French
government passed readaptation legislation for industrial sectors other than coal and steel.[40]

Readaptation in the Italian
Steel Industry

In the postwar period the Italian government
sought to protect the internal market for steel.
This policy failed to stimulate the industry to modernize at a sufficiently rapid rate, so that the
establishment of the Common Market provoked an acceleration of the modernization process and partial
reconversion of the metallurgy industry.

In December 1953 the Italian government requested
aid for 8,000 steelworkers, some dismissed as a result of the establishment of the Common Market.[41]
Final agreement was not reached until May 1956. By
then the number of workers eligible for readaptation
aid had risen to 9,000.[42] The delay was caused by
the difficulties of devising means of using the
funds that would satisfy the exigencies of the Italian
situation and meet the High Authority's standards.

The Italian government invoked line 7 of article
46:

> The High Authority should participate, on
> request of the governments concerned, in
> the study of possibilities of reemployment
> in existent industries or by the creation
> of new activities of manpower rendered
> available by the evolution of the market
> or technical transformations.

The 8,000 discharged workers were a very small part
of the unemployed in Italy, so the Italian government
could neither indulge in favoritism nor afford to
pay allowances to everyone. It held that governmental
aid should not be in the form of indemnity payments
but, rather, that it should aim at procuring the

unemployed new possibilities of employment. It therefore proposed to advance 3.5 billion lire to help
industrial firms of all sectors expand their activities if they would promise to take at least 50 percent
of their new workers from among those discharged by
the steel industry.[43] In this way it hoped to reemploy 1,750 of the 8,000 workers. The High Authority
was not prepared to have its funds used in this way
but agreed to provide an equal sum, destined entirely
for workers, in various kinds of payments comparable
with those made in other cases of readaptation.

The passage of time made it harder to work out
a program for distributing funds. However, an agreement was finally reached between the High Authority
and the Italian government in May 1956, which provided for 3.5 billion lire to be furnished by the
High Authority in the form of regressive allowances
to workers unemployed for not more than fifteen
months.[44] Transport and moving allowances would be
paid to workers obliged to change their place of
residence.

Useful as this distribution of funds was to the
recipients, the psychological advantages of ECSC aid
were reduced by the long discussions between the High
Authority and the Italian government. Because of the
delay readaptation occurred without the benefit of
Community intervention, so that the aid granted appeared as a belated supplementary social security
grant. While the workers were pleased with the provision of indemnities, they considered the only effective solution to such problems to be a policy of
reemployment and policies favoring economic expansion.

Readaptation is of the utmost importance to the
trade unions in their quest for the right to work.
Both the workers and the Assembly's Committee on
Social Affairs have campaigned for the broadest interpretation possible of readaptation provisions
and for the solution of reemployment problems through
regional programs rather than through labor migration.
Although the High Authority deferred to the wishes
of the Assembly and the labor unions in attempting
to improve the execution of readaptation programs,

fundamental differences in interpreting the Paris
Treaty persisted between the High Authority and the
Assembly. The High Authority did not consider itself
competent to control the execution of regulations
concluded at the national level among employers,
workers, and the government--i.e., the maintenance
of wage categories or the provision of appropriate
housing--and it refrained from establishing official
contacts with the employers' organizations and the
trade unions involved, citing its lack of administrative apparatus.[45] However, a major explanation
of the High Authority's lack of vigor in developing
and executing broader readaptation programs lies in
the fact that the initiative in readaptation belongs
to the governments, and they have often proved reluctant to apply these provisions.

Aid to Reconversion

Following the coal crisis of 1959 the problem
of readaptation was viewed within the context of industrial redevelopment and overall regional policy,
areas in which the High Authority's means of action
are largely indirect. Article 46 of the Paris Treaty
allows the High Authority, on request of a member
government, to study the possibilities of reemploying workers laid off because of technological or
marketing changes in either existing or new industries.
As a result, the High Authority has pursued several
studies on regional and economic factors requiring
either the establishment of new industries or the
relocation of existing ones. These studies have
produced an accumulation of important data on regions
where the normal employment growth in coal and steel
is doubtful and have developed formulas for diagnosing
the unemployment potential of a region and for determining appropriate measures to cope with underemploy-
ment. The majority of these studies have focused on
areas affected by pit closures, such as the Borinage
in Belgium.[46]

Actual reconversion plans and their execution
are the responsibility of the member governments;
however, the High Authority can grant financial aid
to these projects as well as participate in studies.

When article 56 was revised in 1960, a new clause
was included permitting the High Authority to finance
new, economically sound activities ensuring employment to workers displaced from other industries.
This provision is aimed at avoiding a delay between
the closure of a mine and the operation of new industrial activities. Delay at such a critical time may
mean emigration from the affected region.

Reconversion was effected for the first time in
the Borinage area of Belgium in order to provide employment for displaced mine workers. Between 1961
and 1967 ECSC efforts in this field allowed the re-
integration of 31,500 former coal- and steelworkers
in various other industries.[47] Subsequently the
Unified Commission has helped create 1,900 new jobs
through its financing of investment projects that
guarantee priority for reemploying coal- and steelworkers.[48] The provision of new employment has
stimulated regional development by helping to diver-
sify the pattern of employment, frequently limited
to one industry, and by stemming emigration flows.

The High Authority's reconversion studies have
served as models for solving the problems of workers
obliged to leave agricultural occupations and as an
aid in coping with the broad problem of the economic
decline of certain regions. At present, however,
policies affecting regional development remain within
national competence.

By the end of 1969 the ECSC had provided
$121,593,730 to help retrain and reemploy 390,679
workers, the majority of whom were coal miners.[49]
Since 1965 the credits allocated and the number of
workers eligible for readaptation have risen appreciably, chiefly because of the acceleration of modernization operations in Germany and because of the
rapid pace at which Dutch pits are being closed.

The principle of readaptation in facilitating
reemployment has become embodied in national law and
has been extended to sectors other than coal and
steel. In addition the financial aid extended by
the High Authority and the European Commission to

ECSC industries has allowed it some influence in re-
orientation operations, for the obligation of employers to submit detailed dossiers in order to qualify
for aid has acted as a spur to developing employment
forecasts, facilitating reclassifications, and often
limiting the number of layoffs.[50] Readaptation has
allowed the ECSC industries to rationalize without
overly serious consequences for their personnel, has
assuaged the legitimate fears of workers, and has
provided a link between closures and industrial
development.

Free Movement of Labor
Within the ECSC

The free movement of labor within the ECSC is
guaranteed by article 69 of the Paris Treaty in which
the member states agree

> to renounce any restriction, based on na-
> tionality, on the employment in the coal
> and steel industries of workers of recog-
> nized qualification

if they are nationals of one of the member states.
However, the same article includes a series of limitations, such as health and public order; and the
High Authority is relegated to the auziliary role of
"orienting and facilitating the action of Member
States." None of the commitments included in this
article could come into effect without the action of
the national governments, which retain the entire
initiative and responsibility in this field.

There was no pressure for a rapid application
of free movement; and, although the Council of Ministers formulated a decision on article 69 in 1954,
ratification was not completed until 1957, more than
six years after the establishment of the Paris
Treaty.[51]

The resulting agreement was hedged with important
restrictions. Only those workers with confirmed
qualifications in coal mining or steel making or who
had worked for two years in an ECSC industry were

eligible for an ECSC labor card, and workers must
have had an offer of employment in order to use the
card. Once in possession of an ECSC labor card, a
worker needed no visa and was exempt from restrictions normally applying to foreign workers. However,
if a government believed that the operation of the
agreement was creating a danger of disequilibrium on
the labor market, it could request the High Authority
to convene the signatories of the agreement in order
to take appropriate steps.

Free migration did not appreciably affect the
already significant international movement of labor
within the ECSC. The extensive employment of Italian
migrants in France and Belgium in the late 1950's
was regulated by a complex maze of bilateral agreements that were not altered by the agreement on the
application of article 69.[52] The latter was largely
irrelevant to Italy's reservoir of unskilled labor,
for only a very few of the Italians migrating to
French or Belgian coal districts had any experience
as miners; and the majority were interested in working only a few years to accumulate savings before
returning home.

Nor did the agreement satisfy the broader economic and social requirements of the ECSC or deal
with the Community's problem of a shortage of coal
miners in periods of high demand. National labor
markets for the coal and steel industries are closely
related to the structure and trends of the labor
market in other sectors, particularly the construction industry. Therefore, in periods of high demand
for steelworkers the unemployed coal- or steelworker
generally prefers readaptation on location, which
means readaptation outside the coal and steel sector.[53] Moreover, national coal and steel industries
are so closely related to the world economic situation that essential differences in employment situations are unlikely. In periods of high demand the
same need will be felt in most countries.

The number of labor cards issued since 1957 is
small, and the results of the agreement on the free
movement of labor remain unimpressive. Generally,

skilled workers are not inclined to emigrate and are
little affected by unemployment. A large number of
workers with "recognized qualifications" employed
in an ECSC country other than their own have obtained
their jobs by bilateral agreements and therefore
have not bothered to apply for a labor card; and for
a native of a Benelux country, working within the
Benelux area, a labor card is unnecessary. The vast
majority of workers eligible for cards never requested
them.

What factors operated in favor of a limited
agreement and a strict interpretation of a seemingly
revolutionary provision? The governments were not
anxious to relinquish their control of labor migration. They feared a large influx of foreign labor
and negative consequences on the labor market.[54]

The majority of trade unions prefer mobility of
jobs to the mobility of labor and believe that any
policy of geographic mobility has fairly narrow
limits beyond which not only the human costs but
also the economic costs make such a policy undesir-
able. While the need for some mobility is generally
acknowledged, most unions condition immigration on
the full employment of nationals and insist that
immigration of foreign workers should not depress
wages or working conditions or diminish the position
of national workers in industrial relations.

The attitude of the trade unions toward mobility
depends upon their nature; craft unions favor geographic but not occupational mobility, whereas industrial unions encourage occupational mobility but
not necessarily other forms.[55] National differences
are also evident in the views of labor unions. The
Dutch and German unions see no advantage in intra-
European migrations and have great difficulty persuading their members that internal economic conditions may warrant migration.[56] In both countries
the reluctance to accept foreign workers is partly
cultural and psychological.

On the whole none of the trade unions complained
that article 69 was overly restrictive; and all

agreed that the free movement of labor should be
limited, as stipulated, to skilled workers. Only
the Common Assembly voiced criticism of the marginal
role accorded the High Authority on this matter.
Its Committee on Social Affairs suggested the establishment of a European Placement Bureau attached to
the High Authority and vested with broad powers,
but the trade unions did not back this proposal.[57]

Free Movement of Labor
in the EEC

In July 1968 a regulation of the Council of
Ministers ensured the complete freedom of movement
for the Community's workers, almost a year and a
half in advance of the date specified by the Rome
Treaties and parallel with the establishment of the
customs union. This is truly a dramatic accomplishment. Labor from any member country may now move
freely within the EEC to accept and even to search
for employment without being subject to any discrimination in the terms of employment.

The establishment of a unified Community labor
market was achieved progressively in three stages.
Regulation 15, governing migration for the first
stage, was drafted in close collaboration with the
trade unions and employers' organizations and was
adopted in 1961.[58] As in the case of the ECSC, there
were no great pressures for application and wide
differences between the European Commission and several governments over the scope of the regulation.
The Bundestag objected to the Commission's proposals
for the priority of the Community labor market, the
admission of families, and the eligibility of migrants
for organs representing workers in the enterprise.
Both the German and Dutch governments wished to render the regulation more restrictive, while the Italian
government sought a broad interpretation of article
48.[59]

Nor was there an identity of views among trade
unions. Fears of wage decreases and job security
were operative along with antipathy toward foreign
workers whose appearance, customs, and habits differ
greatly from those of national workers.

Regulation 15 for the first stage in the liberation of migration was a compromise of these views
and therefore guaranteed the priority of the national
labor markets; any subject of a member state could
work for wages in another member country, provided
the vacancy had not been filled from the national
market concerned after three weeks.[60] The innovation
of the regulation lay in its guarantee of equality
of treatment between national and migrant workers
for all conditions of employment, especially hiring,
dismissal, and payment. Another major improvement
in the conditions of migrant labor stemmed from the
regulation's provisions for the worker's family.
The wife and dependent children of a migrant could
henceforth accompany the latter, provided he had
adequate housing at his disposal, and could also be
employed under the same conditions as the head of
the family.

Regulation 15 had little effect on the already
appreciable flow of workers within the Community.
The most significant effect of its provisions was to
guarantee these migrants equality of status with the
nationals of countries where they were employed.
They were able to settle freely with their families
and enjoy a greater degree of job security than was
possible under bilateral agreements, which could be
revised on short notice with every variation in economic trends.

The second stage in the liberation of labor
movements was achieved in 1964 and terminated the
priority of the national labor market save for certain exceptions and safeguards for regions suffering
unemployment.[61] Measures were also taken to accelerate the full assimilation of the foreign worker to
national worker status by establishing the eligibility of the migrant worker to vote and even run for
office in plant committee elections. In addition
the existing right of wives and minor children to
follow the head of the family was extended to include
all other fully dependent relatives residing in the
same house with the worker. However, the admission
of a worker's family remained conditional on his
ability to house them in a manner considered normal
to workers in his area of employment.

In 1968 all institutional barriers to the free mobility of labor within the EEC were removed. Non-institutional barriers, psychological and cultural, will continue to hinder the flow of labor; but their effect will be diminished by the ease of travel between countries and the exchange of information of labor conditions.

Migrant workers no longer need a permit from the host country in order to work and require only an identity card or valid passport plus a certificate from a prospective employer to obtain a residence permit in any EEC country.[62] The worker's family enjoys the same freedom of movement and employment if they are nationals of a member state. Although a migrant still needs a residence permit, it is valid for five years, automatically renewable, and cannot be canceled in case of interruptions of employment if these are due to accident, layoff, or military service. The new beneficiaries of free movement are the dependents of the worker who are not residing in the same household, provided adequate housing is available in the host country. The waiver of the need for a work permit constitutes a significant improvement in facilitating free migration and the immunity of the residence permit from arbitrary cancellation represents a milestone in the achievement of job security for the migrant worker.

The regulation of January 1968 established freedom of access to employment for the migrant worker.[63] Any worker of an EEC country enjoys the same right to obtain employment as the nationals of that country; he can seek work and make contractual agreements according to the laws and regulations of a member country without any discrimination. Access to employment is no longer contingent upon a vacancy reported in an employment office, and a member state may no longer unilaterally suspend open employment in certain occupations. In fact, all national laws or regulations aimed at limiting or restricting foreign labor are inapplicable to nationals of the EEC, by number, occupation, or region. For all practical purposes all EEC countries must consider nationals of all member states as fully assimilated to their

own labor force and eligible for the same benefits
and protection.

Community workers are guaranteed equality of
treatment in every important field relative to employment. No EEC worker can be discriminated against
because of his nationality with respect to wages,
layoffs, social and fringe benefits, vocational
training or retraining, or the right to own or rent
housing.[64] Nor can any discrimination of this nature
be included in a labor contract resulting from collective bargaining. Migrant labor has also gained
the important social rights to vote and participate
in the trade union organizations of his host country
and in the shop committees at his place of employment.
However, the remaining restrictions on equality of
treatment are important ones, for a foreign worker
may not hold an administrative or managerial position
in a national trade union federation within his host
country and is also excluded from national policy-
making organs.

In January 1970 the European Commission drafted
a proposal aimed at supplementing the free movement
of workers. When it becomes effective, workers who
have ceased to work because of old age or permanent
incapacity may remain in the member state in which
they have been employed; and workers who have been
employed in a member country other than their own
for at least three years will have the right to remain there if they wish to take a job in another
member state, i.e., as a seasonal or frontier worker.[65]
This means that an Italian miner employed in Belgium
could remain there even if he decided to take a job
in France.

In order to implement the mobility of labor and
ensure concerted action among the member governments,
there are three committees to advise the European
Commission. A European Coordination Bureau operates
within the Commission and directs Community procedures in gathering and diffusing information to governments and central employment agencies. At least
once a month each member state sends a memo to the
European Coordination Bureau and national labor

bureaus that includes lists of requests for and offers of employment by occupation and by region. The
data is collated by the European Bureau, which com-
piles and distributes a list of occupations and regions exhibiting a shortage or surplus of labor.
With this information member states and the Commission
meet twice a year to analyze the Community labor market and labor flows from non-EEC countries.

A technical committee composed of governmental
representatives aids the Commission in applying free
migration, and a tripartite consultative committee
on free migration acts in an advisory capacity.

While these achievements may herald the dawn of
European citizenship for the worker, important restrictions on equality of treatment remain; and
trends in the EEC labor markets have created new
problems unaccounted for by article 48.

Because of misgivings expressed by the trade
unions in the Economic and Social Committee, equality
of treatment was restricted and migrant labor was
granted the right to be elected to plant committees
but denied the right to hold offices within trade
unions in host countries.[66] Nor do they share the
right enjoyed by national labor to sit on parity or
tripartite administrative committees, such as the
administrative councils for nationalized industries
or for social security in France. Thus, European
migrant labor has yet to acquire the right to the
social and political achievements of national labor
forces.

The priority of the Community labor market
exists in writing. However, it has yet to be realized, for it conflicts with the priorities resulting
from special relationships between some member states
and third countries. France has a special relationship with her former dependent territories, particularly Algeria, which provides one-fourth of the
migrant labor in France; and Germany maintains bilateral agreements with Portugal, Spain, and Turkey.
Since these two countries are the major employers
of foreign labor within the EEC and account for 87

percent of EEC migrants, their agreements with third
countries and the disparity between Community migrants
and migrants from third countries affects equilibrium
within the EEC.[67] There is no coincidence between
the demand for foreign labor in France and Germany
and surplus labor in Italy; despite free migration
labor requirements are only partially filled by the
EEC, and the traditional migration of Italians to
third countries, especially Switzerland, has not been
affected.

One can conclude that while such measures as
article 48 may facilitate labor mobility, it does
not seem to follow that they will increase labor
flows, for currents of migration depend upon the
economic conditions of the countries concerned as
well as the institutional arrangements for migration.[68]
The movement of labor between countries is of no advantage if the economic conditions, including wages
and employment, are similar. Where economic conditions differ or present a sufficient contrast, mobility of labor is of mutual advantage and may occur
even without such special arrangements as those provided by the EEC. Labor movement between EEC countries can best be explained by focusing upon the
costs and returns of hiring various types of workers.
Workers with experience in industrial employment are
the most economically feasible, because they are more
easily trained and integrated within the national
labor force than are former agricultural workers.
North Italian industrial workers helped fill Germany's
considerable needs during the 1950's; but increased
prosperity in Italy during the early 1960's stemmed
this flow, and German employers had to turn elsewhere.
Present factors influencing immigration to Germany
and France from countries with a high level of employment are distance and the ease with which immigrants can be integrated into the German and French
social and economic structures.[69]

In the Community as a whole, spontaneous rather
than organized migration is increasing; and the
major current of immigration comes from third countries under bilateral arrangements. Of the 1,023,747
foreign workers employed in Germany, 349,717 are from

the European Community; the others come from Spain,
Turkey, Morocco, Portugal, Yugoslavia, Tunisia, and
South Korea.[70] France is heavily dependent upon
Spain, Portugal, Yugoslavia, and Algeria for her
labor requirements; and Belgium has turned to Turkey
to fill the gaps in her labor market. The replacement of EEC migrants by other sources can be explained
by the development of Community and national vocational training and regional policies, which have
reduced the need for workers to leave a locality in
case of unemployment and by the absorption of Italy's
extensive unemployment. In addition one can predict
that as national economic policies become concerted
and the free movement of capital is fully achieved,
the attraction of higher incomes in the more prosper-
ous regions of the EEC will be correspondingly diminished. In each of the EEC countries employing
migrant labor, Community labor is on the decline, although for the ECSC industries the percentage of labor
drawn from Community countries is slightly higher.

Migrant workers from third countries are unskilled or semiskilled and concentrated in sectors
and occupations rejected by national labor because
of poor wages, unpleasant working conditions, and
low social status. They are found in construction,
textiles, heavy engineering, catering, and domestic
service.[71] In contrast, the movement of labor among
the EEC countries consists of the highly skilled,
whose services are required throughout the Community.

The regulations and agreements governing the
legal, economic, and social status of third-country
immigrants differ widely, but the problems assailing
them are all too common: cultural and language barriers, prejudice of the host population, conflicts
with workers in the host country, and economic discrimination. The need for a common EEC policy toward
workers from nonmember countries has been recognized
and is being considered within the Council of Ministers.

The assimilation of European workers to national
labor markets is being completed when there is a
general decline in inter-EEC mobility and a signifi-

cant increase in migration from nonmember countries.
Until the latter problem becomes the subject of new
policies, the regulation on free migration could be
improved by broadening its objectives to include
professional mobility and the creation of a skilled
Community labor force. Geographic mobility could
then be conceived as an element in a European manpower policy rather than as a plug for gaps in the
national labor markets.

European Problems of
Social Security

A European Convention for the
Social Security of Migrant Workers

Article 69 of the ECSC Treaty provides for the
removal of obstacles to the free circulation of
labor that might result from national legislation on
social security. At the time the Paris Treaty came
into effect, many types of discriminatory social
security legislation were in force in the member
countries.[72] Some provisions set strict conditions
to the payment of benefits to foreigners or allowed
the latter to collect benefits only if relations of
reciprocity existed between the countries concerned.
Most national laws on social insurance were based
upon the principle of territoriality, so that the
right to benefits resulting from payments made did
not guarantee full benefits if the eligible person
did not maintain residence in the country of insurance. The acquisition, maintenance, or right to
continuation of insurance was generally subordinated
to a minimum duration of payments, residence, or
employment in the relevant country. This meant that
workers who changed their employment from one country
to another could not maintain the right to benefits
previously acquired if they did not consent to double
payments and that migrant workers were subject to
widely varying and insufficient regulations. Clearly
it was necessary to harmonize and complete the principles governing social insurance so that migrant
workers would be adequately protected.

In 1953 the High Authority assigned a working
group the task of examining the problems of social

security for migrant workers. The International
Labor Organization (ILO) aided this group by submitting several suggestions on the framework of an
agreement for coordinating the social security systems covering migrant workers; and in December 1957,
after three years of repeated revision by the ILO
and repeated examination by the Council of Ministers,
the ministers of labor of the member states signed
the European Convention of Social Security for Migrant
Workers.[73]

By this time, the Rome Treaties establishing the
EEC were signed with special provision adopting the
measures similar to those included in the Convention
of Social Security. The European Commission was
anxious to ensure the application of this provision
without delay, and in April 1958 it proposed that
the Convention be transformed into regulations 3 and
4. These were adopted by the Council of Ministers
the following September.[74]

Regulations 3 and 4 supersede the bilateral and
multilateral agreements that previously governed
social security for migrant workers. They are based
upon three principles: equality of treatment of the
nationals of the Six and of refugees and stateless
persons with respect to social security legislation,
totalization of the periods of insurance completed
in the previous country, and the payment of benefits
in any of the Six.[75] The regulations apply to wage
earners in all sectors of the economy and cover all
branches of social security.

To facilitate the application of the regulations, a special body was created, the Administrative
Committee of the EEC for the Social Security of Migrant Workers, composed of the representatives of
the national governments and the European Commission
with technical assistance from the ILO.[76] It has
been granted wide powers, for it is responsible in
part for settling any administrative questions or
questions relative to the interpretation of the
regulations, as well as for arrangements for settling
claims arising from the payment of benefits under
the Convention. Since its creation it has met every
month and has adopted a large number of measures to

assure the application of regulations 3 and 4, such
as the preparation of forms in four languages to
enable workers and their families to obtain social
security benefits in the special conditions laid down
in the regulations. The Committee has also adopted
certain measures for the evaluation of expenses incurred by the various national institutions on behalf
of corresponding institutions in other countries.[77]

To facilitate relations among the social security
institutions of the member countries dealing with
the application of the regulations and to train specialists in these regulations, the Administrative
Committee prepared a training program for officials
of these institutions and the ministries concerned.
Courses are carried out partly within the Commission
and partly in a social security institution of the
country that employs the trainee.

In collaboration with the European Commission
and the trade unions, the Committee prepared two
regulations concerning social security for frontier
and seasonal workers and containing special provisions
on short-term benefits for the latter. These comple-
ments to regulations 3 and 4 were adopted by the
Council of Ministers in the latter part of 1962.

The trade unions are generally satisfied that
the regulations can produce solutions toward the
harmonization of various national social security
systems, an achievement to which they attach high
priority. However, they have presented suggestions
for revision, including the elimination of restrictions on the duration of the right to payments, the
elimination of all unjustified differences among national systems with respect to scope and rate of payments, and the adoption of provisions of bilateral
and multilateral agreements generally considered
more favorable.[78] A proposal for revision has been
prepared by the Administrative Committee for the
Social Security of Migrant Workers with the support
of the ESC and the EPA, and it is now under consideration within the Council of Ministers.

Studies

The High Authority and the European Commission
have also made important contributions in the field
of social security through their special studies and
proposals and by collating general information on
the development of social security in the Six.

The High Authority has compiled the most complete
and detailed information on the situation of social
security in its publications entitled Social Security
Schemes Applicable to the Coal and Steel Community
and in Great Britain. These monographs are periodically revised. Since 1963 they have appeared as a
joint publication of the EEC and the ECSC and include
all special systems in force in the Six.

Following the initial publication of this reference work, the trade unions repeatedly expressed
their wish to have an outline of the social security
schemes existing in the Community countries presented
in the form of summary tables. In response the High
Authority and the European Commission prepared comparative tables on the social security schemes applicable in the Six. These enable a rapid survey to
be made of the main benefits, the conditions of payment of benefits, and the methods of financing them.

The High Authority also prepared a study entitled Developments and Trends of Social Security,
which attempts to bring out the basic guiding principles of the national social security systems. It
is designed partly as a basis for the discussion of
the harmonization of social security schemes. The
examination of the various trends also enables certain conclusions to be drawn about future developments, since, in order to achieve harmonization, it
is necessary to see that national systems do not develop in divergent directions. The trade unions
have cooperated closely with the preparation of all
of the studies pursued by the High Authority and
the European Commission.

The Harmonization of Social
Security Systems

The trade unions have consistently argued that the coordination of the various national structures of social security systems would accelerate upward harmonization. They therefore requested the European Commission to convene a conference in order to specify measures to achieve the harmonization of social security systems. The Commission agreed and the conference was held in December 1962, under the aegis of the three executives of the European Communities. Its aim was to furnish the governments and the European executives information about the possibilities, methods, and limits of the harmonization of social security rather than to specify the definitive solutions desired by the trade unions.[79] The governments were notably unenthusiastic about such an undertaking and attended as observers rather than as participants, in order to stress that the results of the conference would not commit them in any way. Their reluctance reflected the existence of wide divergencies among national social security systems and the fact that social security occupies an important part of the national budgets, with total costs accounting for 13 percent to 17 percent of the gross national product. Harmonization would involve considerable inroads on national sovereignty. However, their extreme caution proved groundless, for there were wide differences of opinion between workers and employers on almost every topic explored, so that in the final communiqué they could agree only on the necessity of further study of the themes discussed.

The positive result of this gathering was the establishment of guidelines for studies pursued by the European Commission over the years on the costs of social security, for the harmonization of statistics, and for an impressive documentation of the social security systems in force in the Six. The latter was used as a reference in framing medium-term economic policy. These studies have also produced some Community instruments that will serve as aids in harmonizing certain aspects of national systems, i.e., the establishment of a European list of

occupational diseases and a glossary of terminology
in four languages.[80]

Since the achievement of the free movement of
labor in 1968, many problems have arisen in establishing the correspondence of social security benefits for migrant workers. A typical complication is
exemplified by the calculation of pensions. How
does a social security officer determine the pension
of an Italian worker who has spent five years working in France, contributing to the French pension
scheme, and who now returns home for retirement?

In 1970 the Council of Ministers adopted the
framework of a new system that will facilitate the
free mobility of labor and help clarify the problem
of equivalence in social security payments.[81] This
system established the principle that social security
costs are borne by the country that has actually
received the social security contributions and that
social security benefits will be paid in the country
of residence. An efficient procedure is specified
for the prompt reimbursement by the recipient country
to the country from which the benefits are drawn.
The agreement also includes a series of provisions
covering the transfer of unemployment pay, old-age
and other pensions, and family allowances. A newly
created tripartite Committee on the Social Security
for Migrant Workers will function in an advisory
capacity for application problems, although the EEC
Court of Justice has played an increasing role in
the applications of social security regulations in
the past few years.

Housing

One of the most imaginative efforts of the High
Authority in the social field has been its housing
program. Although the Treaty is silent on the matter,
the High Authority secured the full support of the
Assembly, the Consultative Committee, and the Council of Ministers for the very liberal interpretation
of its role in technical and economic research and
its role in financing investments, which formed the
basis of its housing program. By granting funds for

housing, the High Authority intended to supplement national programs by ensuring the construction of housing for workers in the ECSC industries over and above that provided by national housing.

To date the High Authority and its successor, the European Commission, have completed six housing programs for coal- and steelworkers.[82] These include two experimental projects and six loan-aided schemes for large-scale construction. The experimental programs were conducted as aspects of the High Authority's role in technical and economic research and were financed by appropriations from the levy. Experimental Scheme I involved research in low-cost construction methods and aimed to establish criteria for the High Authority's future housing programs.[83] Regional committees composed of representatives of the trade unions, employers' organizations, and public authorities participated in the management of the project.

In order to finance its first loan-aided scheme for large-scale housing, the High Authority reserved one-fourth of a loan from the United States, $2.5 million, in the form of either direct loans to construction companies or future owners, or of guarantees to banks underwriting the loans.[84] It allocated these low-interest credits according to two general criteria: the number of miners and steelworkers in each country and their housing requirements. The first program produced 15,877 housing units and allowed the workers the choice of either purchasing or renting from the construction company, according to the wish of the Assembly.[85]

Since the High Authority's first program proved so successful, it launched a second program for 1957 and 1958, which yielded 20,000 more housing units. Since then new programs have been established on a biannual basis.

A study completed by the High Authority in 1956 on the mobility and readaptation of workers revealed that the lack of adequate housing was one of the most serious obstacles to labor migration.[86] The Assembly's

Committee on Social Affairs wished the High Authority
to pursue the matter and, therefore, in 1958, the
latter conducted a comprehensive survey of the housing conditions of workers in order to improve the
basis of its future housing policy. The results of
the survey were gloomy. Of all the dwellings inves-
tigated, 40 percent were superannuated and lacked
running water, and many were unsuitable for family
residence.[87]

The fourth building program was designed to accommodate the housing needs revealed by the survey
and to respond to the EPA's pressures for the solution of four major housing problems: replacing barracks and makeshift housing with construction designed
to meet modern standards of comfort, sanitation, and
convenience; relieving overcrowding; reaccommodating
workers affected by pit closures and obliged to work
at another colliery; and providing sufficient housing
to keep pace with an expanding steel industry.

From the time of its first building program to
December 1969, the ECSC helped finance the construction of 112,451 dwellings, 61 percent for rental and
37 percent for purchase.[88] A seventh program was
launched in October 1969 and will cover the period
from 1970 to 1974. The first stage of this program
will be financed from the special reserve of the budget for 1971 and 1972.

Although it is modest in scale, the ECSC's
housing program has helped the European Communities
achieve the broader social goals of the free movement
of labor, readaptation, and the harmonization of
social standards.

Social Harmonization in the ECSC

Mixed Committees

Social harmonization is central to trade union
demands within the ECSC. It has been the subject of
great expectations, endless discussions, and a
variety of definitions. The demand for the harmonization of working conditions first assumed ECSC-wide

proportions in 1954, when the Renard Resolution was
passed by the Consultative Committee. The Assembly
promoted the resolution, and the issue was raised
again in 1955 when Jean Rey addressed the Assembly
on behalf of the Belgian government.[89] Belgian trade
unions were pressing for a forty-five-hour week, and
he was concerned about the effect on Belgium's competitive position if industries in other countries
continued to have longer workweeks. Therefore, he
suggested that the ECSC deal with the problem.

After Rey's appeal the Assembly maintained the
discussion of harmonization, focusing its attention
on the establishment of mixed committees. Its Committee on Social Affairs suggested the creation of
one or several joint committees on the ECSC level to
supersede the Consultative Committee, with its limited competence, and to render nonbinding opinions
on working conditions.[90] Their most important role
would be to deal with problems that could not be
solved by one country alone.

The Christian trade unions favored the immediate
creation of a central party organ for the entire Community and one for each industry. The former would
be concerned with studies and research, and the latter would have the power to conclude collective agreements. However, the free trade unions preferred to
wait for the results of the High Authority's efforts
to convene the social partners.

The employers were reticent, because they feared
that such steps would increase pressure on them to
grant benefits and might lead to intervention in
their affairs by either the governments or the High
Authority. They cited the impossibility of dissociating workers of two industries from the economy and
argued that fixing minimum demands for both industries
would isolate them and render their competitive position on the international markets artificial.

Because of the reluctance of the employers, the
opposition of some of the governments, and its own
doubts about what could be accomplished by parity

discussions, the High Authority was slow in organizing
joint committees. However, in 1955, as a result of
discussions within the Council of Ministers and the
pressure of labor groups, the High Authority began a
study of working hours and holidays and published a
number of monographs on the legislation underlying
collective bargaining preparatory to organizing joint
committees.[91]

The first meeting of employers and workers was
convened by the High Authority in 1956 for the steel
industry. The expectations of both parties differed.[92]
The workers insisted that the role of the committee
should not be limited to documentation; it should be
able to conclude framework agreements that would not
only define certain principles but also make them
binding for all cases in which these principles would
involve improvement of national conditions.

The employers objected. They insisted that they
were not ready to be bound by parity agreements at
the Community level and felt that the task of the
committee should be limited to securing information
on national conditions. Any disparities noted during
these meetings should be referred to the competent
national organizations, not to the ECSC.

The result was a compromise in favor of the employers. The High Authority proposed that the Mixed
Committee for Steel begin by examining problems under
the general heading of working time and the organization of work in continuous and discontinuous shifts,
noting differences in regulations among member states.
The Committee accepted this program despite the disappointment of the trade unions. Since then documentation on Sunday and night work, vacations, holidays,
and the workweek has been kept up to date and periodically examined by the Committee. These studies,
and the topics considered, have been broadened to
include the employment situation in the member countries, workers' representation at the enterprise and
industry level, and the effects of technological advance in the iron and steel industry on productivity,
wages, working hours, and employment.

The mixed Committee for Steel has been meeting
regularly at six-month intervals since its creation.
Has its role of compiling, examining, and comparing
documentation borne fruit? Progress has been made
in the reduction of disparities through national collective bargaining agreements based upon the documentation and declarations of the Committee. For example, the findings of the Mixed Committee for Steel
led to the increase in the number of paid holidays
in France, the reduction of working time in the continuous services of the French steel industry, and
an agreement on working time in the Italian steel
industry.[93]

When the High Authority sought to establish a
joint committee to discuss the problems of harmonization in the coal industry, the employers refused.
After a year of discussion they agreed, on condition
that the governments also participate. They felt
that because the governments play an important part
in regulating working conditions in the mining industry it is essential that governmental representatives
attend such meetings.[94] Ultimately, the workers con-
curred, although with reservations. However, months
passed before the governments replied to the High
Authority's invitation, and the Mixed Committee for
Coal met for the first time in 1958, when that industry was experiencing difficulties.

The social partners were unable to agree on an
agenda for the first meeting of the Mixed Committee
for Coal. Therefore, the Committee's activities
during its first year of operation were confined to
the approval of comparative documents prepared by
the High Authority on the various aspects of working
time.[95] Despite the pressure of the miners' unions
and the Common Assembly, the Committee did not recon-
vene until 1961. It has continued to meet at irregular intervals and has required the unceasing efforts
of the ECSC to keep it functioning. The employers
are reluctant to discuss working conditions on the
ECSC level, for they fear that they will be faced
with increasing social demands.

The trade unions are satisfied with the functioning of the Mixed Committee for Steel. It meets regularly and is willing to follow, discuss, and compare
the development of employment problems. They believe
that if the Mixed Committee for Coal met more often,
they could convince the employers of the desirability
of common action. Although the unions recognize that
the High Authority and the European Commission have
no power of decision in this field, they insist that
the ECSC has a particular responsibility to maintain
the dialogue between the social partners.

What are the prospects for mixed committees?
Community-wide collective bargaining is not even a
distant possibility, for there is not enough cohesion
or common interest among the social partners for such
an undertaking. The trade unions themselves differ
in their expectations of mixed committees on the
European level. The German unions take less interest
in the comparative data provided by the ECSC than do
the Italian unions, for the DGB considers its standards the highest in the Community and is therefore
not curious about conditions in the less advanced
member states. On the other hand, the Italian unions
feel that they have everything to gain by studying
working conditions in Germany and France. Disparities
in interest aside, the conceptions of the social optimum vary from country to country, for living and
working conditions are the product of varying economic, sociological, and political factors; and each
country attaches a different importance to family
allowances and other social benefits. Until social
policy within the ECSC is inspired by commonly accepted principles, European discussions in mixed committees will have their main influence on national
collective bargaining and will serve as a means of
generalizing certain minimum standards attained
within a single country.

The documentation gathered by the High Authority
for the mixed committees has been of great assistance
to the social partners in their national activities.
European unions are less well supplied with research

facilities than their American counterparts, and less relevant information is released by the employers or compiled by the governments. Therefore, the High Authority's studies have enabled the unions in each member country to make a comparative assessment of their national standards and to glean ideas for possible goals and ammunition for argument. The reduction of working time in the ECSC industries is partly due to the fact that the trade unions used ECSC documentation on working hours.

Beginning in 1952 the High Authority initiated various statistical studies to provide information on the level and trends of workers' earnings, purchasing power, and labor costs. It also carried out investigations into wage policies and wage systems in Community industries. Its studies on the development of wages and wage policy in ECSC industries cover variations in the cost of living and their repercussions on the development of wages and the influence of production and employment on wages.[96] Another series of studies traces the development of wages, working conditions, and social security in ECSC industries by country; and one of the most important studies of the High Authority compares real wages and wage costs in ECSC industries.[97] In the early 1960's the High Authority initiated an inquiry on the family budgets of workers in Community industries, which furnished important information on the level and way of life of these workers. This was the first time an investigation of this nature was pursued in several countries according to uniform methods and definitions. The ECSC also sponsors continuing research on labor law in the ECSC, since the High Authority considered that a full awareness of national differences in this field is essential to any effort to harmonize living and working conditions.

The High Authority stressed that the purpose of its efforts in gathering documentation was to encourage discussions among workers, employers, and the governments and to promote action for improving living and working standards. Insofar as these efforts have aided national action, this purpose has

been achieved. Without closer coordination of economic policies among the Six, discussions within the
mixed committees and the studies of the ECSC can be
only a spur to national action. The trade unions
are satisfied with the ECSC's activity in this field
and with the modest gains of the mixed committees.
They look to the ECSC to provide a continuous dialogue with management and to create opportunities
for positive discussions, rather than to provide decisions impinging upon the autonomy of industrial
relations.

Social Harmonization
in the EEC

The trade unions have defined harmonization as
the diminution of existing differences in standards
of living and working conditions accompanied by a
constant improvement in the total level of living
and working conditions. By what means do they propose
to achieve this? The trade unions are jealous of
their autonomy and of their role in the achievement
of social progress. They expect the EEC to provide
the framework and the favorable conditions for social
achievements rather than to intervene directly in
social affairs. First, they are interested in having
access to complete information on existing conditions.
When the EEC began to operate, the trade unions suggested that the European Commission extend the documentation of the High Authority on wages to other
branches of activity.

The establishment of mixed committees similar
to those operating within the ECSC would provide a
convenient setting for discussing working conditions,
the substance of harmonization. However, although
the unions profited from the experiences of the mixed
committees within the ECSC and were careful not to
request that the work of such committees culminate
in collective agreements or even in recommendations
to the social partners, mixed committees for sectors
have not yet been established. Because of the reticence of the employers, parity committees were instituted only in those sectors that are the object
of common policy, such as agriculture and transport.

Common economic policies are the indispensable
condition for the progressive harmonization of social
policies. Since the labor unions consider that social
harmonization is a process of social improvement,
which should occur more rapidly for the less privileged groups and areas, they emphasize the importance
of a policy for the structural improvement of less
developed regions with the aid of the European Social
Fund and the European Investment Bank and the establishment of a common cyclical and monetary policy.[98]

The European Commission has promoted the same
conception of social harmonization as that developed
by labor. However, although this matter has been
the subject of numerous declarations by G. Pettrelli
and his successor, A. Levi-Sandri, the Commission
has ventured little and accomplished little in this
area. Its positive efforts have been confined to
gathering relevant documentation, establishing the
Central Group of Workers and Employers for discussing
the goals of article 118, its activities relative to
article 119, and its attention to the social aspects
of common policies for agriculture, transport, and
energy.

Studies

Because the EEC grants the Commission no power
to achieve upward harmonization of working conditions,
the latter has planned its studies to cover all working conditions feasible for harmonization in order
to create awareness of better working conditions in
the member states and to stimulate efforts to gener-
alize these standards. It lent its immediate support
to the trade unions' request for studies on wages,
and in 1960 it began a series of inquiries on labor
costs in EEC industries. Representatives of the labor ministries and the social partners selected the
initial fourteen sectors to be covered. These studies include direct costs (direct wages, grants,
bonuses, remuneration for nonworking days, and advantages in kind) and indirect costs of enterprises,
whether legal, conventional, or benevolent. The
Commission has also prepared synoptic tables on
working hours and has assembled documentation on

the various national policies of capital formation and property ownership for workers. It is currently establishing a series of reports on contemporary developments in collective bargaining. Since national collective bargaining is frequently based on the data made available by these studies, the documentation published by the Commission can be considered a step toward harmonization.

The "Reports on the Social Situation in the Community," published by the European Commission, include a broad range of information on many aspects of social affairs. They deal with developments in social legislation, labor relations, wages, the employment situation, and economic expansion. The Commission has responded to the suggestions of the Assembly on this publication and has attempted to make comparisons and to add its own suggestions and recommendations. Although the problems covered are not treated on the basis of Community criteria, the reports allow the national labor confederations to see where they stand in relation to others and to be kept constantly informed of the state of affairs in all member countries.

Article 119

The harmonization of working conditions is not only a matter of ironing out national disparities, for there exist important differences in incomes between the sexes. Article 119 of the EEC stipulates that equality of wages between men and women shall be achieved within the EEC. The Commission's initial efforts toward this end were focused on defining equality of wages and obtaining agreement on interpretation. It sought to acquire the most complete information on the state of legislation in the Six, collective bargaining systems, and actual conditions and, thereafter, to define in detail the scope and limits of article 119. These efforts culminated in a recommendation addressed to the Council of Ministers in July 1960.[99] The recommendation specified how the provisions of article 119 should be interpreted and suggested that equal pay for equal work should be applied to all the wage systems in force

in the Six, at whatever level the wages may be fixed,
whether they are minimum wages fixed by law, or systems of collective agreements, or wages fixed within
the enterprise. It also stipulated that the criteria
used in the various countries for occupational grading
must be applied impartially to men and women workers,
and that the legislation for the protection of women
must not be allowed to detract from the principle of
equal pay for equal work.

A year elapsed before the Council of Ministers
could come to a decision on the matter, for each
government clung to its own interpretation of article
119. The French government considered that the establishment of a program to achieve equality of wages
should be a condition for passing to the second
stage of the transitional period. The German government pointed out that the constitution of the Federal
Republic guarantees this principle and that, therefore, there was no problem of wage discrimination according to sex. The government of the Netherlands
insisted that the principle of equal pay should apply
only to those occupations and enterprises where men
and women perform the same activities and should not
cover occupations traditionally held by women. Belgium adopted the same attitude as Holland, and Luxembourg claimed that it could not accept the interpretation of the Commission because of its obligation
to the Benelux countries.

These differences in interpretation were resolved
within the Conference of Member States, and a decision
on equality of wages was passed in December 1961.[100]
The decision established a calendar for the progressive elimination of gaps in wages, culminating in
the elimination of all discrimination before December 30, 1964.

Despite considerable progress in attaining
equality of remuneration, the deadline for the removal of all wage inequalities passed without the
accomplishment of the objective. Since then the
Commission has issued biannual reports on the progress
to date and has recently affirmed that important dif-
ferentials and disparities still exist within the Six.

The major obstacles to full equality remain discriminatory job classification, collective agreements containing discriminatory provisions, and the lack of
collective agreements that include equal pay provisions for many sectors.[101] The latest statistics
indicate that women's hourly wages are still considerably lower in Luxembourg, with discrimination among
skilled workers more marked than among the unskilled
and semiskilled.

Regardless of the appeal or idealism of equality
of wages as a goal for the EEC, it still must be attained through the interplay of national interest
groups and the working of national politics; it cannot be achieved from the top down through directives
from the Council of Ministers. Social harmonization
may be a central goal for labor within the EEC, but
the content of harmonization remains the essence of
national politics.

Articles 117 and 118

Although the European Commission has been willing to push hard for the application of article 119,
it has been hesitant in its attempts to achieve the
general provisions on harmonization. In comparison
with the efforts of the High Authority and despite
the pressures of the trade unions and the Assembly,
the Commission has done little to promote harmonization through the confrontation of the social partners
on the European level. It was not until 1961, four
years after the EEC came into effect, that representatives of the social partners met within the Central
Group in order to outline a program of studies to be
pursued by the Commission under articles 117 and 118.
The problems selected for study were social security,
industrial protection of women and young people, and
labor relations. It was the employers who proposed
these topics, for, as in the case of the ECSC, they
were anxious not to commit themselves to anything
smacking of collective negotiation.[102] The choice
of themes also indicated their preference for general
discussions rather than for discussions by sectors.
The trade unions would have preferred a focus on
working time and wages within the framework of the

principal industrial branches. Although the number
of working groups or subcommittees of the Central
Group has increased and now includes groups for wages
and working time, they have convened at irregular
intervals and are highly susceptible to the climate
of relations within the Council of Ministers for
Social Affairs.

Social harmonization is a complex problem, and
there are many factors restraining the action of the
European Commission. This is not a field in which
it can act independently even if it should wish to
do so. The full cooperation of the governments is
necessary, and they are far from unanimous in their
opinions on the matter except in their reluctance to
yield responsibility; and many employers are as reticent as the governments on harmonization. Therefore,
the Commission has defined its role as that of a
catalytic agent, exercising its own activity through
studies, consultations with the member states, and
periodic conferences such as the symposium "Law and
Practice of Collective Agreements," held in 1969,
or the 1970 conference on employment. The dependency
of the Central Group on the disposition of the Council of Ministers has led the Commission to develop
various activities that can serve as a channel of
communication between the social partners and the
governments.

In the late 1960's the Commission shifted the
orientation of its activities in the area of social
harmonization and focused its studies and reports on
the correlation between social policies and other
Community policies.[103] By emphasizing the role of
manpower policies, wages, and social security as
aspects of common economic policies, it sought to
breathe new life into parity discussions on harmonization. As part of this new approach to harmonization, the Commission established joint advisory
committees on the social problems of the fishing industry, for road transport, rail transport, and
inland waterway transport. Discussions among the
social partners within these groups will result in
proposals for Council directives on the harmonization
of certain working conditions. Thus, a step has been

taken toward the trade unions' goal of establishing
parity committees for sectors.

Regional development and the activities of the
European Investment Bank are important tools of harmonization. However, a regional policy for the EEC
is still in an embryonic stage, and the operations
of the European Investment Bank are strictly limited.
The Bank is run on orthodox financial lines and can
deal only with projects that are economically desirable. Although its operations have increased in the
past few years, the development of the less privileged
regions has just begun.

There is also a close relation among wages, employment policy, monetary policy, and a policy on
economic trends. The achievement of social harmonization within the Community will progress with the
development of European monetary and cyclical policies
and common policies for basic sectors.

The European Social Fund

The European Social Fund was created by the Rome
Treaties in order to alleviate possible unfavorable
social consequences expected from the establishment
of the Common Market. In contrast with the readaptation provisions of the ECSC, its interventions are
not conditional on a cause-and-effect relationship
between the creation of the Common Market and the
readaptation of activity. However, the governments
exercise a more direct influence on the conditions
of the functioning of the Social Fund than is the
case with the readaptation fund of the ECSC, and the
conditions for receiving aid from the Social Fund
are more restrictive. The readaptation aid provided
by the ECSC is financed by the levy. The European
Social Fund has no resources of its own and is funded
by contributions from the governments based upon the
total volume of wages paid in each country. Thus,
the Fund operates as a financial organ of compensation between the contribution and expenses of the
member states. It covers 50 percent of the expenses
devoted by a state to three kinds of aid to workers
affected by unfavorable consequences of economic

development: the financing of vocational training
of workers obliged to abandon their occupation, indemnity grants for moving workers who are obliged by
economic developments to change their locality, and
aid to workers whose employment is terminated or
temporarily suspended as the result of the conversion
of an enterprise.[104] The activity of the Fund is submitted to rigorous conditions, for it operates only
a posteriori, on condition that workers benefited
by its aid are effectively reclassified in productive
occupations for a period of at least six months.
This retroactive feature has been severely criticized
by the trade unions.

Regulation 9

The Social Fund did not begin operating until
October 1960, almost three years after the establishment of the Common Market. Despite the pressure of
the Assembly and of labor groups, the Council of
Ministers was slow in establishing the regulations
for the Fund.

Although the Rome Treaties do not require the
consultation of the Assembly on the regulations for
the European Social Fund, the Council of Ministers
decided to request the opinion of the former on the
Commission's proposals. The Assembly was generally
disappointed by the proposal, for it had hoped that
the Fund would be instrumental in achieving European
regional and employment policies, that it would de-
vote special attention to regions suffering structural unemployment. Both the Committee on Social
Affairs of the EPA and the Section for Social Questions of the Economic and Social Committee pressed
for a more European solution than that proposed by
the Commission and suggested the creation of a working fund, carried over from one year to the next,
and the establishment of close collaboration between
the Fund and the European Investment Bank.[105]

The Council of Ministers incorporated in its
decision of May 1960 several important amendments
voted by the Assembly, notably on the tripartite
composition of the Committee for the Social Fund.

However, it retained unchanged the articles of the
regulation governing the scope of, and procedures
for, the intervention of the Fund.

Improving Facilities for Employment

In addition to its activities as an organ of
financial compensation for aid to readaptation, the
European Social Fund also has the more general task
of promoting employment facilities within the Community and contributing to the growth of geographical
and occupational mobility of workers. How has the
European Commission interpreted the role of the Fund
in this field? From its first policy statements the
European Commission stressed the importance of vocational training in attaining a high level of employment and the close relationship between geographical
and occupational mobility. It lost no time in acting
on this premise, and in October 1960, one month after
regulation 9 had come into effect, created a working
group to study the present and predictable disequilibrium in the Community labor markets and to prepare
appropriate remedial measures.[106] The working group
was directed to ascertain unfilled offers of employment by country, sector of activity, and occupational
category and, also, to determine the manpower resources available in the Community and their capability
of satisfying these offers of employment. On the
basis of these studies the Commission established a
Community-wide program of accelerated vocational
training for persons wishing to emigrate but insufficiently qualified, a short-term program to remedy
current labor difficulties. The result was a training program for 10,000 Italian workers destined for
the German and Dutch metal and transforming industries.[107] The program was so successful that the
Commission recommended the introduction of a new
program the following year and the establishment of
a Community training program phased over several
years. These short-term operations for practical
training have affected an average of 22,000 workers
each year, a total of 115,000 by the end of 1968.[108]
Useful as they may be, these measures are temporary
correctives for labor market imbalances and not steps
in the development of the Community manpower policy
desired by the labor unions.

The Balance Sheet

    Despite the hopes raised by the establishment
of the Social Fund, the first five years of its operation proved disappointing. The European Commission
found that rigidities in procedure had prevented it
from applying the Fund toward the more urgent objectives of EEC social policy and that the stimulating
effect of the Fund was reduced because frequently
aid arrived too late to remedy particular needs.[109]

    The great majority of requests for aid concerned
vocational retraining; and, although there were some
requests in connection with resettlement operations,
no country had requested aid for reconversion.[110]
Because of the high level of demand, reconversions
due to the development of the Common Market did not
create problems for workers, who generally found new
employment immediately. Moreover, the economic expansion resulting from the establishment of the Common Market accentuated rather than diminished the
disparities between the most industrialized and the
less developed regions of the Community. Regions
experiencing low employment levels are those lacking
industry; and there the problem is not reconversion
but implantation, a task for the European Investment
Bank or for a Social Fund whose activities are broad
enough to achieve its goals. However, aside from
the favorable economic situation, on the one hand,
and the restricted scope of the Fund's activity, on
the other, there were no requests for aid to reconversion principally because the procedures for granting such aid are complex and difficult to apply, thus
corroborating the Assembly's criticism.

    The European Commission had expected that the
activities of the European Social Fund would constitute a stimulus for national manpower policies.
However, in the first years of its operation the
Fund merely functioned as an organ for refunding the
expenditure of member states on retraining schemes,
the latter dependent upon the financial possibilities,
cyclical situation, and state of the labor market in
the country concerned. Supported by the EPA and the
trade unions, the Commission asserted that the Social

Fund would be more efficient if it enjoyed the power
of initiative, not only to correct cumbersome procedures but also to orient the operations of the Fund
according to an order of priority established at the
European level, rather than being directed toward
those groups most able to pay.[111]

In 1965 the Commission developed a set of proposals for reforming the Fund in order to allow it
increased competence in administering the Fund and
to correct certain inadequacies in the procedures
governing its operations.[112] The Commission, as
well as the EPA, wanted the Fund to be financially
independent in order to be able to advance funds for
preventive measures and to promote plant reconversion
in cooperation with the European Investment Bank.
An improved Fund with sufficient resources could
create a housing construction program to facilitate
readaptation where it involves migration, and it
would have the possibility of constructing and equip-
ping institutes for vocational training and providing
aid for the anticipatory retraining of workers engaged
in trades endangered by obsolescence.

The proposals for reform languished on the Council of Ministers' agenda for three years without resulting in a decision. Therefore, in 1969 the Commission submitted another proposal designed to
broaden the Fund's scope of activities, ensure it an
increased budget, and make its rules more flexible.[113]
It suggested that a radical transformation of the
structure and operations of the Fund would change it
from an inflexible, passive clearinghouse into a
dynamic instrument for a European manpower policy
and an aid in implementing the guidelines on medium-
term economic policy. Until the Fund is revamped so
that the Commission can take the initiative to coordinate the Fund's activities and guide them according
to European priorities, it will have no real impact
on social and economic problems in the Community and
will be unable to adapt to the constantly changing
needs of the member states. When the Rome Treaties
were established, the need to encourage geographic
and professional mobility was less apparent than at
present. Today the principal social problem within

the EEC is no longer the number of unemployed but the
threat of technological unemployment and large-scale
redundancies in such industries as textiles, coal
mining, ceramics, and leather.[114] A reformed Fund
would help retrain workers for new industries before
they lost their jobs instead of partially reimbursing
governments after they have retrained and resettled
the unemployed. The Commission wishes to have the
power to decide when, where, and whom to help instead
of automatically compensating governments for a mul-
titude of uncoordinated projects. It feels that it
should be allowed to help private as well as public
undertakings and relate its activities to the Community's regional and medium-term economic policies.

Increased resources and flexible funding are
needed to carry out these tasks effectively. The
Commission has suggested that the Fund needs an immediate increase to $50 million per year from its
current operating fund of $12 million yearly, and
that ultimately its resources should total $250 mil-
lion per year.[115] Its studies indicate that between
120,000 and 150,000 workers may need help annually
and that a budget of $250 million would enable it to
spend $2,000 per worker. Because needs are rarely
proportional to resources, the Fund's contribution
to the cost of projects should vary from 50 percent
to 80 percent, according to the urgency of the project.
The Commission also proposed the establishment of
independent revenue for the Fund, to accrue from import duties imposed under the common external tariff
and levies on imported farm produce. This reform
would ensure that requests for aid would be motivated
by genuine need and not merely by the desire to re-
coup contributions.

In July 1970 the Council of Ministers for Social
Affairs agreed on the outline for a reformed and
expanded Social Fund. As a result, the Commission
will be able to exercise some initiative in administering the Fund and may act before redundancy occurs.
The Fund will be empowered to finance schemes under
two separate headings: help for workers whose jobs
may be threatened as a direct result of the implementation of the Community's policies and help for

workers threatened with unemployment for reasons not directly linked with the Community's activities.[116] The latter solution was added on the insistence of the Italian minister and is expected to account for at least one-half of the new Fund's resources in the first five years of its operation.

However, no provisions were made for increasing the resources of the Fund, although the amount of aid disbursed annually has increased dramatically in recent years, from $14 million paid out in 1967 to $26 million in 1968 and $36.5 million in 1969.[117] The increase mainly concerns Germany and Italy, whose annual volume of requests for aid grew substantially between 1965 and 1969. The volume of requests from other states remained unchanged.

The modest level of the European Social Fund's activity is out of proportion to the hopes raised when the Fund was established. Therefore, the Fund has been the target of numerous trade union demands for expansion and reform. Aside from the desire for reforms in scope and procedure, the trade unions feel that the operations of the Fund would improve if they could participate in managing it. They have urged that the new Fund be controlled by the new permanent Tripartite Consultative Committee on Employment, established in June 1970 in order to advise the Council of Ministers on employment, and administered by a special management committee chosen from the members of the Committee on Employment.[118]

The difficulties of making the European Social Fund into a genuine instrument of a European employment policy are similar to the obstacles surrounding the development of all European social measures, the lack of political bases. There is neither the institutional framework nor the national consensus available to support the development of a European social policy that would have a significant impact on national life.

TABLE 2

ECSC Readaptation Measures, 1952–June 30, 1969

Country	Credits Provided by the Community (in millions of dollars)*				Estimated Numbers of Workers Affected			
	Coal Mining	Iron and Steel	Iron Ore Mines	Total	Coal Mining	Iron and Steel	Iron Ore Mines	Total
Germany	62.5	3.9	1.7	68.1	193,864	23,501	10,408	227,773
Belgium	18.9	1.8	0.005	20.7	74,003	5,227	37	79,317
France	3.5	2.9	2.5	9.0	11,308	12,644	7,906	31,858
Italy	2.6	10.6	0.8	14.0	6,391	18,331	1,295	26,017
Luxembourg	--	--	0.2	0.2	--	--	220	220
Netherlands	9.2	0.3	--	9.5	24,686	808	--	25,494
Community	98.8	19.5	5.2	121.6	310,252	60,561	19,866	390,679

*The Community's credits were matched by contributions from the member states in-volved.

Source: European Economic Community, Commission, L'action des Communautés en matière de réadaptation et de rééducation professionnelles (Brussels).

TABLE 3

ECSC Readaptation Measures, 1970

Country	Coal		Steel		Iron		Total	
	Workers	Credits (units of accounting)	Workers	Credits (units of accounting)	Workers	Credits (units of accounting)	Workers	Credits (units of accounting)
Germany	1,594	1,176,229.50	--	--	--	150,273.22	1,594	1,326,502.72
Belgium	2,766	1,605,000.00	--	360,000.00	--	--	2,766	1,565,000.00
France	8,177	14,230,697.91	--	--	--	90,922.34	8,177	14,321,620.25
Italy	--	--	--	7,200.00	--	--	--	7,200.00
Luxembourg	--	--	--	--	--	--	--	--
Netherlands	9,210	7,596,685.08	--	--	--	--	9,210	7,596,685.08
Community	21,747	24,608,612.49	--	367,200.00	--	241,195.56	21,747	25,217,008.05

Source: European Economic Community, Commission, Exposé sur l'évolution de la situation sociale dans la Communauté en 1970 (Brussels, February 1971).

TABLE 4

Annual Development of ECSC Readaptation Operations, 1960-69

Year	Readaptation Cases			Estimated Number of Workers Affected			Credits Provided by the Community (units of accounting)
	Coal	Steel	Iron	Coal	Steel	Iron	
1960	3	--	--	2,347	--	--	595,000.00
1961	21	--	2	11,217	--	703	3,139,068.12
1962	25	4	21	18,705	3,881	3,324	7,022,178.04
1963	24	3	21	19,573	928	3,636	4,332,500.77
1964	13	3	8	7,771	1,062	1,355	1,973,604.62
1965	28	11	17	21,582	4,204	4,359	9,134,854.66
1966	37	13	10	51,333	5,425	2,231	16,550,707.30
1967	43	13	16	47,845	4,534	2,822	18,986,744.68
1968	33	16	4	31,937	10,024	761	12,968,367.29
1969 (to June 30)	3	14	1	2,657	11,203	175	15,214,441.85
Total	230	77	100	214,967	41,261	19,366	89,917,467.33
	407			275,594			

Source: European Economic Community, Commission, L'action des Communautés en matières de réadaptation et de rééducation professionelle (Brussels).

222

TABLE 5

Foreign Workers in the EEC, 1961 and 1968
(thousands)

Country of Emigration	1961		1968	
	Total	New Work Permits Issued in Year	Total	New Work Permits Issued in Year
Germany (total)	476	360	1,015	391
Coming from:				
Italy	208	166	287	130
Netherlands	45	--	45	--
Greece	41	37	136	37
Turkey	5	7	139	62
Austria	41	--	56	--
Spain	48	51	112	32
Yugoslavia	13	10	100	77
France (total)*	--	176	--	223
Coming from:				
Italy	--	47	--	8
Portugal	--	8	--	34
Spain	--	106	--	139
Yugoslavia	--	--	--	9
Italy (total)	--	1	33	7
Netherlands (total)	28	12	80	18
Coming from:				
Germany	8	--	12	--
Italy	6	4	10	1
Turkey	--	--	14	3
Spain	1	--	12	2
			(1967)	
Belgium (total)	--	5	182	9
Luxembourg (total)	21	13	29	5

*Unlike the other countries, France has substantial numbers of North African workers.

Source: European Economic Community, Statistical Office, Social Statistics, 1969, Supp. A (Brussels, Commission).

TABLE 6

Differences in Status and Wages of Men and Women in Manufacturing
Industry

Country	Distribution of Workers			Men (as percent of men)	Women (as percent of women)	Percent Difference, Female and Male Wage*
	All	Men	Women			
	(as percent of all workers)					
Belgium						
Skilled	31.4	27.3	4.1	36.7	16.0	-33.2
Semiskilled	29.0	22.2	6.8	29.9	26.4	-28.7
Unskilled	25.3	17.1	8.2	23.0	32.0	-25.0
Other	14.3	7.7	6.6	10.4	25.6	-17.7
All	100.0	74.2	25.8	100.0	100.0	-31.9
Germany						
Skilled	36.3	34.7	1.6	49.3	5.3	-26.8
Semiskilled	36.5	24.2	12.3	34.4	41.3	-25.6
Unskilled	19.7	7.3	12.4	10.4	41.7	-21.8
Other	7.6	4.2	3.5	5.9	11.7	-25.9
All	100.0	70.3	29.7	100.0	100.0	-30.3
France						
Skilled	35.4	31.7	3.6	44.9	12.4	-25.8
Semiskilled	36.5	23.4	13.1	33.1	44.5	-19.4
Unskilled	27.4	15.0	12.3	21.4	42.1	-15.6
Other	0.7	0.4	0.3	0.6	1.0	-18.1
All	100.0	70.7	29.3	100.0	100.0	-27.5
Italy						
Skilled	36.3	30.7	5.6	44.3	18.2	-29.4
Semiskilled	37.6	25.5	12.2	36.7	39.2	-24.0
Unskilled	26.1	13.2	12.9	19.0	42.1	- 9.1
All	100.0	69.4	30.6	100.0	100.0	-24.8
Luxembourg						
Skilled	32.8	32.6	0.2	34.5	3.8	-47.0
Semiskilled	29.1	27.5	1.6	29.2	26.7	-27.7
Unskilled	30.6	28.0	2.6	29.8	43.7	-44.3
Other	7.5	6.0	1.5	6.4	25.8	-48.1
All	100.0	94.1	5.9	100.0	100.0	-45.5
Netherlands						
Skilled	34.0	32.0	2.0	38.5	12.0	-40.1
Semiskilled	38.2	31.0	7.3	37.2	43.3	-39.9
Unskilled	19.4	14.4	5.0	17.3	29.9	-31.3
Other	8.3	5.8	2.5	7.0	14.8	- 7.7
All	100.0	83.2	16.8	100.0	100.0	-39.3

*Average hourly wage. The percentage difference is calcu-
lated as male wage less female wage divided by male wage.

Source: European Communities, Press and Information Service, Trade Union News from the European Community, no. 4 (Summer
1970).

TABLE 7

The European Social Fund's Activities, 1960-68

What Was Spent
(in millions of dollars)

	What Each Country Drew out			What Each Country Paid in
	Retraining	Re-settlement	Total	
Belgium	3.95	0.002	3.95	7.07
France	19.94	0.57	20.51	25.68
Germany	20.19	1.71	21.90	25.68
Italy	23.22	4.00	27.22	16.05
Netherlands	6.65	0.02	6.67	5.62
Luxembourg	0.01	--	0.01	0.16
Community	73.96	6.30	80.26	80.26

Who Was Helped
(number of workers)

	Retraining	Resettlement	Total
Belgium	7,836	13	7,849
France	30,972	78,118	109,090
Germany	57,303	230,101	287,404
Italy	203,310	340,037	543,347
Netherlands	11,243	229	11,472
Luxembourg	96	--	96
Community	310,760	648,498	959,258

Source: European Communities, Press and Information Service, Trade Union News from the European Community, no. 1 (Autumn 1969).

TABLE 8

Aid from the European Social Fund, 1960-69

Country	Retraining		Resettlement		Total	
	Amount (in millions of dollars)	Number of Workers	Amount (in millions of dollars)	Number of Workers	Amount (in millions of dollars)	Number of Workers
Germany	31.54	63,760	2.23	237,409	33.77	301,069
Belgium	4.91	9,063	0.002	13	4.91	9,076
France	22.57	34,002	1.55	91,301	24.11	125,303
Italy	42.48	346,175	4.17	340,196	46.53	686,367
Luxembourg	0.01	96	--	--	0.01	96
Netherlands	7.49	12,032	0.39	231	7.50	12,263
Community	109.03	465,028	7.82	705,046	116.85	1,134,074

Note: To these figures must be added an equal sum paid out by the member governments concerned. It should also be noted that the ECSC Readaptation Fund provides financing for retraining and resettling miners and steelworkers. (See Trade Union News from the European Community, no. 3 [Spring 1970], pp. 14-17.)

Source: European Communities, Press and Information Service, Trade Union News from the European Community, no. 4 (Summer 1970).

TABLE 9

Aid from the European Social Fund, 1970

Country	Retraining		Resettlement		Total	
	Amount (dollars)	Number of Workers	Amount (dollars)	Number of Workers	Amount (dollars)	Number of Workers
Germany	15,604,996	27,767	173,806	13,684	15,778,802	41,451
Belgium	1,426,930	1,775	--	--	1,426,930	1,775
France	3,925,727	3,738	236,693	4,588	4,162,421	8,326
Italy	14,283,477	99,406	238,741	15,163	14,522,218	114,569
Luxembourg	--	--	--	--	--	--
Netherlands	1,149,780	901	1,550	14	1,151,330	915
Community	36,390,900	133,587	650,791	33,449	37,041,701	167,036*

*About 20,000 in this figure are counted twice either because requests for resettlement expenses were submitted by two countries or because requests for retraining expenses were submitted by two institutions.

Source: European Economic Community, Commission, Exposé sur l'évolution de la situation sociale dans la Communauté en 1970 (Brussels, February 1971).

FIGURE 1

Financing and Completion of Construction
of ECSC Labor Dwellings, 1956-70

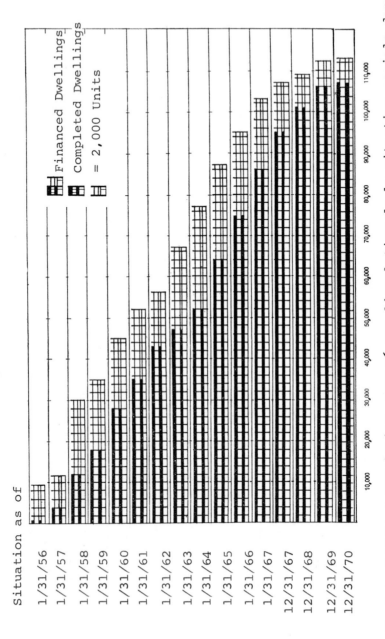

Source: European Commission, Exposé sur l'evolution de la situation sociale dans
la communauté en 1970 (Brussels, 1971).

NOTES

1. William Diebold, Jr., The Schuman Plan: A
Study in Economic Cooperation, 1950-1959 (New York:
Frederick A. Praeger, 1959), p. 3.

2. European Economic Community, European Parliamentary Assembly, Débats de l'Assemblée parlementaire européenne, Compte-rendu in-extenso des séances,
no. 37 (February 27, 1958), 355.

3. "Observations Relative to the Draft European
Common Market Treaty Submitted to the President of
the Ministerial Committee by the Free Trade Union
Organizations of the Community" (Brussels, January
30, 1957). (Mimeographed.) In the files of the New
York office of the International Confederation of
Free Trade Unions.

4. Theo Rasschaert, "Le mouvement syndical
devant la construction européenne," Revue du Marché
commun (January 1960), p. 32.

5. European Coal and Steel Community, High
Authority, First General Report on the Activities of
the Community (Luxembourg, 1953), pp. 79-104.

6. European Coal and Steel Community, Common
Assembly, Débats de l'Assemblée commune, Compte-rendu
in-extenso des séances, no. 9 (Luxembourg, May 10,
1955), 311.

7. Ibid. (May 13, 1955), p. 400.

8. Ibid., no. 7 (May 17, 1954), 228-31.

9. Ibid., no. 26 (June 26, 1957), 630-36.

10. Ibid., no. 16 (February 14, 1957), 336.

11. European Coal and Steel Community, High
Authority, Fifth General Report on the Activities of
the Community (Luxembourg, 1957), p. 232.

12.   Ibid., p. 205.

13.   Ibid., pp. 203-4.

14.   European Economic Community, Parliamentary Assembly, "Bertrand Report," doc. no. 21 (June 1958).

15.   Débats de l'Assemblée commune, Compte-rendu in-extenso des séances, no. 26 (June 26, 1957), 629.

16.   Débats de l'Assemblée parlementaire euro-péenne, Compte-rendu in-extenso des séances, no. 11 (April 10, 1959), 75-77.

17.   Agence Internationale de Documentation, Pharos, Le Marché commun européen, no. 22, D-1-11, doc. 109 (January 1960), 8.

18.   European Economic Community, Commission, Second General Report on the Activities of the Community (Brussels, 1959), p. 109.

19.   European Economic Community, Bulletin from the European Economic Community (January 1960), p. 33.

20.   European Economic Community, Commission, Troisième rapport général sur l'activité des Communautés (Brussels and Luxembourg, 1970), pp. 311-12.

21.   Ibid., pp. 309-11.

22.   European Economic Community, Commission, L'action des Communautés en matières de réadaptation et de rééducation professionelle (Brussels).

23.   European Coal and Steel Community, High Authority, Second General Report on the Activities of the Community (Luxembourg, 1954), p. 166.

24.   European Coal and Steel Community, High Authority, Third General Report on the Activities of the Community (Luxembourg, 1955), p. 153.

25.   Ibid., p. 154.

26. European Coal and Steel Community, High Authority, <u>Fifth General Report on the Activities of the Community</u>, p. 214.

27. A. Bertrand, "Rapport de la Commission des affaires sociales sur les problèmes de la réadaptation de la main d'oeuvre dans les industries de la Communauté," Assemblée Commune, doc. no. 26 (June 1956), p. 21.

28. Alain Girard and Pierre Meutey, <u>Développement économique et mobilité des travailleurs</u> (Paris: Institut National d'Études Démographiques, 1956), p. 53.

29. <u>Ibid</u>., pp. 54-55.

30. European Coal and Steel Community, <u>Obstacles à la mobilité des travailleurs et problèmes sociaux de réadaptation</u> (Luxembourg, 1956), p. 47.

31. Bertrand, <u>op. cit</u>., p. 20.

32. <u>Ibid</u>.

33. European Coal and Steel Community, High Authority, <u>Fifth General Report on the Activities of the Community</u>, p. 215.

34. Girard and Meutey, <u>op. cit</u>., p. 57.

35. <u>Débats de l'Assemblée commune, Compte-rendu in-extenso des séances</u>, no. 13 (June 21, 1956), 714.

36. European Coal and Steel Community, High Authority, <u>Third General Report on the Activities of the Community</u>, p. 152.

37. Bertrand, <u>op. cit</u>., pp. 27-30.

38. <u>Ibid</u>.

39. <u>Ibid</u>.

40. <u>Ibid</u>.

41.   European Coal and Steel Community, High Authority, Second General Report on the Activities of the Community, p. 166.

42.   European Coal and Steel Community, High Authority, Fifth General Report on the Activities of the Community, p. 126.

43.   Bertrand, op. cit., p. 32.

44.   European Coal and Steel Community, High Authority, Fifth General Report on the Activities of the Community, p. 216.

45.   Débats de l'Assemblée commune, Compte-rendu in-extenso des séances, no. 13 (June 21, 1956), 682-83.

46.   European Coal and Steel Community, High Authority, Tenth General Report on the Activities of the Community (Luxembourg, 1962), p. 435.

47.   European Economic Community, Commission, First General Report on the Activities of the Communities (Brussels, 1968), p. 337.

48.   Troisième rapport général sur l'activités des Communautés, p. 320.

49.   L'action des Communautés en matières de réadaptation et de rééducation professionelle.

50.   Ibid.

51.   European Coal and Steel Community, High Authority, Sixth General Report on the Activities of the Community (Luxembourg, 1958), p. 183.

52.   Obstacles à la mobilité des travailleurs et problèmes sociaux de réadaptation, annex IV, pp. 103-4.

53.   Communauté Européenne du charbon et de l'Acier, Actes officiels du Congrès international d'études sur la Communauté européenne du charbon et de l'acier, Milan-Stresa, 31 Mai-9 Juin, 1957, VII (Milan: Dott. A. Guiffre, 1958), 216-18.

54.   Ibid., p. 485.

55.   Manpower Aspects of Recent Economic Developments in Europe (Geneva: International Labor Organization, 1969), p. 76.

56.   Obstacles à la mobilité des travailleurs et
problèmes sociaux de réadaptation, annex VI, pp. 120-
38.

57.   European Economic Community, Parliamentary
Assembly, "Bertrand Report."

58.   Bulletin from the European Economic Community (June 1961), p. 41.

59.   Débats de l'Assemblée parlementaire européenne, Compte-rendu in-extenso des séances, no. 32
(October 13, 1960), 117-21.

60.   Journal officiel des Communautés européennes
(August 16, 1961).

61.   Ibid. (March 24, 1964).

62.   Ibid. (July 2, 1968).

63.   René Bonnet, "L'Europe du travail est-elle
realisée?" Droit social, no. 3 (March 1969), 165-67.

64.   Ibid.

65.   European Communities, European Community
(February 1970), p. 23.

66.   Bonnet, op. cit.

67.   Stephen Castles, "Europe's Migrant Workers,"
European Community (July 1969), pp. 14-16.

68.   Laurence C. Hunter and Graham L. Reid, "Integration and Labor Mobility," in Solomon Barkin
et al., eds., International Labor (New York: Harper
& Row, 1967).

69. Ibid.

70. Castles, op. cit.

71. Ibid.

72. Actes officiels du Congrès international d'etudes sur la Communauté européenne du charbon et de l'acier, pp. 147-50.

73. European Coal and Steel Community, High Authority, Sixth General Report on the Activities of the Community.

74. European Economic Community, Commission, Second General Report on the Activities of the Community (Brussels, 1969), p. 109.

75. European Coal and Steel Community, High Authority, Sixth General Report on the Activities of the Community, p. 184.

76. Journal officiel des Communautés européennes (December 17, 1959).

77. Ibid. (December 21, 1960).

78. Bulletin from the European Economic Community (August 1962), p. 23.

79. Agence Europe, Daily press bulletin, no. 1429 (December 7, 1962).

80. European Economic Community, Commission, Exposé sur l'évolution de la situation sociale dans la Communauté en 1967 (Brussels and Luxembourg, February 1968), pp. 43-46.

81. European Communities, Press and Information Service, Trade Union News from the European Community, no. 2 (Winter 1969-70), p. 17.

82. European Economic Community, Commission, Exposé sur l'évolution de la situation sociale dans la Communauté en 1969 (Brussels and Luxembourg, February 1970), pp. 35-38.

83. European Coal and Steel Community, High
Authority, <u>Third General Report on the Activities of
the Community</u>, pp. 25-27.

84. <u>Ibid</u>.

85. European Coal and Steel Community, High
Authority, <u>Fifth General Report on the Activities of
the Community</u>, p. 206.

86. <u>Obstacles à la mobilité des travailleurs et
problèmes sociaux de réadaptation</u>.

87. European Coal and Steel Community, High
Authority, <u>Seventh General Report on the Activities
of the Community</u> (Luxembourg, 1959), p. 263.

88. <u>Exposé sur l'évolution de la situation
sociale dans la Communauté en 1969</u>, pp. 35-38.

89. <u>Débats de l'Assemblée commune, Compte-rendu
in-extenso des séances</u>, no. 11 (November 30, 1955),
139.

90. M. G. M. Nederhorst, "Rapport de la Commission des affaires sociales sur la création, la fonc-
tion et la composition d'une ou plusieurs commissions
paritaires dans le cadre de la Communauté," Assemblée
Commune, doc. no. 1 (November 1956), p. 14.

91. European Coal and Steel Community, High
Authority, <u>Fourth General Report on the Activities
of the Community</u> (Luxembourg, 1956), pp. 223-25.

92. Nederhorst, <u>op. cit</u>., pp. 20-21.

93. <u>Débats de l'Assemblée parlementaire européenne, Compte-rendu in-extenso des séances</u>, no. 9
(January 10, 1959), 139-42.

94. <u>Ibid</u>., no. 26 (June 19, 1957), 209-10.

95. Intersyndicale CECA, <u>Rapport d'activité de
l'Intersyndicale CECA</u> (Luxembourg, December 1961),
pp. 14-15.

96. European Coal and Steel Community, <u>The Evo-lution of Wages and Wage Policy in the Industries of the Community, 1945-1956</u> (Luxembourg, 1960).

97. European Coal and Steel Community, "Les salaires et les charges sociales dans les industries de CECA," <u>Informations Statistiques</u> (Luxembourg, 1960).

98. Secrétariat Syndical Européen, <u>Déclaration des représentants des centres syndicaux à l'occasion de la réunion avec les parlementaires européens</u> (Brussels, September 25, 1958).

99. <u>Bulletin from the European Economic Community</u> (August-September 1960), p. 56.

100. <u>Ibid</u>. (January 1962), p. 39.

101. <u>Trade Union News from the European Community</u> (Summer 1970), p. 17.

102. Secrétariat Syndical Européen, <u>Troisième as-semblée générale des syndicats libres</u> (Brussels, 1962), "La politique sociale," pp. 8-9.

103. <u>Troisième rapport général sur l'activité des Communautés</u>, pp. 309-11.

104. <u>Treaty Establishing the European Economic Community and Connected Documents</u> (Brussels: Publishing Services of the European Communities, 1961), article 127.

105. Mme. de Reimacher-Legot, "Rapport fait au nom de la Commission des affaires sociales et faisant suite à la consultation demandée à l'Assemblée par-lementaire européenne conformément à l'article 127 du traité constituant la C.E.E. par le Conseil de la C.E.E. sur le Fonds social européen," Assemblée Parlementaire Européenne, no. 81 (December 1959).

106. <u>Bulletin from the European Economic Community</u> (January 1960), p. 32.

107. <u>Ibid</u>. (December 1960), p. 40.

108.   L'action des Communautés en matières de réadaptation et de rééducation professionelle.

109.   European Community (July 1969), p. 12.

110.   L'action des Communautés en matière de réadaptation et de rééducation professionelle.

111.   Troisième rapport général sur l'activité
des Communautés, p. 295.

112.   Mark J. Fitzgerald, C.S.C., The Common Market's Labor Programs (South Bend, Ind.:   University
of Notre Dame Press, 1966), p. 26.

113.   European Community (July 1969), p. 12.

114.   Ibid.

115.   Ibid.

116.   Trade Union News from the European Community
(Summer 1970), pp. 15-16.

117.   Troisième rapport général sur l'activité
des Communautés, p. 295.

118.   Trade Union News from the European Community
(Summer 1970), p. 16.

5

IMPROVEMENTS IN LIVING AND
WORKING CONDITIONS

Indirect Effects of the
Establishment of the
European Communities

The European Coal and Steel Community

How has labor benefited from the establishment
of the European Communities? Workers of the ECSC *(European*
have experienced a steady rise in real income and *Coal +*
improvements in working conditions. Whether the up- *Steel*
ward trend in real wages in the Six is due entirely *Commn)*
to the operation of the ECSC or whether it is the
continuation of trends already evident at the establishment of the ECSC is debatable. [What is lacking
is an accurate balance sheet of the operation of the
Common Market for coal and steel from the point of
view of the development of social policy and the economic and social situation of miners and steelworkers.]
However, as far as labor is concerned, it is important
that there were no complaints on this score. There
was no mass unemployment as a result of the implementation of the Common Market; and, where there has
been localized, temporary unemployment, the High
Authority made full use of its possibilities for readaptation. Moreover, coal- and steelworkers have
the benefit of shorter working hours. The studies

of the High Authority played an important role in
the movement to reduce the workweek. In 1953 the
workweek for underground miners was 48 hours in Belgium, France, and Italy; 46 in the Netherlands; and
45 in Germany. Reductions took place in all these
countries between 1953 and 1968. Germany and the
Netherlands introduced a 5-day, 40-hour week; Belgium,
a similar arrangement; and France, 40 hours of work
every other week. (See Table 18.) Similar improvements have occurred in the iron and steel industries.

However, by 1969 the leveling up of living and
working conditions expected to result from the operation of the ECSC had not fully materialized; and,
while there has been substantial progress toward the
harmonization of working hours, there remain considerable disparities in paid vacations and wages.
(See Tables 12, 13, 16, and 17.) Although the documentation of the High Authority and the findings of
the Mixed Committees for Coal and for Steel have resulted in certain social improvements, overall harmonization remains conditional on a coordination of
economic and social policies.

The European Economic Community

Living standards and working conditions have
improved within the EEC, and there have been a substantial rise in wages and a marked decrease in unemployment. While the size of the Community's labor
force has been increasing, unemployment throughout
the EEC in 1968 ranged from 1.2 percent of the working
population in Germany to 3.5 percent in Italy, with
the latter displaying the most striking changes in
unemployment within the EEC. (See Table 10.) The
overall upward movement of wages in the EEC in the
past few years has been higher than in third countries of comparable industrial level: The average
rise in wages for the EEC as a whole between 1958 and
1970 was more than 50 percent. In Italy the increase
amounted to 92 percent, while France, Germany, and
the Netherlands experienced a rise between 54 percent
and 95 percent and Belgium and Luxembourg, 56 percent
and 62 percent, respectively.[1] Since the highest
wages initially were found in Belgium and Luxembourg

and the lowest in Italy and the Netherlands, differences among the Six have indeed narrowed. Improvements within the EEC also include a general trend
toward extending the application of social security
to categories of workers not covered or incompletely
covered, such as farmers and the self-employed, and
a general rise in benefits paid.

However, balanced social progress has not been
achieved, for social harmonization is still problematic, both at the European level and within each
member country. The highly industrialized regions
have benefited the most from economic growth, while
those regions where a large part of the active population is engaged in agriculture have derived only
attenuated advantages. Moreover, expanding economic
sectors are experiencing higher rates of increase in
living standards than those industries in a state of
decline. Regional disparities are especially apparent in Italy, where economic development has pro-
gressed rapidly in the Northwest, to a lesser degree
in the Northeast-Center, and at a much slower rate
in the South. Generally, the larger industrial zones
of the Community have achieved a high level of employment and productivity. In these regions standards of living (bearing in mind different habits of
consumption) are relatively close, at least for workers in large cities. However, if labor costs, including wages and social charges, have converged in
the past few years in the main industries of the
Community, this does not necessarily mean that real
wages and average standards of living of various countries have developed toward uniformity. Italy continues to lag behind the other member countries with
its low standard of living, and sociological and economic factors influence the development of living
standards along divergent paths.

Today one of the main social problems plaguing
the EEC is the shortage of skilled labor in key industries throughout the Community contrasted with
zones of unemployment in certain depressed areas.
This problem must be solved in the framework of a
Community regional policy, for the progressive integration of nations along the lines of free competition

cannot ensure a balanced economic and social development among and within these nations. The harmonization of social policies is also essential: an active
collaboration of governments for the coordination of
policies and for the alignment of legislation. These
efforts have not been forthcoming, for certain governments do not agree that harmonization is necessary
or desirable. The harmonization of collective negotiations is also problematic, since employers are
generally unwilling to confront labor on the European
level; and in some instances labor itself is not convinced of the desirability of European bargaining.

Direct Effects of the European
Communities: Social Policies

The indirect effects of the European Communities
on wages and working conditions are debatable. It
can be argued that in some instances social improvements would have been achieved without the benefit of
the EEC or the ECSC and that the favorable social
results observed in the Six can be traced to a complex
of causes ranging from trade union action to national
economic policies, as well as to the economic growth
following the establishment of the Common Market.
However, progressive social policies have been directly fostered by European activity and, in varying
degrees, the social policies pursued by the High
Authority and the European Commission have immediately
benefited labor. In drawing up a balance sheet it
must be borne in mind that there are gaps in information on the effects of Community social policies
on the economic and social situations of the workers
in the Six. It must also be recalled that the European Executives are politically dependent on the
national governments and that for certain policies,
such as readaptation, the governments retain the
entire initiative.

Although readaptation has been less important
in the operations of the ECSC than expected, it has
been regarded with favor by the trade unions, for it
is an important factor in their struggle to have the
principle of the "right to work" recognized in national legislation. In France it was the inspiration

for similar legislation applying to other sectors of
the economy. Owing to favorable economic conditions
and the reticence of the national governments, readaptation aid was directed to only 1 percent of the
ECSC labor force during the transition period.[2] It
assumed fair proportions after the revision of article 56 because of persistent difficulties in the coal
industry and, since 1965, has been benefiting an increasing number of workers, chiefly because of ac-
celerating modernization operations in Germany and
the rapid closure of Dutch pits.[3] Thus, readaptation
is helping the ECSC industries to rationalize, without negative consequences, for their personnel and
has scored a number of small-scale successes. However, although the workers have been pleased with
readaptation payments, in many cases they have
achieved productive reemployment without the benefit
of Community aid; and, when Community aid is applied
to situations of general unemployment or to cases
involving large-scale migrations, it has proved ineffective. As long as industrial redevelopment, vocational training, and regional and employment policies
are determined at the national level, readaptation
aid can only be a palliative to technological unemployment.

The agreement covering free migration within
the ECSC did not result in a dramatic increase in
migratory movements among member countries, nor did
it alleviate Italy's problems or satisfy the requirements of the ECSC, for it is restricted to workers
with confirmed qualifications. The results of this
agreement for the ECSC remain unimpressive, since
skilled workers are not inclined to emigrate and are
infrequently affected by unemployment.

In July 1968 the complete freedom of movement
for the European Community's workers was achieved,
and labor from any member country may now move freely
within the EEC to accept and even to search for work
without being subject to any discrimination in the
terms of employment. This means that no EEC worker
can be discriminated against because of his nationality with respect to wages, layoffs, social or
fringe benefits, or the right to own or rent housing.

The equality of treatment guaranteed by the 1968 regulation includes the immunity of the migrant's residence permit against arbitrary cancellation, a milestone in the achievement of job security. Migrants have also gained the important social rights to vote and participate in the trade union organizations of the host country and in the shop committees at the place of employment. However, important restrictions on equality remain with respect to holding office in trade unions and participation in national policy-making organs. The European migrant has not become a European citizen. Moreover, the assimilation of European workers to national labor markets is occurring at a time of general decline in inter-Community migration and of significant increase in migration from third countries. Community migrants represent little more than 30 percent of the foreign workers employed in the EEC. The extent of migration from third countries and the social problems attending this current of labor have precipitated the need for a new EEC policy in the field of labor migration.

The European Convention of Social Security of Migrant Workers facilitates labor migration, for it has supplanted widely varying and insufficient national regulations on social security and has guaranteed migrant workers adequate protection. The regulations apply to wage earners in all sectors of the economy and cover all branches of social security. They guarantee equality of treatment of the nationals of the Six with respect to social security legislation, totalization of the periods of insurance completed in the country of previous employment, and the payment of benefits in any of these countries.

However, the trade unions have received little satisfaction in their demands for the harmonization of the various national social security systems. Although harmonization is occurring in the field of application of social security, the nature and degree of risks covered vary and there is great diversity in the level of payments. The Conference on Social Security was a failure for labor in this respect, for the employers refuted the trade unions' demands for the raising of grants to the highest level and the

governments showed their reticence by refusing to
participate. Under the circumstances the European
Commission refused to commit the EEC to further action. However, as a result of the Conference, the
Commission outlined a series of studies on the costs
of social security and the harmonization of statistics
and began to build up extensive documentation in the
social security systems in force in the Six. Some
of these studies have produced Community instruments
that will help establish uniformity in coverage and
harmonize certain aspects of national systems, such
as the establishment of a European list of occupational diseases. Although the list has been the subject of two recommendations to the member states by
the Commission, they have been only partially incorporated into national legislation.[4] While the harmonization of social security systems may not be
feasible, given the complexity of national systems
and their importance for national politics, the EEC
has made genuine progress in furthering free migration by establishing the correspondence of social
security benefits for migrant workers. In 1970 the
Council of Ministers adopted the outline of a new
system to assure migrants of full equivalence in
social security payments.

Workers in the ECSC have benefited from the High
Authority's direct aid to housing. From the date of
its first building program to January 1970, the High
Authority contributed to the construction of 114,000
low-cost housing units for the ECSC labor force.
(See Figure 1.) Although the trade unions have demanded similar measures of the EEC, and although the
European Commission has expressed its interest in a
housing program, it lacks an independent source of
funds for this purpose.

The studies and research of the European Executives in wages, working conditions, and social security have been of great assistance to labor at the
national level. They have provided labor with information it has previously been unable to secure because
of inadequate research facilities. Community sponsored studies enable national unions to see where
they stand in relation to others and provide ideas

for possible goals and ammunition for arguments.
Since national collective bargaining in the Six is
frequently based upon data gleaned from the documentation published by the Community, these studies can
be considered as a step toward harmonization of living and working conditions. The reduction of working
time within the ECSC is partly owing to the fact that
the trade unions had access to the documentation of
the ECSC. The trade unions are also pleased with the
former High Authority's efforts to encourage regular
discussion of its studies within the Joint Committee
for the Coal and Steel Industries, although they have
been disappointed by the European Commission's slow
and limited response to their requests for joint discussions by sector in the EEC.

The European Social Fund is the EEC's version
of aid to readaptation and was designed to alleviate
unfavorable social consequences resulting from the
establishment of the Common Market. Its modest activity has been out of proportion to the hopes raised
when the Fund was established, chiefly because the
procedures for granting aid are cumbersome and because
aid is granted only after the eligible workers have
been effectively reclassified in new employments for
a period of at least six months. Unlike the former
High Authority, the Commission has no resources of
its own to finance social policies, and, therefore,
the Social Fund is financed by governmental contributions and operates as an organ of financial compensation between the contributions and expenses of member
states. Because of the rigid procedures for applying
aid, the manner of financing the Fund, and the fact
that the European Commission enjoys no initiative in
administering the Fund or in establishing European
priorities for aid, the Fund has had a minimal impact
on national economic and social problems. The reforms
outlined by the Council of Ministers in July 1970 will
introduce a measure of flexibility to the operations
of the Fund and allow the Commission some initiative
in administering the Fund. However, no provisions
were included for increasing the resources of the
Fund, although the amount of aid disbursed has risen
considerably in recent years. (See Tables 7-9.)

The difficulties of developing an effective
Social Fund, operating according to European priorities, are similar to the obstacles facing the success
of all social policies within the European Communities. In the case of readaptation and the Social
Fund, the initiative lies with the member governments,
so that Community organs exercise minimal control
over their operations. Where the Commission may
exercise initiative, such as in the field of labor
migration, it enjoys a modicum of influence but no
decision-making power. Nor does the Commission have
recourse to an independent source of revenue to finance its social policies. Within the chief rule-
making organ of the Community, the Council of Ministers, there is no consensus on the desirability of
developing EEC social policies that could have a
significant impact on national life. Although they
are dedicated to the construction of Europe, members
of the Council of Ministers are primarily responsible
for the most feasible preservation of their national
priorities in the European compromise.

Prospects and Possibilities

Can labor's objectives be realized in the present
European structure? The ECFTUC believes that a progressive social policy can be achieved only when the
requisite economic conditions exist and not within
the framework of economic liberalism. A European
planning board to coordinate the action of member
states in order to promote balanced economic expansion is a necessary condition of the free trade
unions' demands for a Community social policy. Although the Christian trade unions believe that much
can be accomplished within the existing institutional
framework, they have also regarded the orientation
and control of investments necessary for a high level
of employment and a rise in living standards.

What is lacking for economic expansion to
proceed as we wish are the organs and procedures for orderly and efficient intervention. The present dispersal of powers
among European institutions, among the

latter and the governments, and among the
governments themselves does not favor
either efficient action or reasonable coordination.[5]

It was stated at length in Chapter 2 that the institutional complex of the European Communities does
not correspond to the wishes of labor. The coordinated monetary, cyclical, and sectoral policies that
they seek and that are conditional for a progressive
social policy cannot be achieved without a central
political authority.

What does labor expect from the European Communities in their present form? Both the Christian
labor unions and the free trade unions accord the
harmonization of living and working conditions a
primary place in their demands at the European level.
The European Executives have satisfied their requests for statistical surveys, studies, and monographs on living and working conditions in the various
branches of the economy. However, the European labor
groups have been disappointed with the other possibilities of contributing to harmonization provided
by the European Treaties, notably with mixed committees, the European Social Fund, the European Investment Bank, and regional policy. The High Authority
made a considerable effort to establish and maintain
the Joint Committee for the Coal and Steel Industries.
On the other hand, the Commission was more cautious
in promoting harmonization through discussions between
the social partners on the European level. It took
a late start in organizing these discussions; and
when they were established, they occurred on the general level, rather than for sectors, and were confined to noncontroversial problems.

However, labor's disappointments on this score
must be qualified, for the trade unions have differing expectations of mixed committees on the European
level and the conception of the social optimum varies
from country to country. Because living and working
conditions are the result of varying economic and
sociological factors, and because social policy within

the Six is not inspired by commonly accepted principles, discussions within mixed committees will continue to have their main influence on national collective bargaining. Bearing in mind that trade unions
vary in the amount of governmental or European intervention they are willing to tolerate, the unions are
generally loath to relinquish their power and are
jealous of their autonomy in obtaining social benefits for their members. Thus, while the trade unions
have been disappointed with the efforts of the European Commission to promote organized discussions between the social partners, they agree that in the
present and foreseeable state of integration indirect
methods in social affairs are preferable to direct
intervention. The extension of European regional and
agricultural policies and improvement of the European
Social Fund and of a European vocational training
policy offer greater hope for the achievement of
harmonization.

EUROPEAN LABOR ORGANIZATIONS

In order for the trade unions to achieve their
goal of participation in the development of European
policies, they need an effective organization, capable of decision and initiative. Do the structures
of the European labor confederations fulfill these
requirements? Both labor groups suffer from material
obstacles--a lack of financial means and a shortage
of personnel--and this has limited somewhat their
initiative. However, the European structures developed by the free trade unions and the Christian
trade unions have ensured them a sufficient amount
of cohesion to define European programs and to defend
them within the Communities.

The ICFTU and the WCL have developed differing
structures in response to their European needs. The
Christian trade unions created independent federations in order to deal with the ECSC and the EEC.
Decisions reached by a two-thirds majority within
these organizations are binding on all, ensuring a
greater degree of unity than the free trade unions
were able to command before their reorganization of

1969. Their secretary-generals enjoy broad powers
of discretion and the capacity to bind their organizations by effective patronage power. Consensus on
European questions is broad in scope within the
Christian trade union organizations and covers various
aspects of economic and social policy with a commitment to political unity. However, although the
Christian labor federations are characterized by a
more tightly knit organization than their free trade
union counterpart, they are numerically weaker than
the latter and are at times compromised by their centralized organization and ideological leanings. Because the bulk of the WCL's membership is in Western
Europe, there exists considerable friction between
the WCL and its European Organization, compounded by
an ineffective division of resources and responsibil-
ities between the two. The EO has encountered similar problems with the WCL's international secretariats,
which are highly jealous of their autonomy at the
European level. Difficulties in forging close links
with the international secretariats and the problem
of overlap with the WCL inspired the 1969 decision
to form a European Confederation of Christian Trade
Unions. The newly formed confederation is strengthening its organizational ties with the international
secretariats and has attempted to ensure close cooperation with the ECFTUC's industrial committees in
order to compensate for the limited resources of its
own industrial groups.

The free trade unions' European Trade Union
Secretariat possessed no federal characteristics or
central powers of decision making for important matters. Because of their differing national situations
its affiliates had difficulty in agreeing on the
structure of their mutual relations and were unwilling to cede a significant part of their national competencies. The result was a congress of equals, with
an executive committee operating as an international
organization and industrial committees functioning
almost independently. The limitations of a loosely
structured trade union organization appeared painfully evident to its leadership in the late 1960's.
Labor leaders were demanding federal features for
European institutions while they themselves retained

organizations with the characteristics of coordinating
boards.   Therefore, in order to solve the problems
of strengthening the structure of the Trade Union
Secretariat, endowing its Executive Committee with
greater competence and improving its relationship
with the industrial committees, the General Assembly
of the free trade unions in Europe revised the statutes of the Secretariat to form a genuine confederation of its national membership.   The General Assembly
was transformed into a congress with weighted representation and the power of taking decisions by a
majority vote.

The reorganization of both labor groups has
facilitated the development of the internal cohesion
necessary for effectively conducting lobbying and
representational activities within the European Communities.   Although there remain important problems
of material resources, personnel, and contacts with
grass-roots membership, these problems are not peculiar to labor and are shared by other European interest groups.   In spite of them labor groups have been
able to define European programs, to present common
stands in the consultative organs of the Communities,
and to participate in developing policy proposals.

The industrial committees of the ECFTUC and the
EO have displayed considerable vitality and have
managed to influence the formulation of European policies for agriculture and for transport.   The agricultural committees of both labor confederations have
acted as pioneers in European industrial relations,
for they were parties to the first collective agreement negotiated within the Community in 1968.   These
committees have not only proved themselves in developing joint discussions within the Communities but
have also surpassed their respective European secretariats in forging unity of action among affiliates
of the ICFTU, the WCL, and the WFTU.

Although a trade union plurality anchored in
separate international affiliations and differing
ideologies has prevented the creation of a single
trade union organization for Europe, the ECFTUC and
the EO have developed a common labor program for the

European Communities. From initially divergent attitudes on European affairs, the Christian trade unions
and their free trade union counterparts have developed common policies on the institutional structure
for an enlarged Europe, on social affairs, and on the
need to ensure a greater degree of democracy at all
levels of the economy. Both European labor groups
are convinced that the social policies they are promoting can be achieved only within the framework of
European regional and sectoral policies. They are
deeply concerned with their minimal influence in the
integration process, and, therefore, they have cooperated closely in developing and promoting European
labor programs.

Although the creation of genuine European labor
organizations is being directed by a determined and
highly competent leadership, it promises to be a long
and difficult task, for labor's power remains operative chiefly at the national level. Nevertheless,
the achievement of a European policy is an even more
perplexing and long-term political task, and in the
interval the labor confederations have proved their
value as permanent bodies for contacts with the
European institutions and as channels for the exchange
of views and information.

Although the Paris and Rome Treaties restrict
the formal participation of interest groups in policy
making to membership in consultative organs, labor
has managed to develop a variety of channels to the
sources of policy and to exercise its influence at
several points in the decision-making process.

Since the establishment of the ECSC labor's direct involvement in the Communities' decision-making
structure has declined. Labor enjoys an important
role in the Consultative Committee and the Economic
and Social Committee, and labor leaders are also
members of the European Parliamentary Assembly. However, these organs play a marginal role in the European policy process and are useful chiefly as platforms for labor's programs and as sources of information on all aspects of European activity. Elite
representation is more important to labor in the

Communities' executive organs than in its consultative bodies. However, while the High Authority included a coopted member from labor's ranks, the trade
unions did not succeed in having a representative of
the labor movement admitted to the original European
Commission or in obtaining a coopted representative
of labor in the unified Commission established in
1967, although Wilhelm Haferkamp of the DGB was named
to the latter.

Labor has penetrated the decision-making process
through its participation in the proliferation of
study groups established by the Commission's directorates. Because the Commission enjoys the initiative
in rule making but has no power, it has directly
stimulated a vigorous consultative activity with interest groups in order to increase its influence in
its dealings with the Council and to marshal political
mediators in the national capitals. In addition to
the establishment of study groups to plan policy
proposals, the Commission has fostered the activity
of labor groups through round tables, conferences,
and its participation in European trade union gatherings. Thus, it has helped stimulate the growth of
a group of labor leaders well versed in European
problems and able to convey the importance of European activities to their membership. However, the
operations of joint study groups, such as the Central
Group, and the scheduling of tripartite conferences
are dependent upon the will of the governments in
the Council of Ministers to proceed with integration.
In fact, the intervals between the meetings of these
study groups constitute a fever chart of the integration process, for periodic disruptions or decelera-
tion of European activity radiates from the Council
of Ministers to the Commission and its directorates
and acts as a damper on their activity and the
activity of interest groups.

The legislative organ of the European Communities, the Council of Ministers and its Permanent
Representatives, is not subject to the control of
the consultative organs of the Community or to the
EPA, where trade union opinion might have an indirect
impact on its decisions. Nor have the unions proved

TABLE 10

Labor Force, Employment, and Unemployment, 1967-70
(thousands)

Country	1967	1968	1969	1970 Estimates
Belgium				
Total labor force	3,701	3,714	3,760	--
Employed	3,609	3,604	3,672	--
Including salaried	2,814	2,812	2,884	--
Unemployed	92	110	88	--
Unemployment rate	2.5	3.0	2.3	--
Germany				
Total labor force	26,262	26,188	26,516	--
Employed	25,803	25,865	26,337	--
Including salaried	20,691	20,853	21,435	--
Unemployed	459	323	179	--
Unemployment rate	1.7	1.2	0.7	--
France				
Total labor force	20,147	20,224	20,494	20,826
Employed	19,782	19,793	20,154	20,470
Including salaried	14,922	15,040	15,501	15,930
Unemployed	365	431	340	356
Unemployment rate	1.8	2.1	1.7	1.7
Italy				
Total labor force	19,611	19,568	19,336	19,371
Employed	18,922	18,874	18,673	18,755
Including salaried	12,248	12,371	12,554	--
Unemployed	689	694	663	616
Unemployment rate	3.5	3.5	3.4	3.2
Luxembourg				
Total labor force	138,4	138,8	140,4	--
Employed	138,4	138,8	140,4	--
Including salaried	102,6	103,5	105,7	--
Unemployed	0	0	0	--
Unemployment rate	--	--	--	--
Netherlands				
Total labor force	4,454	4,493	2,543	4,736
Employed	4,364	4,409	4,477	4,539
Including salaried	3,559	3,619	3,702	--
Unemployed	90	84	66	56
Unemployment rate	2.0	1.9	1.5	1.2

Note: The unemployment rate is the percentage of unemployed in the total active population.

Source: European Economic Community, Commission, Exposé sur l'évolution de la situation sociale dans la Communauté en 1970 (Brussels and Luxembourg, February 1971).

TABLE 11

Standard Workweek, Selected Industries, 1963-70

Industry	Month	Bel-gium	Germany	Italy	Lux-em-bourg	Neth-er-lands
Automo-	Oct. 1963	45	41.25-42.50	46-46.50	--	45
tive	Oct. 1967	44	40	43.50-44	--	43.75
	Oct. 1968	43	40	43.50-44	--	43.75
	Apr. 1970	43	40	42	--	43.25
Electri-	Oct. 1963	45	42-42.50	46-47	--	45
cal	Oct. 1967	44	40	44.50-45.50	--	43.75
	Oct. 1968	43	40	44.50-45.50	--	43.75
	Apr. 1970	43	40	43.50	--	43.75
Textiles	Oct. 1963	45	42	46	--	45
	Oct. 1967	45	41	45	--	45
	Oct. 1968	45	41	44	--	43.75
	Apr. 1970	36.50-44	40	43	42-44	43.75
Artificial	Oct. 1963	45	42.50	46.50	--	45
and syn-	Oct. 1967	45	41.25	45	--	45
thetic	Oct. 1968	45	41.25	45	--	43.75
fibers	Apr. 1970	--	40	42	42	42
Rubber	Oct. 1963	45	42-43	46	44	45
	Oct. 1967	45	40-41.50	45	44	45
	Oct. 1968	43-45	40-41.50	44	44	43.75
	Apr. 1970	44	40	43.50	44	42.50
Chemical	Oct. 1963	45	42.50	46.50	--	45
	Oct. 1967	43	41.25	44	--	45
	Oct. 1968	43-45	41.25	43.50	--	43.75
	Apr. 1970	44	40	42	42	42.50
Clothing	Oct. 1966	45	40-42	45	--	45
	Oct. 1967	45	40-41	45	--	43.75
	Oct. 1968	45	40-41	45	--	43.75
	Apr. 1970	44	40-41	44	45	42.50
Glass	Oct. 1966	45	40-42.50	45.40	--	45
	Oct. 1967	44-45	40-41.25	45.50	--	45
	Oct. 1968	44	40-41.25	44.50	--	45
	Apr. 1970	40-44	40	44.50	--	42.50
Ship-	Oct. 1966	44	41.25	46	--	45
building	Oct. 1967	44	40	46	--	43.75
	Oct. 1968	43	40	46	--	43.75
	Apr. 1970	43	40	44	--	43.75
Construc-	Oct. 1966	45	Apr. 1-Oct. 31:42	45	45	45
tion	Oct. 1967	45	Nov. 1-Mar. 31:40	44	45	45
	Oct. 1968	45	--	44	45	43.75
	Apr. 1970	43.75	40	42	44	42.50
Steel	Dec. 1957	45	45	48	44	48
	Jan. 1964	45	41-42	44-45	42.33	45
	Apr. 1968	43	40	42-42.50	41.50	43.75
	Apr. 1970	42	40	41	41	43.75

Note: France is excluded. The legal workweek is set at 40 hours by the act of June 21, 1936. There is no labor contract deviating from the legal workweek, although special agreements on this matter may be negotiated.

Source: European Economic Community, Commission, Exposé sur l'évolution de la situation sociale dans la Communauté en 1970 (Brussels and Luxembourg, February 1971).

Table 12

Basic Annual Paid Vacations, Selected Industries, 1963-68

| | | | | Working Days | | | |
Industry	Year	Bel-gium	Ger-many	France	Italy	Lux-em-bourg	Netherlands
Automotive	1963	12	15	24	12	--	15 working days
and electri-	1965	18	17	24	12	--	15 working days
cal	1966	18	17	24	12	--	3 weeks
	1967	18	18	24	12	--	3 weeks
	1968	18	18	24	12	--	3 weeks
Textiles	1963	12	18	24	12	--	3 weeks
	1965	18	18	24	12	--	3 weeks
	1966	18	20	24	12	--	3 weeks
	1967	18	24	24	14	--	3 weeks
	1968	18	24	24	14	--	3 weeks
Synthetic	1963	12	18	24	12	--	15 working days
and artifi-	1965	18	18	24	12	--	15 working days
cial fabrics	1966	18	18	24	12	--	15 working days
	1967	18	18	24	13	--	15 working days
	1968	18	18	24	13	--	15-16 working days
Rubber	1963	12	15-18	24	12	8-18	15 working days
	1965	18	18	24	12	--	3 weeks
	1966	18	18	24	12	18	3 weeks
	1967	18	18	24	12	--	3 weeks
	1968	18	18	24	12	--	3 weeks
Chemical	1963	12	18	24	12	--	15 working days
	1965	18	18	24	12	--	15 working days
	1966	18	18	24	12	--	15 working days
	1967	18	18	24	12	--	15 working days
	1968	18	18	24	12	--	15 working days
Clothing	1966	18	21-24	24	13	18	3 weeks
	1967	18	24	24	13	--	3 weeks
	1968	18	24	24	13	24-28	3 weeks
Glass	1966	18	18	24	12	--	15 working days
	1967	18	18	24	13	--	15 working days
	1968	18	18	24	13	--	15 working days
Shipbuilding	1966	18	15-17	24	12	--	3 weeks
	1967	18	18	24	12	--	3 weeks
	1968	18	18	24	12	--	3 weeks
Construction	1966	18	15	24*	15	18	15 working days
	1967	18	15	24*	15	--	15 working days
	1968	18	15	24*	15	24-38	17 working days
Steel	1957	12	12	18	12	12	15 working days
	1961	12	12-18	18	12	12	15 working days
	1964	15	16-22	18	12	12	15-18 working days
	1968	24	18-24	18	12	15	15-20 working days

*Salaried workers with less than 1,800 hours per year: 18 working days.

Source: European Economic Community, Commission, Exposé sur l'évolution de la situation sociale dans la Communauté en 1968 (Brussels, February 1969).

TABLE 13

Living Standards in the European Communities,
1967 and 1970
(1958 = 100)

Country	Consumer Price Index		Hourly Gross Wages Index		Real Rise in Wages (percent)
	1967	1970	1967	1970	
Belgium	123	137	170	214	56
France	140	164	183	252	54
Germany	123	133	199	259	95
Italy	137	148	206	284	92
Luxembourg	118	130	161	215	62
Netherlands	137	159	203	275	73
Britain	129	151	151	196	30
United States	115	161	134	135	19

Note: Indexes show trends within each country. They do not indicate comparative living costs and wage levels among countries. Increase in wage index is adjusted to account for rise in consumer price index.

Source: European Communities Statistical Office.

TABLE 14

Financing Social Security, 1968

Country	Sources of Finance (percent)		
	Employer	Employee	State*
Belgium	50	23	27
France	69	22	9
Germany	49	31	20
Italy	66	17	17
Luxembourg	40	23	37
Netherlands	46	39	15

*Includes interest on invested funds.

Source: European Communities Statistical Office.

TABLE 15

Average Hours Worked in Industry, Including Overtime, April 1970

Country	Manufacturing, Industries	Manufacturing, Building, Extractive
Belgium	43.1	43.1
France	44.9	45.8
Germany	44.1	44.2
Italy	42.6	42.5
Luxembourg	43.8	45.1
Netherlands	44.5	44.6

Source: European Communities Statistical Office.

TABLE 16

Paid Holidays, April 1970

Country	Legal Minimum	Minimum Laid Down by Collective Agreement	Public Holidays	Total*
Belgium	3 weeks	--	10	25-28
France	2 working days/month	24	8-10	32-34
Germany	15-18	16-24	10-13	25-37
Italy	--	13-21	17	30-38
Luxembourg	18-24	--	10	28-34
Netherlands	10-12	15-24	7	17-31

*Care should be exercised with these figures, since the workweek may be five or six days. Twenty-four days a year may mean four weeks' holiday in the case of a six-day workweek.

Source: European Communities Statistical Office.

TABLE 17

Paid Vacations, Coal Industry, April 1, 1968

	Germany	Belgium	France	Italy	Netherlands
Underground					
a	15	18	24	12	17
b	21	30	30	18	23
	over 15 years of seniority	depending upon performance	over 20 years of seniority	over 20 years of seniority	over 20 years of seniority
Surface					
a	15	18	24	12	15
b	18		30	18	21
	over 15 years of seniority		over 30 years of seniority	over 20 years of seniority	over 20 years of seniority

a = Basic number of vacation days.

b = Maximum number of vacation days, considering seniority, age, or performance.

Source: European Economic Community, Commission, Exposé sur l'évolution de la situation sociale dans la Communauté en 1968 (Brussels and Luxembourg, February 1969).

TABLE 18

Normal Work Periods, Coal Industry, April 1, 1968

	Germany	Belgium	France	Italy	Nether-lands
Under-ground		System A			
a	8 hours	8.25 hours	8 hours	8 hours	8 hours
b	40 hours	41.25 hours	40 hours	40 hours	40 hours
	(5 days)	(5 days)	(5 days)	(5 days)	(5 days)
	during		during		
	40 weeks		32 weeks		
	32 hours	33 hours	48 hours		
	(4 days)	(4 days)	(6 days)		
	during	during	during		
	12 weeks	16 weeks	20 weeks		
		System B			
a		8 hours			
b		40 hours			
		(5 days)			
		32 hours			
		(4 days)			
		during			
		8 weeks			
		System A			
Surface					
a	8 hours	8 hours	8.25 hours	8 hours	8.75 hours
b	40 hours	42.50 hours	41.25 hours	(44 hours	45 hours
	(5 days)	(5 days)	(5 days)	during 26	(5 days)
	during		during	weeks, 5	
	40 weeks		32 weeks	days-a-	
	32 hours	34 hours	49.50 hours	week	
	(4 days)	(4 days)	(6 days)	system)	
	during	during	during		
	12 weeks	16 weeks	20 weeks		
		System B			
a		8.25 hours			
b		41.25 hours			
		(5 days)			
		31 hours			
		(4 days)			
		during			
		8 weeks			

a = Workday.
b = Workweek.

Source: European Economic Community, Commission, Exposé sur l'évolution de la situation sociale dans la Communauté en 1968 (Brussels and Luxembourg, February 1969).

successful in their numerous attempts to establish
direct and regular contacts with the Council of Ministers of Social Affairs. Although they have managed
to engineer joint meetings with the Council on a
yearly basis, they have been unable to engage the
latter in discussions on broad policy issues and are
frequently referred to the national capitals. Having
endured pressure-group activity at the national
level, the Council considers European pressure groups
an impediment rather than an aid in building consensus during ministerial sessions.

Because the rule-making procedures employed by
the Council of Ministers deny labor groups the opportunity of participating in Community building at the
European level, the labor groups have become the
radical democrats of the European Communities. They
have complained that their influence in Europe compares unfavorably with their national influence, and,
therefore, they have campaigned for a revision of
the European institutional structure that will lend
greater competence to the consultative organs.

NOTES

1. European Economic Community, Commission,
Exposé sur l'évolution de la situation sociale dans
la Communauté en 1967 (Brussels and Luxembourg, 1968),
p. 8.

2. Jacques Tessier, "Les aspects sociaux de la
Communauté européenne," Revue d'économie politique,
special issue, "Le Marché commun et ses problèmes"
(1958), p. 5.

3. European Economic Community, Commission,
L'action des Communautés en matières de réadaptation
et de rééducation professionnelle (Brussels).

4. European Economic Community, Commission,
Exposé sur l'évolution de la situation sociale dans
la Communauté en 1969 (Brussels and Luxembourg, 1970),
p. 178.

5.   Roger Reynaud, "La CECA, réflexions sur un traité," Revue de l'action populaire (February 1960), p. 150.

BIBLIOGRAPHY

Documents from the International
Confederation of Free
Trade Unions

Confédération Européenne des Syndicats Libres dans
la Communauté. Concentrations economiques et
industrielles: Réponse syndicale. Brussels,
October 1970.

_____. Premier Congrès: Discours, décisions,
résolutions. Brussels, April 1969.

European Regional Organization of the International
Confederation of Free Trade Unions. European
Integration. Report of the European Trade Union
Course held in London, September 2-11, 1959.
Brussels: European Regional Secretariat, 1959.

_____. European Regional Conferences. Biennial.
Brussels: European Regional Secretariat, 1950,
1952, 1954, 1956, 1958.

_____. Observations Relative to the Draft Euro-
pean Common Market Treaty Submitted to the President of the Ministerial Committee by the Free
Trade Union Organizations of the Community.
Brussels, January 30, 1957.

_____. The Problems of the European Unification.
Report of the European Trade Union School, held
at Egmont-on-Sea at the Trade Union Training
Center of the National Free Trade Union Organi-
zation of the Netherlands, September 12-25, 1954.
Brussels, 1954.

_____. Social Aspects of European Integration.
Report on the European Trade Union School, held
at Hengenburg, Austria, June 18-30, 1956. Brussels, 1956.

International Confederation of Free Trade Unions.
Activities Reports of the World Congresses.
Biennial. Brussels, 1949, 1951, 1953, 1955,
1957, 1959.

_____. Economic and Social Bulletin. Monthly. Brussels, 1950-70.

_____. Information Bulletin. Bimonthly. Brussels, 1950-70.

Intersyndicale CECA. Rapport d'activité de l'Intersyndicale CECA. Luxembourg, December 1961.

Secrétariat Syndical Européen. Avis sur l'accélération. Brussels, April 22, 1960.

_____. Déclaration des représentants des centres syndicaux à l'occasion de la réunion avec les parlementaires européens. Brussels, September 25, 1958.

_____. Déclaration sur la politique sociale de la Communauté. Brussels, January 12, 1962.

_____. Deuxième Assemblée générale des Syndicats libres des états-membres des Communautés européennes. Luxembourg, November 1959.

_____. Notice on the Possibilities of a Trade Union Representation in the European Economic Community. N.p., n.d.

_____. Prise de position du Comité exécutif du Secrétariat syndical européen sur les dispositions sociales du traité de la CEE. Brussels, June 9, 1960.

_____. Rapport d'activité du Secrétariat syndical européen à la Troisième assemblée générale des syndicats libres des états-membres des Communautés européennes. Brussels, January 12, 1960.

_____. Rapport du secrétariat à la Deuxième assemblée générale des syndicats libres des états-membres des Communautés européennes. Luxembourg, November 10, 1959.

_____. Résolution. No. 75. Brussels, April 28, 1969.

_____. Résolutions. Luxembourg, November 6, 1959.

_____. Sixième assemblée générale: Rapport d'activité, 1966-1968. Brussels, April 1969.

Documents from the International
Confederation of Christian
Trade Unions

European Organization of the International Confederation of Christian Trade Unions. Deuxième conférence européenne des syndicats chrétiens. Brussels, May 10, 1962.

_____. Motion adoptée par le Comité restreint de l'Organisation européenne de la CISC. Brussels, February 21, 1963.

_____. Quatrième conférence européenne des syndicats chrétiens, Amsterdam, October 6-8, 1966. Brussels: Organization Européenne de la CISC, October 1966.

_____. Résolution concernant un programme d'action syndicale dans le cadre européen. Brussels, May 10, 1962.

European Organization of the World Congress of Labor. Premier congrès: Cinquième rapport d'activité. Brussels, May 1969.

_____. Résolution. No. 22. Brussels, May 9, 1969.

Gerritse, G. Premier congrès, la place des travailleurs dans une Europe en mutation. Brussels: European Organization of the World Congress of Labor, May 9, 1969.

International Confederation of Christian Trade Unions. Le syndicalisme chrétien, sa nature et sa mission, XVIIème congrès. Brussels, 1951.

Documents from the European
Communities

European Coal and Steel Community. Actes officiels
    du Congrès international d' études sur la Com-
    munauté européenne du charbon et de l'acier,
    Milan-Stresa, 31 Mai-9 Juin, 1957. III and VII.
    Milan: Dott. A. Giuffre, 1958.

_____. Bulletin from the European Coal and Steel
    Community. Bimonthly. 1953-62. Monthly before
    1953.

_____. The Development of Wages, Working Condi-
    tions and Social Security in Community Indus-
    tries in 1959. Luxembourg, 1960.

_____. The Evolution of Wages and Wage Policy in
    the Industries of the Community, 1945-1956.
    Luxembourg, 1960.

_____. Informations Statistiques. Monthly.
    1956-70.

_____. Obstacles à la mobilité des travailleurs
    et problèmes sociaux de réadaptation. Luxem-
    bourg, 1956.

_____. Réadaptation et Réemploi de la main-
    d'oeuvre: Rapport de la mission aux Etats-Unis
    des syndicalistes de la Communauté. Luxembourg,
    1960.

European Coal and Steel Community, Common Assembly.
    Débats de l'Assemblée commune, Compte-rendu in-
    extenso des séances. Serial. Luxembourg.

_____. Report of the Committee on Social Affairs.
    1953-57.

European Coal and Steel Community, High Authority.
    General Report on the Activities of the Communi-
    ty. Annual. Luxembourg.

European Communities. European Community. Monthly.
     1967-70.

European Communities, Press and Information Service.
     Informations syndicales et ouvrières, notes
     rapides. Serial.

_____. Trade Union News from the European Commu-
     nity. Quarterly, 1961-64. Monthly, 1965-68.
     Quarterly, 1969-70.

European Economic Community. Bulletin from the Euro-
     pean Economic Community. Monthly. 1959-70.

European Economic Community, Commission. Exposé sur
     l'évolution de la situation sociale dans la Com-
     munauté. Annual. Brussels and Luxembourg,
     1959-69.

_____. General Report on the Activities of the
     Community. Annual. Brussels, 1958-66.

_____. General Report on the Activities of the
     Community. Annual. Brussels and Luxembourg,
     1967-69.

_____. Memorandum of the Commission on the Action
     Program of the Community for the Second Stage.
     Brussels, October 1962.

European Economic Community, Economic and Social Com-
     mittee. Bulletin d'information. Quarterly.
     Brussels, 1961-70.

_____. "Ten Years of Activity of the Economic and
     Social Committee of the European Communities."
     Speech delivered by Louis Major, chairman of
     the Economic and Social Committee of the European
     Economic Community, at the Committee's tenth
     anniversary celebration. Brussels, 1968.

European Economic Community, Parliamentary Assembly.
     Cahiers mensuels de documentation européenne.
     Monthly. 1959-70.

_____. Débats de l'Assemblée parlementaire européenne, Compte-rendu in-extenso des séances. Serial.

_____. Report of the Social Committee. 1958-70.

Journal officiel de la Communauté européenne du charbon et de l'acier. Serial.

Journal officiel des Communautés européennes. Serial.

Treaty Establishing the European Economic Community and Connected Documents. Brussels: Publishing Services of the European Communities, 1961.

Wigny, Pierre. Un témoignage sur la Communauté des Six. Luxembourg: European Coal and Steel Community, Common Assembly, 1957.

_____. L'Assemblée parlementaire dans l'Europe des Six. Brussels: European Economic Community, European Parliamentary Assembly, 1958.

European Press Service

Agence Europe. Daily press bulletin. In the files of the European Community Information Services, Farragut Building, Washington, D.C. 20006.

Agence Internationale de Documentation, Pharos. Le Marché commun européen. Monthly. 1959 and 1960.

Books

Barkin, Solomon, et al., eds. International Labor. New York: Harper & Row, 1967.

Blackmer, Donald, L. M. Unity in Diversity: Italian Communism in the Communist World. Cambridge, Mass.: MIT Press, 1968.

Clark, W. Hartley. The Politics of the Common Market. Englewood Cliffs, N.J.: Prentice Hall, 1967.

David, Marcel. La participation des travailleurs à
    la gestion des entreprises privées dans les
    principaux pays d'Europe occidentale. Paris:
    Librairie Dalloz, 1959.

Diebold, William, Jr. The Schuman Plan: A Study in
    Economic Cooperation, 1950-1959. New York:
    Frederick A. Praeger, 1959.

Fafchamps, Joseph. Les conventions collectives en
    Belgique. Brussels: La Pensée Catholique, 1961.

Fejto, François. The French Communist Party and the
    Crisis of International Communism. Cambridge,
    Mass.: MIT Press, 1967.

Fitzgerald, Mark J., C.S.C. The Common Market's
    Labor Programs. South Bend, Ind.: University
    of Notre Dame Press, 1966.

Freidrich, Carl J. Europe: An Emergent Nation? New
    York: Harper & Row, 1969.

Germino, Dante, and Passiglio, S. The Government and
    Politics of Contemporary Italy. New York: Har-
    per & Row, 1967.

Girard, Alain, and Meutey, Pierre. Développement
    économique et mobilité des travailleurs. Paris:
    Institut National d'Etudes Démographiques, 1956.

Haas, Ernst B. The Uniting of Europe: Political,
    Social, and Economic Forces. Stanford, Calif.:
    The University Press, 1958.

Kapteyn, P. J. G. L'Assemblée commune de la Commu-
    nauté européenne du charbon et de l'acier: Un
    essai de parlementarisme européen. Leyden:
    A. W. Sythoff, 1962.

Kassalow, Everett M. Trade Unions and Industrial
    Relations: An International Comparison. New
    York: Random House, 1969.

LaPalombara, Joseph. The Italian Labor Movement:
    Problems and Prospects. Ithaca, N.Y.: Cornell
    University Press, 1957.

Lindberg, Leon N., and Schiengold, Stuart A. Europe's
    Would-Be Polity: Patterns of Change in the Euro-
    pean Community. Englewood Cliffs, N.J.: Pren-
    tice-Hall, 1970.

Lorwin, Val. The French Labor Movement. Cambridge,
    Mass.: Harvard University Press, 1954.

Manpower Aspects of Recent Economic Developments in
    Europe. Geneva: International Labor Organiza-
    tion, 1969.

Le Marché commun: Chômage ou prospérité. Paris:
    Editions du Monde Ouvrier, 1959.

Spinelli, Altiero. The Eurocrats: Conflict and
    Crisis in the European Community. Baltimore:
    The Johns Hopkins Press, 1966.

Spiro, Herbert J. The Politics of German Codeter-
    mination. Cambridge, Mass.: Harvard University
    Press, 1958.

Weil, Gordon L. The Benelux Nations: The Politics
    of Small Country Democracies. New York: Holt,
    Rinehart and Winston, 1970.

MARGUERITE BOUVARD, founder and codirector of the European Studies Program at Regis College, Weston, Massachusetts, has taught political science there since 1966. Her courses include political theory, comparative politics, and international relations. In 1971 she was appointed a Fellow at the Radcliffe Institute. Dr. Bouvard attended Northwestern University and Radcliffe College and received her Ph.D. from Harvard University in 1965. She has traveled extensively and resided in Europe, where she completed much of the research that is the background for this study.